I0621623

Southbound as Told by Number 2

I'll Get There When I Get There

Margie Sanders

Wild Apple Press

Cover design by Melissa Moore.

Cover inspired by original photo courtesy of Leah Holt.

SOUTHBOUND AS TOLD BY NUMBER 2

This is my retelling of memories and characters I experienced on the Appalachian Trail in 2013. In an effort to retain anonymity, I have changed conversations, names, and likeness of most people in my story.

With the recent official name change to the mountain Kuwohi (formerly known as Clingmans Dome), located in Tennessee and North Carolina, I want to recognize and acknowledge the sacred territories of all the Indigenous Nations that led to the assembled form of the Appalachian Trail. Full credit given to Mr. Trey Adcock (Cherokee Nation) and the Appalachian Trail Conservancy for their incredible work on the following list of Native Land Territories along the Appalachian Trail:

Wabanaki

Penobscot

Nanrantsouak

Arosaguntacook

Pequawket

Abenaki

Pocumetue

Nipmuc

Mohican

Wappinger

Paugussett

Munsee Lenape

Lenni-Lenape

Susquahannock

MARGIE SANDERS

Piscataway

Massawomeck

Manahoac

Monacan

Moneton

Tutelo

S'atsoyaha (Yuchi)

Cherokee Nations (Tsalagi Ayehli)

Adcock, Trey. (2021, February 23). *Native Lands*. Appalachian Trail Conservancy.

https://appalachiantrail.org/official-blog/native-lands/

Contents

Dedication   VII

Acknowledgements   VIII

Introduction   IX

1. Practice Makes Perfect-ish   1

2. Maine, Part One: 100 Mile Wilderness   13

3. Maine, Part Two   43

4. New Hampshire, Part One   85

5. Vermont   97

6. Massachusetts   126

7. New Hampshire, Part Two: The White Mountains (Wobanadenok)   136

8. Connecticut   152

9. New York   160

10. New Jersey   175

11. Pennsylvania   183

12. Maryland and West Virginia   215

13. Virginia   220

14. Tennessee (and North Carolina)   254

15. North Carolina   288

16. Georgia   301

Appendix   319
Glossary, iPod Playlist, Gear List

Dedication

This book is dedicated to my Mom, my Great Aunt Doris, and to anyone who feels stuck.

To my Mom,

I dedicate this book to you because you are my adventure mentor with hawk eyes. You are always going camping and fishing, whether with friends or by yourself – it's happening! I have the same urges towards "running away" and feel like you are cheering me on every step of the way. I love you days and nights and nights and days. You know this. Can't talk about it too much.

To my Great Aunt Doris,

I have always kept your magic with me ever since I was a child. Your talent as a writer and your appreciation for childlike curious charisma are not lost on me. I also want you to know that I promise to date every entry. It is important!

To anyone who feels stuck,

I'm with you, my friend. It's time to start doing the things that make us happy.

Acknowledgements

To Mom, Dad, Tony, and Cathy, thank you for all your love, support, wisdom, and laughter. Remember, everybody needs support: me, Momma, Daddy...Aunt Frances.

To BK, Al, and Robs, thank you for listening to me go on and on about this writing process every single day. I cherish your friendship. We are the party.

To Melissa, thank you for your encouragement, patience, and creative prowess that brought the book and website to life.

To Casey and Tara, thank you for your connections. They gave me the direction I needed to pull this off.

To my editors, Sara Thomas and Abigail Campbell, you two made this way better than I ever could have on my own. I'm grateful for everything you brought to the table.

An extra special thank you to Abigail Campbell for all the extra time and energy you gave to this project. We learned a lot together, and I'm forever grateful for you and your talents. Now, let's meet up at Casey's and go build our boat.

Introduction

Hey there!

Let me start by saying I'm no Shakespeare, but I did have a shake for breakfast and a pickle spear at lunch.

It's about damn time I shared the true story of my experience on the Appalachian Trail. It's only taken me 11 years to finish this process, which is wild to think about because it has played a huge role in my life every day since starting way back in May of 2013.

I've actually got to back it up even further to set the scene: in 2009, my partner, Carey, and I got together, and we dove headfirst into cycling, rock climbing, kayaking, and backpacking. We were an unstoppable adventurous duo always on the go. I planted this one little seed about hiking the Appalachian Trail, and she started researching it. It became our obsession. There was no dilly dally! In 2011, we made the decision to go for it, and spent the next two years aggressively saving, researching, planning, and executing our plan.

What you are about to read are two versions of the story: the sugar-coated version known as the "original trail journal," coupled with my retrospective, revealing stories of what really happened out there.

Here we are over 11 years later, and my mind is chock full of stories and details I want to share with you. If you were following along with us in real time through the trail journal, you might have noticed there were entries that weren't telling the whole story. Reason being, I was trying to protect my mother. I would type up the journal entry at the end of every evening out on the trail using the notes section on the phone. When we got to town or somewhere with good cell service, we'd email it to my mom who would then update the online trail journal.

Who besides my family would be reading those journal entries? Turns out there was a whole community of people who were following along. At the time there weren't many dedicated southbound journals listed on the Trail Journals website, so I guess that's what made this journal stand out. The more I wrote, the more readers became interested and followed along. I address them a lot throughout the book, and so enjoyed reading their clever and witty comments all the way to Georgia. At the end of every journal entry, I tried to come up with the silliest segues to Carey's two cents. It became my personal challenge to never repeat myself and it was the highlight of my evenings. I have my personal favorites to this day.

Being from the family who invented worry, I decided to keep things positive in hopes of reassuring them that everything was "nice" and people were "great" all along the trail. As a whole, the experience was truly amazing and positive and wonderful, yadda yadda; *but* over the past few years, I've heard this voice inside my head telling me to share what *really* happened out there because it's worth telling!

I can only tell this from my perspective, even though I have to believe Carey and I had the same emotions at certain times along the way. She and I split up about five years after we hiked the A.T. We accomplished great things together, and I can definitively say that I would not have made it through the A.T. without her. So, here's to Carey! Thank you for all your calculations, determination, perseverance, and support throughout our time together.

To those who kept up with the trail journal, I hope you find this story to be as exciting as the first time around. Boy, didn't we have fun with that, America?! This version is going to have the original journal entries with the dates and locations just the same as before but now in italics (oooo, ahhhh!), and I have added a section at the bottom I like to call "What Really Happened." But wait, that's not all! Included in the Appendix you'll find a homespun glossary of terms, my iPod playlist from 2013, and my gear list.

Some of the things I'm going to expound upon in this book are how we almost drowned, fought hard against hypothermia, acquired a gun, survived some shady characters, delayed our journal entries out of fear of being followed, mental warfare, the death of a fellow thru hiker, and much more. I ran through every emotion during this five month and three weeks adventure of a lifetime. On this 11 year anniversary, I feel it is time to retell it without hiding any details. My mom will be fine.

This whole thing started small and grew into this book. All in perfect timing. This is me reaching back out to those original readers, my dear friends, and celebrating what we created and shared. To the new readers, I hope you'll find the rhythm and magic that sparked this multitude of campfire stories.

So go ahead and make a pot of coffee and a campfire; we have *much* to cover, my friends.

From the Outside,

Number 2

Chapter One

Practice Makes Perfect-ish

Monday, January 21, 2013 – Practice Makes Perfect-ish

Location: Nashville, Tennessee – 118 days until starting the A.T.

Here we go! To start the trail journal, I am writing about one of the many practice backpacking trips that we've done since deciding to hike the Appalachian Trail. Our gear is working out really great; we use everything we bring. Today, the trail gave us our first opportunity to ford some raging waters. I was doing real good until I wasn't...got to hike with soaked socks and shoes and gaiters for a bit. Practice makes perfect-ish.

We ran into some folks I knew from days gone by. I said, "Hey Folks! I know y'all!" They all smiled and laughed, and we reminisced about the good old days of Catholic parochial school and big group camping trips out on the lake. Carey was not at all surprised that I ran into someone I knew.

For dinner we had a big pot of mac'n cheese, some string cheese, sausage bites, and a couple of Fruit Roll-Ups. Carey also made me a perfect cup of coffee. Camp life comes so naturally. We love it.

This is our first post for the journal. Many more to come! Thanks for checking in with us, and in the words of my dad, "Y'all be good, and I'll be better." Bye!

Now it's time for Carey's two cents:

We have to get out there to get it right.

Wow, I had no idea what I was getting myself into or how much joy this online trail journal would bring me for five months and three weeks, let alone 11 years. I didn't know how dedicated I would become to this daily practice of summarizing my day. I've always liked journaling, but it comes in waves. I'll get excited about something and do it for a little while then get bored and move on to something else. Boredom is my biggest enemy.

This trail journal became my therapist, my support group, my friend. My separate paper journals held my secrets, fears, frustrations, mistakes, and healings. They were my confidants. Ever wish you could bear your soul to a stranger on an airplane and never see them again? The trail journal was not that. This became a connection between writer and reader, a shared love for the Appalachian Trail and all that goes with it.

Thursday, January 31, 2013 – Preparing for the A.T.

Location: Nashville, Tennessee – 108 days until starting the A.T.

Hello again, this is journal entry #2, if anyone is keeping count. We are getting closer and closer to our departure date of May 17. We shall arrive to the trail via sea plane, thanks to Katahdin Air and my parents. The Delta tickets to Bangor, Maine, will be booked in the next week. All of the planning and anticipation is paying off as our departure date grows near. We're going to do a couple more weekend practice trips – practice makes perfect-ish, remember that.

Until then we are soaking up our time with the fur babies, family and friends. We are looking forward to getting our trail names.

I was making ready and thinking about all that was to come. We thought signing up for numerous "fun runs" with obstacle courses that would drag us through the mud might serve as good training exercises. My future muddy experiences on the A.T. were not quite as intense as being covered in mud from my ears down to my toes but damn near at times. It was a good practice experience for hiking the trail.

So, what are some other ways to prepare? I don't think there is a way to truly physically or mentally prepare for this thing. It comes with the experience. But I do think it was helpful for me, both physically and mentally, to get outside of my comfort zone and literally test the mud. I'm talking about hiking in bad weather, testing my gear, and staying in cold wet clothes for the day. The best tip is to be okay with come what may. Everybody's different, and this is such a personal experience. I can't tell you how to do it; I think part of the journey is figuring it out for oneself. I can make recommendations about gear, but these companies are improving their products all the time.

I had the gear, the savings, the house and fur babies covered, and I had the excitement for the adventure. That was key for me! I could not ignore my curiosities about the A.T. Everything was in motion.

A word on trail names. Trail names are magical. Most often, they happen organically out on the trail, usually because of a funny or frequent experience, a preference, or a conviction; they are a truly inspired moment of magic when they are revealed. The puns are fun! Thru-hikers are an interesting group of people; they willingly walk away from society to be free in the woods and become a new version of themselves. Sometimes in my head, I play around with trail names for my coworkers without them knowing it: Coleslaw, Broccoli Rob, Ja'Mall Bangs.

At my previous job, there was a whole lunch crowd with nicknames that could have easily been trail names: Sassafrass, Mrs. Winners, Hot Puddin', Bruce (she was the boss), Baby Momma, Manders, Sh'Merle, Baby Lewis, TCrunk, and Ginja' Spice. Trail names are sacred, and I think everyone should have one. In order to get one, you just have to get out there and hike. More to come on the rules of trail names. One of my editors took a rafting trip down the Salmon River in Idaho and gave everyone "river names" inspired by this book. Now I want a river name!

Saturday, February 2, 2013 – Chop, Chop, Lettuce and Tomato

Location: Nashville, Tennessee – 106 days until starting the A.T.

It is possible to step out of the norm to do something incredible. If we can do it, you can do it! In the words of my dad, "chop chop, lettuce and tomato." Translation: LET'S GO!

Carey's two cents:

Don't over plan. It's going to happen the way it happens.

Carey was in overdrive with the logistical plans of this adventure, while I was in heaven with all the gear research. We bought and tested different types of water purifiers and I read everything I could about the best lightweight backpacking gear options on the market. We were both consumed by our tasks and it was all we could talk about.

Thankfully we trusted each other's suggestions and information. I knew the planning part was Carey's forte, and she knew my obsession with gear was very real. Altogether it took us two years to fully prepare for this adventure, and I think that's a realistic amount of time to save up enough funds, nail down the perfect gear, and allow family to stew over the decision.

The hard part was waiting. I was working at a non-profit in town and was not giving it my best efforts. I was so distracted by my goal and timeline. Surely this is the norm for anyone about to embark on a big adventure. I had to keep reminding myself to stay the course. It was like standing at the starting line, revving my engine, and seeing this never-ending countdown...

Tuesday, February 19, 2013 – Introductions

Location: Tracy City, Tennessee – 89 days until starting the A.T.

Hi folks, I'm Margie. Born and raised in Nashville, Tennessee. The first time I heard about hiking the trail was when I was about nine years old on a visit to Kentucky with my parents, and I met my mom's cousin Phil. He had a ton of tiny boxes stacked up in this one room of his home; I asked him what they were for, and he said, "That's my food for hiking the Appalachian Trail. You should do it one day when you're older."

Well, it's here! I'm finally doing it! I mean, the start date is coming up in less than 13 weeks. Carey and I have been preparing for our thru hike for over two years, but we talk about it every day.

And I'm Carey. Originally from up north, which is why I moved down to Tennessee. I'm pumped to be taking on this incredible journey. I didn't know anything about the A.T. until Marge mentioned it. After constantly thinking about it for two years straight, I'm ready for the adventure.

No emails, no office phone, no dress code, no deodorant, ha! We can't wait to be outside! Thanks so much to our families and close friends who have helped us prepare. There's sure to be stories to share along the way.

Happy Trails, Marge & Carey

Carey's Two Cents:

Marge is the one who will be writing the most. I'm good with my two cents. That's all I need.

It's true that I had taken the reins for the journal entries, and Carey kept her parts brief. She is a very efficient individual, and I appreciated that. You'll see, though, that we switched roles in social situations on this adventure. A fun and natural social experiment! Someone once told me that authors are generally introverts, and I agree with that for myself. I mean, my moon and ascendent are both in Scorpio if that tells ya anything (i.e., big emotions, intensely private, Gemini mask). It's like I'm over here with one hand waving a fancy sparkly distraction while living in a dark hidden cave at the same time. Good luck analyzing that one.

One thing's for sure, the journal entries are consistent. They were sugar-coated just enough to tell a good story but kept my parents from picking me up off the trail for safety reasons.

Friday, March 1, 2013 – Ain't Gonna Be As Long As It Has Been

Location: Nashville, Tennessee – 79 days until starting the A.T.

It's going to feel so surreal the morning we board our plane and say "see ya soon" to loved-ones. We're ready. We've talked about it for so long. Looking forward to our A.T. Send-off Party! In the words of my dad, "It ain't gonna be as long as it has been."

Carey's two cents:

I enjoyed working my 9 to 5; got us free flights to Maine.

At this point we were looking at two and half months before we said, "see ya soon." I was dying! It was like that feeling of getting one of your training wheels caught on something and just pedaling so fast but going nowhere. I couldn't sleep; I was over-eating; and I was a terrible listener.

I remember being in meetings at work feeling a hundred percent disconnected. I had become totally committed to this idea and felt a nearly uncontrollable drive to pursue it. I had the single-minded determination to make this big shift of uprooting my life, and there was no way of stopping it. Also, everything was falling into place, and I could see that this was really happening. I can be extremely patient in some regards, but when I'm excited about something – forget it. On long family car rides to the beach, my dad would say, "We're halfway there" when we were actually almost there. It drove me nuts!

Carey traveled full time for work; every week she was flying out to another state racking up those frequent flyer miles from Delta Airlines. I was always amazed when she talked about the amount of points she and her coworkers had saved up. I wonder what it's like to have over 200,000 points? Sometimes I'll give myself one point for various reasons, but this game of frequent flyer miles and points and status can get real competitive. I'm grateful that we were able to use her points to our advantage. We even got to walk across the fancy red SkyMiles carpet like "royalty" or even worse. I felt and looked like one of the Clampetts.

Saturday, March 30, 2013 – Be Extreme

Location: Nashville, Tennessee – 50 days until starting the A.T.

Just got back from the West Coast visiting family and had an awesome time. The trees and the mountains were so majestic and beautiful, and the snow was crazy deep. We hope Katahdin isn't that bad. If it is, we'll never get started.

There were 67 inches of snow at Crater Lake near Klamath Falls, Oregon, and we walked to the edge just to scare the pants off my dad. It worked (DO NOT DO THAT!). Although the West Coast was amazing and different, we could not stop thinking about hiking the A.T. We saw the sign for the P.C.T. (Pacific Crest Trail) on the way up to Crater Lake and that only fanned the flame. Our start date is nearing, as is our retirement from the good old 9 to 5.

Now let me tell you this, the state of Oregon rocks because there is no sales tax. We stopped in the local REI and found our tent we plan to use for the A.T.; we used both our dividends combined with one 20% discount and no sales tax and saved $325.50!

It's really starting to feel like the beginning is finally getting close. In the words of my dad, "Be extreme." Translation: Be good and have a good time.

Carey's two cents:

None of this would be possible without my parents. They agreed to move in and look after the house and fur babies while we are gone. I love my parents!

A huge thank you to Carey's parents. They were living our dream as full-time RVers. They could come and go as they pleased and earned the right to do so. It worked out perfectly. They took great care of our fur babies and the house while we were gone. We had all the bills on auto-draft. We didn't have to worry about anything back home, which was great because we had enough to think about out on the trail. It was such a gift to walk away from the house for almost six months worry-free.

Thursday, May 2, 2013 – There's No Going Back

Location: Nashville, Tennessee – 17 days until starting the A.T.

Two weeks and counting! Since our last entry, we have both retired from our jobs, sold the car, set up our finances, and practiced fording a river. Today's adventure had us waist high in water, and it was a great test for our gear and our mental state.

*We'd like to give special shout outs to the following people: Emily Culpep-
per, our banker; Alexander Hamilton, our financial advisor; Baby Lewis,
just because; JMAC, for the bar-b-q; Sahara Divine, for being awesome;
TCrunk, for life; and all our friends and especially our families…and our
pets.*

Now, I'd like to pass the mic over to Carey for her two cents:

*These next couple of weeks will be over before we know it. All that is left
is to fly to Maine and hike home. Thanks to all of those who are thinking
about us. We appreciate you.*

Here's the inside scoop: An absolute and total meltdown happened
to both of us. Somewhere in this timeframe, Carey was on a flight home
from a work trip and got super emotional thinking about quitting her
lucrative job to hike in the woods. Walking away from the stability of
steady incomes gave us nervous breakdowns. For days, I wept holding
my dog so close that I almost suffocated him.

We had been so programmed for worry and fear that pulling the plug
on a great job to do something that has no guarantees of security felt
scary and foolish. We had to fight all the "what if" scenarios that tried to
get in the way of our leap of faith.

I was walking away from a career that spanned almost eight years, and
I did not have a plan for what to do next. I'd saved up enough money
to auto-draft my mortgage for a few months; Carey had a general idea of
how much we could spend on this adventure despite not knowing exactly how long it was going to take to cross the finish line. No major health
insurance! Who did I think I was? A rich person with endless funds?
What *if* something terrible happened out there? It was a hard pillow to
sleep on not having answers to these questions, but this adventure was
already in motion.

There was no going back.

Sunday, May 12, 2013 – The A.T. Send-off Party

Location: Nashville, Tennessee – Seven days until starting the A.T.

What a great party! We had so much fun having all our friends and family over for our A.T. Send-off Party! You all made us feel so loved, and you encouraged us with your questions and curiosity about the trail. We've got plenty of toilet paper now, thanks to y'all.

Five more days until we fly out of Nashville, and we will be updating our trail journal along the way. Y'all keep checking in from time to time and be sure to leave us a message on the guestbook.

Happy Trails,

Marge and Carey

Carey's two cents:

To everyone who wasn't there, we could feel your excitement as if you were there. In this short time we have before leaving, I want to go rock climbing and mountain biking as much as possible. Let the countdown begin!

The send-off party was really fun. Both our families came, friends from work, and even our banker joined the party. My buddy, JMAC, catered the event with his delicious bar-b-q, and we had a lovely spread of sides, salads, and chips. My sister somehow got her hands on a huge vinyl banner and painted a sign for us. We also had fun activities and games about the Appalachian Trail. It was the perfect way to express appreciation, make sure everyone knew we loved them, and provided closure to the old life before embarking on this new adventure.

For some reason everyone thought we were going to bring our entire supply of toilet paper with us from the start. Roller board luggage full of toilet paper.

Freedom and nerves had started settling in; I was already free from my 9 to 5 job, and I was putting all my focus on the adventure...and hugging my dog, Peejay. I spooned him a lot before I left – more so than usual. I think he was ready for me to go too.

Tuesday, May 14, 2013 – Twenty Thousand Calories and Twenty Thousand Tears

Location: Nashville, Tennessee – Five days until starting the A.T.

We have a total of 20,000 calories for both of us for our first stretch of Maine. Good thing we're starting out fat and happy. Carey and I always bring way too much food on our backpacking trips, but this time we feel like we hit the nail on the head. It feels good to have all that packed up...we're really getting close now! We're ready to start hiking.

Carey's two cents:

My backpack feels lightweight minus the food. We can always eat more to lessen the load. Praying for Plan A.

Tears. Tears upon tears for me.

I have lived in close proximity to my parents for all of my life. I went to college in Chattanooga, Tennessee, graduated in 2004, and came right back to Nashville, Tennessee. Started my career in July 2006, and I bought a townhouse two streets down from my parents' house in October that same year. Everything had been right here in my safe little bubble.

Hell, I'd never even been to Virginia before, and now I had one-way tickets to Maine so I could walk home. The sheer enormity of what was ahead felt daunting to say the least but like I said, it was already in motion, and there was no going back.

I was caught in the middle of being incredibly ready to go and scared all at the same time. My emotions were intense but brief. I don't like feeling sad or negative; and I don't do well in that space. I'm a master of distraction and was hiding from my fears. I needed to get going.

So, here we go, folks! Welcome to the beginning of the actual adventure; I hope you feel enticed enough to press on and find out what actually happened out there. I have done my best to fully tell all the stories from this point on, and I can't wait to talk with you about them.

Chapter Two

Maine, Part One: 100 Mile Wilderness

Friday, May 17, 2013 - Three One-way Flights to Millinocket, Maine

Location: Millinocket, Maine – Two days until starting the A.T.

The alarm clock was set for 4 a.m. but Carey and I got up at 3:57 a.m. Our wonderful parents dropped us off at the airport, and we hugged and cried just a little bit saying, "See ya real soon!"

It took three one-way flights to get us all the way to Abol Bridge Campground just outside of Millinocket, Maine.

We'd like to give a shout out to Gary, our cab driver, who dropped us off at Katahdin Air, which is where we connected with our last flight of the day on the fantastic seaplane! The owner of Katahdin Air was our seaplane pilot, and he was so funny and so helpful; we strongly urge everyone we know and don't know to hook up with Katahdin Air for a seaplane adventure. It was the absolute best way to get to Millinocket! Our camp is set up, our bellies are full, and we are anxious for the next part of our adventure. Tonight's low is 41 degrees.

Now it's time for Carey's two cents:

My final meal in town was a Big Mac Combo Meal from McDonald's with a creamy milkshake. Extra calories. And Marge said it, go check out Katahdin Air. You won't regret it!

This was my first time flying first class anywhere, and it felt...embarrassingly special. I was enjoying my orange juice as other passengers were steadying their carry-on luggage to keep from knocking my armrest on their way to their seats in the back. I looked and felt out of place, for sure, but it was a nice gesture of a "final luxury" before this unfolding of the unknown in the woods.

I, of course, recognized one of the passengers who was making her way towards the back of the plane. She is a well-known fly-fishing instructor and was thrilled to see us embarking on our A.T. adventure. In true native Nashvillian fashion, we hadn't even left the ground yet and already saw someone we knew.

This was also my first ride in a seaplane. It was very compact, loud, and minimal compared to the big planes. I felt way more engaged with the actions of flying, similar to the feeling of riding a rollercoaster. Every drop, turn, twist, and bump was exposed and absorbed by my body. I loved it! We were given headsets to put on once we got settled inside the tiny space, and he had Pink Floyd's "Hey You" playing in between his commentary. I could barely understand a word he said through the headset – not because of the noise from the engines but rather because of his thick Maine accent. I felt like there were a lot of hard "r's" in just about every word; plus, he spoke so fast that it took me a full uncomfortable pause to work out the translation in my head before I could respond.

The owner of Katahdin Air was not only our seaplane pilot, but he also drove us in his work truck to Abol Bridge Campground. I felt nervous getting out of his truck thinking about how this was our last bit of security, and the trail was really upon us now. I also remember reading about the dreaded black flies which were in their peak season with our arrival into Millinocket. I kid you not, as soon as we hopped out of his truck, he was wishing us good luck on our trip with three or four tiny black flies swarming at each of his eyelids and nostrils. It didn't bother him one bit.

My final thought was, "Shitballs, we're really doing this."

Saturday, May 18, 2013 – Katahdin Stream Campground

Location: Millinocket, Maine, 1 day until starting the A.T.

Katahdin was calling our names today, so we packed up our packs and hiked the Blueberry Ledges Trail to Katahdin Stream Campground. We kept our eyes peeled for moose along the way, but only found moose poop. Hey, we'll take what we can get!

The daytime high was about 63 degrees and tonight's low is forecasted for the 20s. We met a guy named Mike who was car-camping, and he was asking us about all our plans and excited for us to summit Katahdin in the morning; then, we got word from the park ranger that the trails would not open for a "few more days." That's why we are heading for the 100 Mile Wilderness in the morning.

You might have heard about "trail magic" on the A.T. It's a beautiful thing! We might have experienced some "trail barter" this evening...we found some firewood and I thought if we brought it over to the folks who were car camping across from us that they might offer us some of their food; it worked. We got a bunch of food and a couple of Kahlua Mudslides! Even though we have to skip Katahdin first, we're still having an amazing experience up here in Maine.

Now, over to Carey for her two cents:

There's a small chance Katahdin will be open in the morning; if not, then we move to Plan D. I'm good with the plans. Something that's important for me out here is talking with good people along the way. I'm excited to see who else we meet.

So, yeah, we got to the base of Katahdin and it was still closed. We had traveled all that way to be told we couldn't hike up to the top due to all the snow melt, and the park ranger couldn't give us any further information other than it would take "a few more days" to open. I had failed to read the part about Katahdin typically not being accessible until the very end of May or early June in my research. On May 18, we were still at least a week out from it's opening.

Having only packed a certain amount of food to get through the 100 Mile Wilderness, waiting around was costing us time, money, energy, and...well, food. We had to make the decision to go ahead and start the 100 Mile Wilderness and plan to come back to complete Katahdin afterwards. The 100 Mile Wilderness starts after about a 13 mile stretch within Baxter State Park, so we got ourselves in the right frame of mind for it and got a "good night's sleep."

The nervous and excited feeling in the pit of my stomach was keeping me awake all night. We were now facing the start of our hike, no more procrastination or distraction. It was go time.

Rumor has it we stayed where Mr. Henry David Thoreau stayed during his quest for the summit of Katahdin. I sat and meditated about that very thought for a good while. His book *Walden* is one of my favorites. I find it very inspiring, along with everything Mr. John Muir wrote, and I realize I'll never write as profoundly as they did. For me, it's as simple as, "We're out here, and we're doin' it."

Sunday, May 19, 2013 – Caution Sign for the 100 Mile Wilderness

Starting Location: Katahdin Stream Campground → Destination: Hurd Brook

Today's Miles: 13.40 – Total Miles: 24.40

We accomplished our first actual miles on the A.T. today! Got a little teary eyed when we first saw the A.T. southbound caution sign.

Today was beautiful. We forded two rivers that were moving pretty fast. Couldn't begin to pronounce the rivers by their actual names. Lots of crazy names up here in Maine. We ran into two guys carrying their kayaks on the trail who were very nice and excited for us to be heading southbound.

They pronounced the name of the river that we had just crossed, and I swear I thought he said "Nana-kissed-a-kuala" river. I could be totally wrong, but that's what I heard, and it made us laugh all afternoon.

Two cents from Carey, ready go:

Three blisters and a near wipeout on day one. All I could think is at least I'm not hiking with my kayak.

The southbound caution sign for the 100 Mile Wilderness reads: CAUTION! IT IS 100 MILES SOUTH TO THE NEAREST TOWN AT MONSON. THERE ARE NO PLACES TO OBTAIN SUPPLIES OR GET HELP UNTIL MONSON. DO NOT ATTEMPT UNLESS YOU HAVE A MINIMUM OF 10 DAYS SUPPLIES AND ARE FULLY EQUIPPED. THIS IS THE LONGEST WILDERNESS SECTION OF THE ENTIRE A.T. AND ITS DIFFICULTY SHOULD NOT BE UNDERESTIMATED.

My gut reaction to that sign was, "Mercy Sakes Alive!" That is a true statement made by me, and I believe it could also be a shorter paraphrased version of the sign made by the Maine Appalachian Trail Club. This section is *not* to be underestimated.

Our first night in the 100 Mile Wilderness took some adjustment. We stayed in our tent instead of the three-walled shelter. This shelter looked like something out of a reenactment scene, like I was allowed to look inside to get a sense of what hikers' lives were like but it was only for show. This particular shelter had a bunch of round logs laid together as the floor, which I imagined would be like laying down on a big box of crayons. I thought, "Maybe it's good for the back muscles?" I will admit that I never got used to the shelters being open in the front. At the time, I felt more secure in my thin four-walled nylon tent.

It was also my first introduction to the darkest dark night I had ever experienced out in the woods. We decided to sleep in earplugs and take a Benadryl to help us get through the first night. The thought was, "Well, if something is gonna get us, we don't want to know about it."

I also didn't realize all the shelters had a notebook and pen for hikers to sign and write a little something during their stay. Like a guestbook but referred to as a logbook. I sure had a good time signing and reading those all the way down to Georgia. Thru hikers are an entertaining bunch.

Hanging from the ceiling was a string with a twig tied to the end and a plastic barrier in the middle. This was for hanging backpacks. The plastic piece in the middle made it harder for the mice, rats, and squirrels to get to the bag and chew through it. It takes some impressive rat acrobats to maneuver around those plastic pieces to get to the goods, but they are professionals.

Thinking back, I'm nostalgic about the sight of an A.T. shelter. It marked our whereabouts on the trail, provided a temporary safe zone against the elements, and served as an authentic stamp of approval for the day's work. There was something unique about each shelter out there on the trail whether design, shape, size, or smell. I think what I really miss is the need to rely on one.

Man, I wish I was there right now...

Monday, May 20, 2013 – Rainbow Stream and Meeting Lieutenant

Starting Location: Hurd Brook → Destination: Rainbow Stream Shelter

Today's Miles: 11.50 – Trip Miles: 35.90

We got our trail names today! Marge is now Number 2, and Carey is now Puma.

Today was hard. Super muddy, rainy, cold, but awesome! We saw 32 piles of moose poop, and Puma asked what the difference was between moose poop and human poop on the trail? I said, the difference is that we speak English and know better.

We also met our first fellow Southbounder; his name is Lieutenant. He was so excited to see other hikers and is going to hike with us a little bit.

We've got a big day tomorrow and need some rest. We love our families so much and think about you often. Talk to you soon!

Puma's two cents:

Announcing four blisters so far. Also I fell today, and I saw it coming and shouted, "Number one!" Number 2 got confused.

I was actually given my trail name by the park ranger back at Katahdin who told us that it was not going to open and had us sign the hiker log when we decided to go ahead with the 100 Mile Wilderness section. He said to me, "You are Number 2," meaning that I was the second Southbounder to start the A.T. in 2013. Lieutenant was the first hiker to start heading southbound in 2013.

For Carey's trail name, you should know that she has always been tough. I mean, she has three older brothers, so the name "Puma" came naturally to her. And I will say that it fit her the whole way. Pumas can do it all. They are great climbers, can handle all types of weather, and are very agile and powerful.

The tradition of the trail name is that you may veto up to two times for your trail name. If you don't like the trail name by the third try, it's too late, and that is your given trail name. We both accepted our first round names.

So, here we are into our second full day on the A.T. It was rainy and cold and wet, the usual forecast, and we were hiking along when we came to this very large tree that had fallen and blocked the path. The girth of this tree was comparable to the size of a large pillar. While we were deciding whether to try to climb over it or push our way under it through the mud, we heard gun shots...close by. We looked at each other in disbelief and gave a nervous holler of, "Hikers! Hikers here!" No response. We dropped to the ground and crawled under the tree scraping our packs and water bladders on the bark and our knees through the mud. We didn't have any orange on at the time, just perfectly blended greens and a "Touch of Grey." No other shots were fired, but the woods are so dense up there that we never saw or heard any other signs of human activity.

Crossing the slippery bog bridge across Rainbow Stream to get to Rainbow Stream Shelter was interesting. A bog bridge is typically two logs laid side by side with a width of about one foot across. These logs are very slippery, even with the added chainsaw scratches for traction. Another key element to bog bridges is that there is no handrail. That water was moving fast and splashing up onto the skinny little bridge making me really have to focus on my task. My eyes were trying not to cross while looking at this raging water right under my feet. It felt like it took me forever to reach the other side, and I sure was thankful for a successful crossing. It must have been 25 yards! The water was very deep in addition to moving swiftly. We could not use our trekking poles as a steady guide because they would have been washed away, and for that to have happened on our second night would have totally sucked.

Now, let's talk about Lieutenant. He was in his early 20s, from the West Coast, and he had a tattoo of a dishwasher on his chest. Very friendly and approachable. He was in his sleeping bag inside the shelter watching us cross the bog bridge. He'd been there for at least a day waiting for someone, anyone, to show up on the trail. We did use caution realizing that we'd be staying with our first fellow Southbounder ("SOBO" for short), but we quickly embraced him as one of our own.

His pack must have weighed at least 75 pounds. He wore canvas pants, like a Carhartt or Dickies brand, and he and I had the same exact navy blue Bass Pro Shop hat. I was thrilled! He had brought a collapsible fishing pole thinking he'd be able to catch some fish along the way, but in that fast-paced water, there was zero chance of that happening.

Puma and I had more than enough food to get us through the 100 Mile Wilderness, so we took Lieutenant under our wing and fed him along the way. He was so helpful, too. In his appreciation of us sharing our food with him, he'd go filter the water at the end of each day. I must note that the water was always down a steep hill or was an additional half mile or more away, but he was always up for the challenge.

We were grateful for each other, and I'm so happy we got to share the trail with him all the way to the end of the 100 Mile Wilderness.

Tuesday, May 21, 2013 - Nahmakanta Stream

Starting Location: Rainbow Stream → Destination: Nahmakanta
Stream

Today's Miles: 14 – Trip Miles: 49.90

*Another rough and tumble day! We are so happy to have our buddy,
Lieutenant, with us! We're a team now. This evening, we made our first
fire and dried out our wet socks. There are bog bridges, roots, rocks, mountains, and streams that we battle every day. Another week and we'll be
through the 100 Mile Wilderness.*

Puma, you got any change?

*My blisters are healing. The secret is keeping my socks dry. It's tough out
here, and everything I was hoping for.*

Meanwhile at the shelter, hanging from the rafters was my backpack
and my navy blue Bass Pro Shop hat. Lieutenant hung up his pants, shirt,
and camo jacket, and Puma added her backpack, our tent, and tarp all in
an effort of drying things out. Thank goodness for paracord and long
johns.

I remember sitting in the shelter and feeling uneasy about...well,
everything. I was adjusting to my new reality, and it took me some time to
get there, I'd say at least the entire 100 Mile Wilderness. I was physically
fit enough, but this was a new level of extreme for me. I was working through getting comfortable with the uncomfortable (i.e., relentless
ruggedness and cold rainy weather). Also, the high-water crossings were
making me extremely nervous, but I reached a level of comfort that I
could hang out with for most of the day.

Day three of hiking the Appalachian Trail, and Puma's already providing medical care to her feet like that of a nurse in the Civil War. She
was so smart about it. At the end of our day, she would take her soggy

socks off and soak (i.e., ice) her feet in the frigid mountain streams. I tried it but felt like I was gonna lose a toe if I left it in that ice cold water. Good thing she got her trail name early on, too, because she might have wound up with a third time's the charm trail name like "Twisted Blister" or "The Movie Blister" or "Sister Blister" or "Are You There, Blister? It's Me, Blister."

Wednesday, May 22, 2013 – Coopers Brook

Starting Location: Nahmakanta Stream → Destination: Coopers Brook

Today's Miles: 16 – Trip Miles: 65.90

We saw a MOOSE today! It was standing on the trail about 100 yards staring at us then it ran off down the trail. It was so awesome and BIG...no antlers.

Today was a lot of miles and very eventful. We did eight miles before stopping at a shelter for lunch and got the chance to use "Fort Relief," which is the famous two-seater privy. Me and Puma peed at the same time!

We had to cross many streams today. For one of them we had to get down on all fours to crawl across a bridge that was super skinny and about six feet up from the water. Another time, we had to hold on to a climbing rope that stretched across the river. We saw old timey farm equipment, lots of rocks, tons of slippery bog bridges, and the Sun for a little bit.

The shelter is wonderful tonight! We're drying out our gear. We have a nice fire, and we've eaten really, really good. Thank you, Mountain House meals...and Cumberland Transit.

We think about all our support back home and appreciate all your prayers. I promise to catch up with you when we get to Monson! I can feel that we are getting stronger every day. Onward and upward!

Signing off,

Number 2

Puma's two cents:

One more blister on the underside of my large toe. All the other blisters are healing okay. Our thinking process has changed so much out here in this short time. Back home, we'd step around dog poop, but now we hike through moose poop. I love this life.

Maine often did not provide a bog bridge over the water crossings. Instead there would be a long, weathered string of climbing rope with worn, fuzzy knots that'd been tied between two trees. Sometimes we used it, sometimes we didn't, but every time was an adventure. There was no rock hoppin' across the creeks; we were in it up to our knees, thighs, hips, or chest. We found out the hard way how snow melt can make all water sources swell to the hazardous size of "oh shit!"

Within the bowels of the 100 Mile Wilderness is the famous two-seater privy. We definitely used it, and I *did* write in the hiker logbook while using it. It was so cold and wet outside on the trail; I will admit that I had thoughts of wishing we could have hung out inside the privy for just a couple of hours to recharge. You know it's crazy weather when the thought of hanging out inside the composting toilet seems like a good idea.

Thursday, May 23, 2013 – Rivers to Ford and Feeling Fussy

Starting Location: Coopers Brook → Destination: Logan

Today's Miles: 11.20 – Trip Miles: 77.10

Today started our climb towards White Cap Mountain. We did just over 11 miles and took our time getting to 2,400 feet elevation. Only had to cross a couple of rivers.

For dinner, we had some awesome macaroni and cheese to keep us warm in the shelter up here in the clouds. Tonight we're sharing the shelter with a couple guys from Tampa who are heading to Katahdin. Guess we caught each other at the midway point in the 100 Mile Wilderness.

We're ready to crank through these next five days to get to Monson. Y'all keep praying for us, and we'll keep on climbing. We've formed a team with our good friend and fellow hiker, Lieutenant, and our team's name is MEGA SOBO (Get it? Maine to Georgia Southbound). Thanks for reading.

Love,

Number 2

Puma's two cents:

Nothing much to say right now. We'll see about tomorrow after conquering White Cap Mountain.

Wrestling with hard hiking, I remember being "in it" at this point. My feet and knees and body were very achy, and we were starting to get quiet. By that I mean no more silly chit-chat while hiking because we were tired and hungry and cold and a little fussy. This is day five in the 100 Mile Wilderness with five more days to go.

I remember sitting in the shelter with the "Tamp Guys" (that's the name they gave themselves) and feeling zapped of all human connection. If memory serves, they were just doing the 100 Mile Wilderness, and I was feeling pushed to my physical and emotional limits making me at the very least anti-social. Wrestling with this harder level of hiking right out of the gate, I separated myself from the group. Foolishly, I started hiking faster no matter if I was going up or down; I was moving and not waiting on anyone. Big mistake.

Friday, May 24, 2013 – White Cap Mountain

Starting Location: Logan → Destination: Shelter

Today's Miles: 7.20 – Trip Miles: 84.30

Well, we can definitely kiss the flat and flowy terrain goodbye. We conquered not three but FOUR three thousand foot plus mountains today. My knees were screaming at me by the end of it all. Puma and Lieutenant helped me out.

Today was very windy and very cold and very wet...but we're getting closer and closer to Monson. All is well! We're turning in early tonight to rest up for another day in paradise! Wish you were here! Send us your prayers.

Love,

Number 2

Puma's two cents:

I might have cussed out loud today, but it actually means I'm having a good time.

White Cap Mountain was one of these big "up and overs" for the day. The trail maintenance was incredible on this mountain. The trail crew had built hundreds of stairs made of rock all the way to the top, and I reckon doing four sets of these stairs got the best of my knees.

I kept apologizing for having to take breaks in the wind and rain and cold. I was just as frustrated as Puma and Lieutenant were about this, but it felt like a knife was being dug into both of my knees with every step. My knees started to swell up which made me look even more awkward since I have my mother's skinny "chicken legs," as she likes to call them.

Hiking super fast uphill was probably my downfall. I learned to rise above my fussiness and told myself, "Go slowly up the hills." I conserved my energy and let my mind have the most amazing daydreams while taking in the natural beauty of Maine's backcountry.

This was the absolute most rugged hiking I had ever experienced. There was standing water everywhere. Just right there on the trail, knee-high water on top of White Cap Mountain. No designated stream, just water *everywhere*. I was cold and wet and flirting with hypothermia. Conditions like that bring perspective, and it was clear that we had to band together to get through the 100 Mile Wilderness.

Saturday, May 25, 2013 – West Branch Pleasant River and Chairback Mountain

Starting Location: Shelter → Destination: Chairback Mountain

Today's Miles: 9.90 – Trip Miles: 94.20

Unbelievable adventures today! We locked arms and crossed the West Branch Pleasant River. It was moving fast and was up to our waist most of the time AND it was about 30 yards wide. We communicated and worked as a team the whole way. As soon as we got to the other side, we hollered and screamed with joy and relief; then I cried again.

The trail has opened the emotional floodgates for me, and the rain tries hard to disguise my tears, but my puffy red eyes give me away every time. I am so incredibly proud of my teammates, Puma and Lieutenant.

The second hairy situation was conquering Chairback Mountain with its elevation gain, strong winds, and hand-over-hand boulder climbing. When we actually reached the real summit of Chairback Mountain, we could see for hundreds of miles. The wind was blowing so much that it filled up our rain jackets, so we looked like marshmallow people waving at the clouds. So stupid and awesome.

Y'all, I am telling you right now that this adventure is hard and totally, totally amazing. We are two nights and three days away from walking into Monson. Your encouraging messages and prayers keep us going. We love all of you!

Still crying,

Number 2

Puma Power Hour:

Dang! What...a...rush!

What was it really like crossing the West Branch Pleasant River? It was our first *big* ford not only because it was a long distance, but it was also waist-high freezing cold water. Everything went numb from the waist down. Lieutenant was upstream, Puma in the middle, and me at the downstream end of our chain link formation.

The water was moving so swiftly that it was definitely *not* a good idea to lift our feet too far up off the rocky bed. It was more of a shuffle move than taking a step. Let's just say that I learned to adopt this method very quickly because when I did try to take an actual step, the power of the current made my leg go all "Elvis-like" under water. It was hard to get myself back under control, but thankfully, I did.

I learned then that strong currents are not to be underestimated. Especially when one is out in the remote wilderness, it is not a good idea to get overpowered by the rushing current. Still pretty scary for me to think about even 11 years later. But we did make it across, and we don't have to worry about that anymore.

I have this condition that affects the blood flow in my hands called Raynaud's Syndrome. Basically, my fingers turn white and sting real bad if they get too cold. I remember when we made it to the other side of the river, we did hug, and I did cry some tears of relief. I also remember joking that someone stole my gloves because I couldn't find them. This made us all laugh pretty hard because we hadn't seen a soul going in our direction in over a week. "Great. Someone stole my gloves..."

A word about Chairback Mountain: This one had a bunch of false summits for me. I'd start to get my hopes up thinking we were nearing the top, but noooo. The wind was very strong, and we were just shy of bouldering up the side of this mountain when the wind gusts would completely fill our rain jackets and pack covers. We really did look like marshmallow people up there. Just big puffed pieces of candy stuck to the rockface, like we belonged in Harry McClintock's song "Big Rock Candy Mountain."

Sunday, May 26, 2013 – Cloud Pond Shelter

Starting Location: Chairback Mountain → Destination: Cloud Pond Shelter

Today's Miles: 6.90 – Trip Miles: 101.10

What an adventure today! We saw our first black bear, prolly weighed about 250 pounds. He was on the trail a ways up from us and I stopped and showed Puma. She went straight into safety mode and said, "Okay! Wave your arms and holler!" So immediately we sounded like two ranch hands and the bear just trampled off. It was so cool to see the bear in his natural habitat. We took about a five to seven minute break to give the bear time to get ahead of us. We didn't see him again. We did continue to sing all 79 verses of "She'll Be Comin Round the Mountain When She Comes" just to make our presence know.

The climbs were intense today, but we are stronger for it. The wind and the rain are with us all the time, and the trail is full of standing water and mud...BUT we're almost to Monson! Being out here for over a week has been so rewarding and hard and awesome all at the same time.

Today, we started what I like to call "dirty talk" and by that I mean we started talking about FOOD! Here's a strand of dirty words; chicken pot stickers BLT pizza with goat cheese and a little more bacon.

We have been rewarding ourselves at the end of the day with bite size sausages, and we call these "victory sausages." It truly is the best part of the day.

Sure, I've cried a good bit of this trip, but we've laughed a lot, too. Thanks for following us, and please don't stop sending us your thoughts and prayers.

Holler at y'all soon!

Number 2

Now, make some noise forrrr Puma Pump:

I knew it was smart to make ourselves known to the bear, but I missed my opportunity to get a picture. We played it safe, and that's what counts.

Thinking back on this morning and giving my advice to future A.T. hikers, one of the best ways to prepare for the A.T. is to wake up and put on cold wet clothes. Then make sure to stay in these clothes until just before dinner time.

Physically putting on cold wet clothes never got easier, but mentally knowing this *will* happen a bunch of times in a row made me stronger. Imagine waking up in a toasty sleeping bag with a beautiful view of pristine nature. Now, imagine having to change out of those toasty long johns into the cold shorts and shirt that never dried out from the day before...oh, and your shoes and socks are frozen, too. I guess you could put your socks, shoes, shorts, and t-shirt in the freezer overnight, and then put them on first thing in the morning. If I can do it, you can do it. It helps if you make up some silly bluegrass call and response song while doing it like, "It's a mighty cold sock (That's a mighty cold sock!)."

One of the best gear purchases we made were the Sea to Summit dry compression sacks. I kept my sleeping bag and my long johns dry the entire hike. Thank you very much.

We ended up seeing a total of 11 bears during our whole experience on the A.T. I will say that I did get used to seeing them in the woods, and we never had any problems with them either.

Hanging a bear bag to keep our food safe from bears at night, which we did a lot of, sometimes gave us a problem. You can research exactly how to hang a bear bag, but let me tell you what they don't tell you...there's never a perfect limb off a perfect tree. Most of the time, we just had to work with what we had, and tossing the bear bag was entertainment for the evening. Equivalent to binge watching three episodes of your favorite show on Netflix.

Lieutenant decided that he was going to finish the 100 Mile Wilderness with us and fly back home to the West Coast. I guess he realized that a thru hike was going to take a lot more resources than he could afford at the time. So, he asked us if we wanted to buy the handgun he had with him so that he could put that money towards the cost of his plane ticket back home. Puma and I agreed that it was a fine idea, especially since I had my carry permit with me for this trip. Yes, you read that correctly, I brought my carry permit with me but no gun. And now we found ourselves with a handgun. Crazy.

Lieutenant had so many boxes of ammo, too. His backpack was unbelievably heavy. So we spent one of the evenings out on the trail shooting the extra rounds of ammo at this mound of dirt. It felt exhilarating, foolish, and smart all at the same time. I apologize to any hikers who might have heard a bunch of gunshots that one night, but I'm pretty sure we were alone out there. Although that's what Puma and I thought back on our second day of the 100 Mile Wilderness when we heard gunshots and hit the ground.

Monday, May 27, 2013 – Wilson Brook

Starting Location: Cloud Pond Shelter → Destination: Wilson Brook
Today's Miles: 8.70 – Trip Miles: 109.80

What a day it has been, my friends. We woke up to blue sky and sunshine...and 35 degree air. The first part of the day was just spectacular! We climbed up to the top of Barren Mountain, which had a lookout tower held down by four cables. For just a minute we thought it was a telephone tower, but that would have been ridiculous. We'd been out of civilization for so long that the tower stole our attention away from the trail for a few minutes as we discussed what it could have possibly been used for waaaay up on the tippy top of Barren Mountain. Puma said it was a lookout for wildfires...I heard her wrong and thought she said it was a lookout for "wildflowers." I'm sure it's the latter of the two.

After Barren Mountain, we had a lovely lunch at a shelter that was about halfway through our mileage for the day. Again, the sun was shining, and we were relatively warm. After lunch, we knew we had to ford a few streams, ponds, and brooks to get to our final destination for the night. Let me tell you something, the ponds are way bigger than the streams and the brooks can knock you down. Let's just say that after one particular ford of a particular "brook," we were all crying and hugging. It was insane. We have a video that we'll share in a presentation at the end of this adventure. Please stay tuned.

Y'all, we're walking into Monson tomorrow. Only 11 more miles until we get to enjoy some of the things we all take for granted (like a shower, or even a door, or a cup of orange juice, or...a shower, you know what I mean!).

We have thoroughly enjoyed this experience, especially the fox squirrel that glared at us for making our "home" the other night in the Chairback Mountain shelter. That squirrel was so mad I'm pretty sure I saw his cute little middle finger go straight up in the air.

We love reading your wonderful posts on our journal, and yes, Cousin Maureen, we have plenty of toilet paper. Thanks for asking!

So great to hear from all our family and friends. You all keep us going. Truly, you do. Everyone gets a hug today...a virtual hug.

With everything I have,

Number 2

Live and in concert, Puma performs:

Blister update, all of them are almost healed. Between my duct tape and torn pieces of bandana, I am getting by. That one on the underside of my large toe is sore; brushed it against my sleeping bag this morning and it hurt. I hate when there's no trail sign letting us know we made it to the top of a mountain. Feels wrong without it.

It was a beautiful day. The sun was shining, and it was perfect hiking weather. We had a lovely day all the way up to the bank of the Big Wilson Brook...and this is where things got dicey.

This was white water rapids. I mean, it reminded me of the Ocoee River down in Cherokee National Forest, which is where they held the 1996 Olympic kayaking event.

So here we were, standing on the bank, watching this super-fast water rushing by us. Lieutenant had barely made it across, but he was made of rubber bands and magic. Puma and I stuffed excess items inside our backpacks and strapped them tightly to our backs. I secured my hat, locked arms with Puma, and we started across.

The water was very strong, so we were both doing the shuffle move instead of trying to lift our feet up too far off the rocky streambed.

Rushing water was at our shoulders. We got about three quarters of the way to the other side, and the water started to overpower us. I was getting pulled away from Puma's armlock, and the panic started. The water was just too strong for us to hold on to each other anymore. Right before I lost my grip, I looked at Lieutenant standing on the rock maybe five feet from me and hollered his name. I saw his eyes go big and full of fear right before I got swept away by the current.

I remember being tossed and jostled, banging my body against big rocks. I remember holding my breath for what felt like forever. I remember hearing my inner voice asking, "Is this IT? Is this my *dying moment?*" The scariest part was being unable to gain control of my own body. I wasn't strong enough to pull my arms in or put my feet first. Hell, I couldn't even find my feet!

Then a very brief moment of respite when my head came to the surface. It was less than a second, but in that moment, I can still remember seeing the sun shining over top of the tree line with the gorgeous blue sky behind it. In my nano-second of relief, I took a breath and whispered out loud, "Save me." I didn't shout it, I didn't sing it, I didn't say it in my head, I just said it calmly as a request.

Back under the water I went, but only for another second. It was like an immediate answer to my request. I felt my body get pushed out of the strong current and back to the brookside where I started. I was crying and threw up a little bit. My knees were bloody, and I was definitely in shock for a minute. I crawled to the bank and heard Lieutenant yelling, "Where's Puma?" I looked down stream and saw her going through a similar "pull together" since she, too, had gotten swept away by the current. Puma and I reconvened back on the original side of the trail, and we both decided that we would respect the waters from here on out.

We yelled at Lieutenant to come back across to our side. He made it, but it wasn't easy. I couldn't watch. This experience gave me nightmares for many nights and even years after. I will never forget the moment I asked for my life. It was a very special and powerful moment.

Tuesday, May 28, 2013 – Shaw's in Monson, Maine

Starting Location: Wilson Brook → Destination: Shaw's in Monson, Maine

Today's Miles: 3 – Trip Miles: 112.80

To wake up this morning to blue skies and the sun shining was the best gift we could have received. The mileage was cut short today because the rivers were just too dangerous to ford. So, we called the lovely ladies at Shaw's in Monson, told them our exact location, and they told us to follow the railroad tracks until we reached Elliotsville Road. Jen picked us up after about a two hour hike along the tracks in her green Honda CRV. It was such a wonderful sight for our tired eyes.

The first thing I did when we arrived at Shaw's was have a bag of Doritos and a Coke as the owner showed us to our rooms. Hot showers followed by laundry, and then pizza and beer to hold us over until dinner at the Lakeshore Pub just up the street.

The Lakeshore Pub was really, really great. Tiny, wooden bar filled with locals who were all drinking and telling stories. There was another hiker there who we invited to join us at our table; her name was Reign. She had just gone for an afternoon hike, but we swapped stories with her while chowing down on our bacon cheeseburgers.

The owner of the bar was hilarious. And everyone in the entire place ended up telling stories about all the funny hikers they have seen and met over the years. We're looking forward to the "all you can eat breakfast"

tomorrow morning at Shaw's. I've been thinking about a cup of coffee for a long time...

This is just the beginning, folks. We have a long way home, but the experiences have been absolutely incredible. I'm looking forward to another day of rest tomorrow, which will also allow us time to plan our next jaunt.

We've laughed, we've cried, and we're still here pushing towards our first state line. Thank you so much to all who are cheering us on along the way by sending us messages on our guest book. We LOVE hearing from you!

There really are great people in this country, and we have definitely found some in the great state of Maine. Thanks for reading and y'all be good to each other. This has been a really great day.

All our love,

Number 2 and Puma

When Jen picked us up, I could feel my tail go between my legs. She didn't have to say anything about how foolish we were for trying to cross Wilson Brook. She drove us to Shaw's hostel in Monson and nobody said a word. We just looked out the car windows at the beautiful scenery, and I was in my head realizing that we missed a good chance of dying out there. The miles were not worth our lives.

Arriving at Shaw's was surreal because we were...inside. We were the only hikers because it was still a little early for the hustle and bustle of the thru-hiking season. Ms. Shan, the owner, was a no-nonsense kind of lady, and as she was showing us the place and telling us the rules, I guess she could see the tears welling up in my eyes. She knew what had happened since word travels fast around a small town, and she asked if we had told our moms about it. That was enough to send me over the edge, and she just wrapped me up in the most amazing stand-in mom hug of my life. I crumbled in her arms, and it was exactly what I needed.

I grabbed a bag of Doritos and ate them while I sniffled and listened to the rest of her instructions for our stay.

Ms. Shan also told us that we were real lucky to have landed back on the original side of the Wilson Brook because if we had made it across, we would have been stuck between the Big Wilson Brook and the Little Wilson Brook. She said the Little Wilson was even worse than the Big Wilson.

I want to thank Ms. Shan for that much needed hug. It was everything I needed to feel restored.

Wednesday, May 29, 2013 – Still at Shaw's

Starting Location: Shaw's → Destination: Shaw's

Today's Miles: 0 – Trip Miles: 112.80

Another day of rest is in order for us. We had a great bargain come our way with splitting a shuttle up to Katahdin on Friday with a couple of hiker friends from Tampa who we met in the 100 Mile Wilderness. We worked out all those details earlier this afternoon.

Today, we ate food, watched television, elevated and iced our knees and ankles. We did go to the local outfitter for better rain gear and food rations for our next little bit to Caratunk, which we will start on Saturday.

The people here in Monson are absolutely wonderful. We even scored free pepperoni pizza from the lady working behind the counter at the local gas station.

According to Puma's calculations, we should be crossing into New Hampshire in less than 21 days. Boy, it'll feel so great to have our first state line under our belts!

Sitting around during the day today was very hard because we want to keep moving forward, but it was real important to ice and elevate and rest.

We're feeling good and ready for the next leg of this adventure. Y'all keep reading and checking in and we'll keep the journal entries coming. Thanks for following us!

Y'all are awesome,

Number 2

Now, here's your very own copy of The Puma Press:

Anyone who knows me absolutely knows how much I dislike wasting time. We've been resting for about three days. Ready to get to the top of Katahdin.

I needed to process. We paid extra to have one of the upstairs bedrooms in Shaw's hostel. There were two twin beds and two chests of drawers, and the room was slathered in the pinkest pink color from floor to ceiling. Being in this bedroom, as pink as it was (pink has never been my color), brought me so much comfort. I took some time to myself to write in my personal journal about almost drowning. I just needed to sit alone in the bed, under the covers, with some tea, and write down all the emotions I was having inside. It was a much-needed release.

I kept my own personal journals throughout the trail in addition to the online journal. Once I filled up one of my personal journals, I mailed it to a dear friend of mine for safekeeping. He probably still has them somewhere safe to this day.

I also called my sister on the phone and had to come clean about what had just happened. I couldn't call my parents because, remember, I was trying to protect them from all the scary details. I couldn't call my brother because I missed him too much. My sister is the baby of the family and is also a travel nurse, so she was used to emotional scary shit. I cried telling her all about it, and she made me feel so much better. I was like, "Mermz, I almost died!" And she was all, "*WHAT!*" Then she said,

"If you can cough, you can breathe." Trauma nurses have the best senses of humor. Probably make for seriously good thru hikers, too.

Thursday, May 30, 2013 – Spring Creek Bar-B-Q in Monson, Maine

Starting Location: Shaw's → Destination: Spring Creek Bar-B-Q in Monson, Maine

Today's Miles: 0 – Trip Miles: 112.80

I'd like to dedicate this journal entry to my good buddy, JMAC. Today we stopped in at Spring Creek Bar-B-Q in Monson, Maine. Puma and I just split a large pork bar-b-q sandwich with pickles and onion. In the words of my mother, "It's so good, it'll make you wanna slap your mother!"

They are also famous for their "fiddlehead salad," which we missed by a week. We're gonna put that on our list of things to do when we get back up this way on future flyfishing trips with family.

Well, we'll be heading out bright and early tomorrow morning for Katahdin!

We're gonna pack our bags tonight, keep staring at the A.T. maps all over the walls in Shaw's, and eat some more food until we fall asleep tonight.

Peace, love, and brisket,

Number 2

Order Up! Puma, scattered and smothered:

That bar-b-q sandwich cancels out any weight I lost in the 100 Mile Wilderness.

I'm always down for some good bar-b-q, and this place was making my mouth water as we walked up the drive. The smell of that bar-b-q was so good; it was worth the struggle of the 100 Mile Wilderness. This place was fun, unique, quaint, and delicious. I was super bummed to miss out on the fiddlehead salad, but we were too early in the season. Fiddleheads really do look like tiny green fiddle heads; a fact that makes me squint, ponder, and smile. It was later on that I found out Mr. Anthony Bourdain had found his way to this very bar-b-q joint back in 2010. This place was delicious, and I would love to make a special trip to Monson to have that bar-b-q sandwich again – this time with a side order of the fiddlehead salad.

I wasn't feeling homesick. I loved exploring the town of Monson so much, and everything was new and different. The three of us, Lieutenant, Puma, and myself, had just completed an extreme backpacking experience together, and he was heading home. We really bonded with him, and I will never forget his agreeable demeanor, terrible gear selections, and lovely smile. I was grateful to have shared the experience with him. Lieutenant played such an important role in this adventure. We needed him and he needed us.

Friday, May 31, 2013 – Mount Katahdin

Starting Location: Spring Creek Bar-B-Q in Monson, Maine → Destination: Katahdin

Today's Miles: 5.20 – Trip Miles: 118

Put a fork in Katahdin because it is DONE, folks! We shuttled up to Katahdin Stream Campground with our friends, the Tampa Guys, and all of us got our pictures with the famous sign. That was no easy hike; they start ya out easy, then throw in some steps and a detour (special circumstance, I guess), and they finish you off with some awesome boulder climbing with the wind at your back.

At the top Puma said, "We're only a few thousand feet from approved inflight use of electronic devices on an airplane." That really spoke to me.

The Tableland was really cool, too; that's the part where you think you're close, but then you figure out that you still have about one-ish more miles to the actual sign at the top. We both inhaled a Snickers, took a swig from our water bladders, and focused on the rocky trail to the top. I could have sworn someone kept pushing the sign back for fun, but they didn't. When we finally reached the top and the beloved sign, we got some really great pictures of ourselves.

On the way back down Katahdin, we could see two storms brewing and coming our way fast. I told Puma, I said, "Puma, we gotta' scoot!" We did not want to be exposed above tree line with those storms. Coming down was a lot faster than going up! It was incredible to see how Katahdin has its own weather bubble. Felt bad for the young folks still working their way up to the top. I'm sure they were fine.

We took our time...slow and steady...started hiking at 8 a.m. and finished at 4:38 p.m. Felt really great to get my knees moving again and get some miles under our belts.

Tomorrow, we're off to Caratunk! We feel so special reading everyone's posts on our journal. Thanks a bunch!

Overjoyed that Katahdin is complete. Thinking of you, our friends.

Sincerely,

Number 2

Now, give me a P! Now, give me an UMA! Puma's in the house! Seriously, she's laying down on a twin mattress right now. What you got to say, Puma?

I'm so relieved Katahdin is done. Switching my brain to the rest of the trail now.

Going up Katahdin is no walk in the park. I mean, you got to *want* to get to the top of this thing by climbing up and over boulders using sketchy rusted rebar that juts out from these massive rocks, and watching your footing. We heard of this fellow hiker who had gone up Katahdin shortly after us, and he ended up having to get life-flighted off the mountain because a boulder broke loose and roughed him up pretty good. We had *just* come through there!

There are warning signs about how dangerous it can be on top of Katahdin in bad weather. It has its own weather system up there, and I think we were lucky to have had the time to snap some silly photos. After we were done, Puma wanted to sit down and have a snack on the mountain top. I guess she didn't feel her hair starting to stand up on her head from the electrical currents that were growing stronger and stronger. I looked up and gave the signal that we needed to get out of there fast. We literally ran down this mountain to get out of the lightning storm and made it to the tree line just as the rain hit.

Chapter Three

Maine, Part Two

Saturday, June 1, 2013 – Sir Moxie and the Mosquito Buffet

Starting Location: Bald Mountain Road → Destination: Bald Mountain Brook Lean-to

Today's Miles: 8.70 – Trip Miles: 126.70

Man, was it hard to get going this morning after our restful stay at Shaw's. Puma and I both had butterflies in our stomachs as we were getting our backpacks on and all the familiar aches and pains of those first couple of miles were reminding us about our goal.

We must dedicate this entry to the wonderful Sir Moxie Bald, the cutest Pomeranian mix you ever saw. Sir Moxie belongs to Ms. Shan who runs Shaw's. You absolutely MUST meet Sir Moxie when you stay at Shaw's. The reason we dedicate this journal entry to Sir Moxie Bald this fine day is because we successfully made it over Moxie Bald today JUST before a thunderstorm arrived. We actually made it all the way down the other side when the rain fell, and it was glorious.

The bugs have come out in full force, my friends. We are sleeping in our bug nets and hoping not to drool in them too, too bad. Puma sneezed inside

her bug net on the way down Moxie Bald, and I laughed a little bit inside. It really does stink when you do that. A word to the wise, don't forget to lift up your bug net before you sneeze, burp, or spit.

It feels good to be back on the trail, and we look forward to meeting more friends out here. All the best to you who are just getting started! We look forward to crossing paths with you. And a special thank you to those people who we don't even know who have signed our trail journal. It's just really so cool to hear from you. We do take requests, so if there's a song or a movie that you would like for me to reference in some silly or cheesy way during the "pass the mic over to Puma" segment of our show, please don't hesitate to tell us and I'll see what I can do. In the words of my dad, here's a "great big huge large voluminous" HUG to all our friends and especially our families. We really, really love YOU!

Everyone gets a free bug net tonight,

Number 2

Make way for Puma Cottontail, comin' down the Appalachian Trail (I always thought my dad was the one who wrote "Peter Cottontail." He also always told me he used to cook chicken with Dolly Parton). Puma, now back to you:

A million thank yous to all the volunteers who maintain the trails. This is a tough trail and without you it would be awful.

You would have to see it to believe it. This was the day I counted 86 mosquito bites on the back of my thighs. That's right, folks, 86 mosquito bites. I wasn't able to count them until we got to the Sterling Inn the next day, but June 1 was the day I acquired all 86 of them. I actually lost count at 86, so likely there were around 93 or so.

The trail was very marshy, the weather during the day was humid, and the mosquitos were living their best lives. I felt like an all-you-can-eat buffet at a mosquito casino. I even put on my raincoat, hood cinched down tight, bug net over top, just to try to keep them off me. That's how my legs got annihilated.

Hiking in a raincoat in humid conditions is probably close to what one of those sweat suits feels like. I remember seeing guys in high school wearing trash bags under their sweatshirts while working out so they could cut weight for wrestling or whatever. I was hiking hard to get through that cesspool of mosquito larva because it was nasty and irritating. Their bites stung like a shot on the back of my thighs, and I felt every one of them over and over again. They were relentless, and we had to keep moving in order for it to stop.

And oh, the itchiness drove me nuts. Pretty sure I bathed in Calamine lotion the next day. Just painted it on the back of my thighs. Never in my life have I had another bug bite experience like that. I've been stung by a wasp a couple of times over the years, and I *might* take that over getting that many mosquito bites ever again.

Sunday, June 2, 2013 – Caratunk and The Sterling Inn

Starting Location: Bald Mountain Brook Lean-to → Destination: Sterling Inn

Today's Miles: 14.70 – Trip Miles: 141.40

Left the shelter at 6:30 a.m. and headed for our first small victory, the top of Pleasant Pond Mountain. We thought we were close to the top and decided to take advantage of our clear cell phone reception. I called my parents and my dad said, "We just started cooking the eggs, y'all come on by!" I started crying.

The sky was clear, and the sun was hot on top of those rocky balds. During our break on the side of Pleasant Pond Mountain, Puma and I shared a Snickers, drank lots of water, and checked our trail journal to see if we had

received any messages. We had! Those messages also made us cry in a really great sort of way.

It took us a while to get over Pleasant Pond Mountain, but comin' down wasn't too bad. The rain had started on our way down, but we were not far from the Pleasant Pond lean-to. We stopped for some lunch, dried out our socks, filtered some more water, and suited back up again to push on to our next town, Caratunk.

It was a great decision to hike into town because 1. I got a bar-b-q cheddar burger 2. Puma got a little bit of ice cream 3. We're resting at the Sterling Inn 4. Today is my 31st birthday. I will never forget this birthday for as long as I live.

It rained most of the day, but we handled it well and made it to town. I'm pooped. Thank you to all who have been praying for us to have safe travels, it's working. I love you all.

Thanks for reading,

Number 2

Now, quietly turn your attention to the side stage for Puma's story time hour:

I'm working harder now than when I had my 9 to 5 job.

Let me give you the scoop about the Sterling Inn way back in 2013. It was a sleepy and spooky kind of place. The big wrap-around porch was lovely, but there was an eerie feeling inside. The dining room had probably four or five round tables set for a dinner party, but all the glasses and dishes were covered in dust. No lights were on, and for some reason, I felt like I was walking through the dining room of the Titanic – complete with ghosts.

The floors were uneven and every step we climbed to our second-floor room creaked. There was one other hiker staying there and nobody else.

He gave me and Puma the heebie geebies. I think we put a chair up against the doorknob that night, just to be safe.

Killing time and reflecting on our day, I remember sitting on the front porch looking out over the sprawling landscape. There was a two-lane road that stretched on out of sight, a small house across the street, and the dense green belt of evergreens that stared back at me. I'd get lost in thought and then grasp my pearls when these massive logging semi-trucks would blast through the scene at 90 miles per hour down this modest road. They'd appear out of nowhere! Good luck to all the humans, turtles, and chickens trying to cross that road. Funny how we had come to feel safer in the woods versus in civilization, and I still feel that way.

Monday, June 3, 2013 – The Sterling Inn and Tornado Warnings

Starting Location: Sterling Inn, Caratunk, Maine → Destination: Sterling Inn

Today's Miles: 0 – Trip Miles: 141.40

Sometimes it's hard to say goodbye. We had a funeral today. A funeral was held for Puma's big toenail and my toenail of the toe next to my big toe. It happened early this afternoon. I sang my best rendition of "Go Rest High on That Mountain" as Puma simply brushed the toenails off the front porch and into the grass.

One can totally survive without a toenail, I just never had this happen before. You've heard of "trail maintenance" but this was full on "toe maintenance." When Puma was done removing her nail, I had the same amazement as I did when I found out what was behind the wardrobe doors in "The Lion, the Witch, and the Wardrobe."

We rested up pretty good today and mapped out our next plan to Stratton – heading for the "Bigelows." With a healthy plan of attack; I know we shall conquer.

I forgot to tell you folks about how we made it to the Sterling Inn. Here's the skinny (yeah right, y'all already know I ramble): we had JUST walked down the trail to US 201 and stood in the rain for maybe 45 seconds when a lady named Sam pulled to the side and asked if she could give us a ride.

We gladly took her up on the offer, threw our packs and sticks in the back of her lovely new Suburban (after we figured out how to open the hatchback – nothing's easy in the rain), and she took us to the Sterling Inn. On the way, Sam told us that there had been tornado warnings in the area. Touching base with parents was the first order of business when we got to a phone (my dad watches the weather like a hawk). Thank you so much to Sam for bringing us in from the rain before it started to blow sideways.

During our stay, we've enjoyed the food at Northern Outfitter's Kennebec Pub and Brewery. The burgers and fries were excellent.

Alas, it's time to keep pushing onward, my friends. The trail journal needs to be fed and the only way to do that is to keep on hiking. Your posts mean the world to us, and we thank you from the bottom of our hearts for following along.

I'd like to give a special shout out to my work family. Somebody tell Baby Lewis that I already listened to one Christmas carol.

Family and friends, we love you so much.

Respectfully Yours,

Number 2

And now, a reading from the Book of Puma:

I'm missing my kitty cats this evening, but it's a little bit easier when the place we are staying has polydactyl cats. Ready for our canoe ferry in the morning.

We had been hiking in the rain most of the day, and it's really not bad under the cover of the trees. When we reached the road, we weren't really looking for a ride, just trying to spy the marker for the trail, when this big black Suburban pulled up. Sam was concerned, and we were clueless. She told us to get in because of the tornadic activity in the area. We never questioned her instruction, just followed her orders. It amazes me now how trusting we were in certain moments out on the trail.

She filled us in on the weather warnings that had surrounded us all day. She was also the one who said we needed to call our parents to check in with them. Thanks, Sam! I also remember getting the backseat very muddy and apologizing for it. She was just a lovely human who had no hesitations about helping us out, even though we didn't know we needed it. I hope that kind of trail magic still exists after all these years.

Tuesday, June 4, 2013 – West Cary Pond Lean-to and Muddy Temper Tantrums

Starting Location: Sterling Inn → Destination: West Carey Pond Lean-to

Today's Miles: 14 – Trip Miles: 155.40

It was a late start today by our standards, but today was the day that we got to be canoed across the Kennebec River by our wonderful canoeing guide, Darren. We had his number listed in "The A.T. Guide" book and called him up. All A.T. hikers use this service because the Kennebec is considered too dangerous to ford due to fluctuating water levels and currents thanks to the Harris Dam.

Our instructions were to meet him at the river by 9:00 a.m., but the cool part is that both parties were a little bit early. We actually started hiking at 9:00 a.m. on the other side. Way to go, Darren!

Canoeing across the Kennebec, I had hoped we could sing a couple of verses of "What Shall We Do with a Drunken Sailor" in unison but no dice. Puma took the front of the canoe, I had the middle seat, and Darren steered us across as Puma paddled her heart out. It was moving pretty swiftly, so Darren had us paddle upstream a good bit then cut out into the channel. I did my best to sit still and follow orders, which were to sit still. It was smooth sailing, and we truly appreciate Darren and his canoeing expertise.

The rest of the day was flowy terrain with parts of it still super muddy. You know, the kind of mud that suctions your entire shoe off. Good ol' American mud. Every day, Puma and I hike through thick mud. We've come to expect it, and it can slow down our stride at times, but we just keep on truckin'.

I had a hard time finding my stride this morning and had a weak moment after the hundredth time I slipped into the thick mud. Puma stood back as I stabbed the mud with both trekking poles about 20 times very quickly, then she said, "Did you want that recorded?" The moment had past but I'm sure it will happen again, like prolly tomorrow.

I'm proud of us for making it to the West Carry Pond lean-to from the Kennebec today. We were spent by the time we got here, but we set ourselves up for easier miles through the Bigelows.

I'm so thankful to be hiking the trail and to be sharing this trail journal with all of you. Does anyone have any questions, comments, jokes, or testimonies? (I had a professor in college who would end every class with that question; funny how things stick in my brain.)

Y'all are fantastic! Keep checking in on us. We're heading for the Bigelows tomorrow. Stay out of the mud.

Yours truly,

Number 2

And now, a letter from Puma:

To Maine,

A thief has taken your first layer of dirt uncovering all of your rocks and roots.

Good luck finding who did it,

Puma

It's true, I was in a funk having a hard time finding my stride with all the mud. It would suck my shoe right off my foot, and it wasn't like I hadn't tied my shoes with double knots. I double knot my shoes to this day. I'd had enough and made a bunch of stabby jabs at the mud. I felt better after my release, and I seem to recall pulling out my iPod to listen to a song or two.

Rarely did I pull out my iPod because I was paranoid about it dying out there when I really needed it. I had about 25 songs on it. That was it, and they seriously helped me get through some of the tougher moments. My brain has a large library of songs, but sometimes I needed to tune everything out and just listen to an artist who could help me recenter and refocus.

Who was I listening to? Kenny Chesney and Jimmy Buffett. Yes, those two helped me get through the cold, the mud, and the rain by transporting my brain to the warm sunny beach. I felt warmth from their tunes, and they reminded me to be happy with every moment.

Puma was patient with me and graciously understood that I just needed a moment to get myself back on the path. We had one rule for backpacking and that was allowing for unlimited timeouts. Anyone could call for a timeout as many times as they needed. I still uphold this rule to this day.

Wednesday, June 5, 2013 – Safford Notch Campsite and the Perfect Bear Bag

Starting Location: West Carey Pond Lean-to → Destination: Safford Notch Campsite

Today's Miles: 13 – Trip Miles: 168.40

Our greatest gift today was the amazingly beautiful weather we had all day long. This time our socks and feet stayed dry from start to finish.

Originally, our plan for today was to only do seven-ish miles and stop at the shelter, but we reached the shelter around 12:30 p.m. We ate some lunch, called my parents on my super powerful flip phone, and decided to push on past Little Bigelow. I am SO glad we made that decision because now we've only got five miles over Avery Peak and Bigelow West Peak to get to our next shelter tomorrow. Granted, it's gonna take us about three hours to do the first two miles, but I'm just focusing on the fact that it's only five miles.

We met a very nice lady today on top of Little Bigelow; her name was Lynn, and she was just doing a day hike. Let me tell you folks that Ms. Lynn was trucking right behind us and smiling the whole way. I started to joke with Puma about how funny it would be if by the time we had huffed and puffed our way to the top Lynn might just be sitting there chilling out. And it was almost the case! As soon as I opened my big mouth, here comes Lynn! She was a serious hiker and likes to hike out west, too. We told her about our trail journal and gabbed more than we prolly should have about things that were just side notes (i.e., like how we got our trail names and such). Lynn, if you're out there, ma'am, you are a great hiker and I hope I keep hiking like you have. (I might be "hiking" using a 4x4 Segway after this adventure).

Today's views were outstanding, and I am just so incredibly thankful for the nicer weather. The plan is to bag the next two mountains before more rain comes in tomorrow evening...remember, we've only got five miles.

My belly is full, we're in our tent tonight, and I'm ready to hit the night night trail so that we can get it done tomorrow. Y'all are in our thoughts all the time, and we LOVE hearing from you. It truly makes a difference in our day.

Dreaming of a catapult over the mountains tomorrow.

Fat and happy,

Number 2

Please welcome our next guest, Puma Pume McPumerson:

Newsflash: An entire day of dry socks! Doesn't matter though, I still got one additional blister. The remaining blisters are all better, though. Also, we successfully hung the inaugural bear bag this evening. Textbook form.

I was shocked rereading that this was our first evening hanging a bear bag. I know we had hung them in the shelters, but I'm just as surprised as you are about having been out there on the trail for a few weeks already and just now getting to hang the bear bag. Hmm!

A specific food hanging method recommended by the A.T.C. is called the P.C.T. (Pacific Crest Trail) Method. We did not know about this method at the time and simply tied our paracord off around the tree. Bears have figured out how to swat at the knot tied around the tree resulting in the food landing in their laps. The P.C.T Method eliminates that situation by using a carabiner and a toggle to hold the food bag at the perfect distance from the tree and the ground. There's a lot more information about how to successfully rig the P.C.T. Method online, and I will be using this method on my future adventures.

I can tell you that we had many, many more times hanging the bear bag along the way. I would make the sound of the *SportsCenter Top 10 Plays* when we got it hung. It was the little things.

Thursday, June 6, 2013 - Horns Pond Lean-to and My Great Aunt Ruth

Starting Location: Safford Notch Campsite → Destination: Horns Pond Lean-to

Today's Miles: 5.30 – Trip Miles: 173.70

Well, y'all, we made it over top of three big peaks today: Avery, West Peak of Bigelow, and the South Horn...and we did all of this by 12:45 p.m. The rain started falling at 1:00 p.m., but we were already enjoying our victory sausages by that time. God bless the victory sausage.

The climbs were pretty intense today; many times, when we came to the base of another climb, we'd just stop and look up thinking, "This goes up forever," but we make it every time, slow and steady. We've had amazing cell service over the past couple of days, and I got a real treat today during one of our breaks where we stalled before going up a really long climb. Puma said, "We got a post from Aunt Ruth?" I stopped right then and teared up a little bit because I immediately knew that was from my Great Aunt Ruth. Oh my word, Aunt Ruth, your post meant the world to me!

Puma had to listen to me rekindle all my wonderful memories and stories I have of Uncle Jimmy and Aunt Ruth and then pretty much the rest of the Sanders genealogy for a good while as we were walking down the other side of that particular mountain. Thanks be to Puma for puttin' up with me and my stories.

It felt so nice coming into the shelter early today, early enough for me and Puma to take a nap before dinner. We have a tight schedule and like to get as much rest as we can before our next day begins.

Tomorrow, we've only got 5.3 miles to our next town of Stratton, and that means we get in early and have almost two days to just eat and eat and eat. The "hiker hunger" appetite might have started today. We accept any and all food challenges.

We are tucked in for the night and look forward to tomorrow. Y'all stay with us, and we'll keep the journals coming. Thanks for reading, I love my family! I also love beef stew from Mountain House meals.

Signing off with beef stew breath,

Number 2

Now it's...one for the muddy, two for the snow, three to get leggy, now, go! Puma go:

Another day of dry socks. We'll see how long it lasts.

Aunt Ruth's message on the trail journal guestbook: *I am enjoying all your blogs. I don't think I will be making the trip. At 87, it tires me out just reading about it. Take care of yourselves and come home safe. Love you, Aunt Ruth*

My Aunt Ruth lived to be 94 years old. I remember going to see her and Uncle Jimmy down in Vero Beach, Florida, when I was a kid. Their home had the perfect lanai, or "Florida room" as we called it, and there were coconuts carved into pirate faces in every corner. My parents always told me that Uncle Jimmy was a real pirate, and Aunt Ruth was his muse.

Matter of fact, he was a very talented painter in addition to being a pirate, and I infamously assisted him with his unfinished portrait of Aunt Ruth by taking the initiative of painting her ruby red lips. As a two-year-old, what I lacked in a balanced brush stroke, I made up for with the vibrance of color choice. With love, to Uncle Jimmy and Aunt Ruth, and all the family.

Friday, June 7, 2013 – Maine Roadhouse and the Wolf Burger

Starting Location: Horns Pond Lean-to → Destination: Maine Road-house in Stratton

Today's Miles: 5.30 – Trip Miles: 179

Today's first three miles were pretty much straight down over rocks and roots. Puma and I had our air brakes on most of the way down, and you really gotta' concentrate when everything is wet. Those rocks were pretty much like stepping on wet slate in a downward direction. The last couple of miles into Stratton flew by, and we had Liz from the Maine Roadhouse pick us up from the trail by 9:50 a.m.

The Maine Roadhouse is just too cute, I'm talkin' even the toilet paper holder is adorable. We're in a lovely room with a DOOR, and we pretty much have the place all to ourselves. After laundry, hot showers, and a nap, we headed into town for our next food supply and some treats (i.e., Doritos, pizza flavored Combos – Puma refers to them as "combinations"...cute). We were also on the hunt for the famous Wolf Burger from the White Wolf Inn.

On the way into town, Puma checked our trail journal for any new posts for the day and saw one from Pamela, Milkman's wife. She put us on the lookout for him in Stratton today, so we thought it was a shot in the dark to find him, but we DID! I kid you not, as soon as we got into town, I heard a gentleman introducing himself to another hiker as "Milkman" and told Puma, "That's him!"

He seemed a little surprised that we knew his agenda so well, but then Puma showed him the post from Pamela, and he lovingly said, "That's my wife!" We explained that she gave us the tip on his arrival today. It was just so funny how that all worked out. We plan on catching up with him and swapping stories tomorrow. There you go, Mrs. Pamela! Ain't that just too funny.

A couple of days of rest for our knees is a good plan so we can get ready for the tough stretch ahead. We're closing in on our first state line, y'all!

As always, thanks for following us along the trail. Now, I gotta' go because my Wolf Burger is talkin' back to me. Thank goodness for adorable toilet paper holders.

All my love,

Number 2

In Maine, the Secretary of Slate, Ms. Puma Pumerton:

Today, I learned that there is nothing easy about this trail. Yesterday, I was assuming today would be an easy day, but it was tough. I won't make that mistake again.

Let's talk more about this Wolf Burger at the White Wolf Inn. What a great little bar and restaurant! I am a sucker for all things wolf-related. So, you can imagine how excited I was to find out about a wolf burger. No, it is not made of wolf meat; it is, however, big and mighty, just like a white wolf. The burger patty comes with bacon, sausage, mushrooms, lettuce, tomato, onions, *and* cheese. I think it stood six inches high off my plate. I was singing Duran Duran's "Hungry Like the Wolf" while eating this beast of a burger.

The extreme satisfaction that a long distance hiker feels when a large plate of food arrives to the table can be likened to that of a wolf catching its prey. I was depleted on fuel, and the Wolf Burger eased my ravenous hunger. On the appetizer menu (a.k.a. "Wolf Snacks") were "Curly Wolf

Whiskers" which are fried fiddleheads. Let's *all* go and get a few orders of these next time.

The Inn was cozy and quaint. It's a two-story building with a wrap-around porch, complete with flower boxes. The restaurant was downstairs. A little bit biker bar, a little bit diner, a great deal of delicious food and drink with an absolutely wonderful name.

Saturday, June 8, 2013 – Hike Your Own Hike

Starting Location: Maine Roadhouse → Destination: Maine Roadhouse

Today's Miles: 0 – Trip Miles: 179

We had the most enjoyable evening of dinner and conversation with Liz and Ralph Eustis of the Maine Roadhouse. Ralph made a delicious meal of grilled chicken, potatoes, carrots, and Liz made an arugula salad and treated us to her homemade bar-b-q sauce for the chicken. My heart skipped a beat when she offered us homemade bar-b-q sauce. I heard them snicker a little bit when I sopped up the chicken juice and leftover sauce on mine and Puma's plates with an entire loaf of bread.

We got lost in talking about Southern cuisine and travels. Liz and Ralph are two very cool people who we have thoroughly enjoyed hanging out with this past day and half. If you ever get the chance to stay in the storybook town of Stratton, Maine, we highly recommend the Maine Roadhouse. They will take great care of you.

Well, y'all, we head out bright and early tomorrow morning for our next town of Rangeley. We're getting into what some call "the hardest part" of the trail in southern Maine, but we are ready to rock! That state line is calling our names.

Hope you'll follow us to Rangeley; I'm sure there'll be stories to tell along the way. From our cell phone to your computer, we enjoy bringing you with us. Keep the posts coming.

Cornbread, crowder peas, homegrown sliced tomatoes, and turnip greens, that's what I'm talkin' 'bout!

Love y'all,

Number 2

Here now to sing her entire message, please welcome, the artist formerly known as Puma:

Got to speak with Milkman for a while today. Sounds like we are all heading out in the morning. We'll probably see him and Pamela in Gorham, New Hampshire. I found out how important it is to stretch out here. It actually works.

I remember Milkman was a really nice guy and fellow hiker, and he was committed to hitting every mile. I think Puma also appreciated his dedication to hitting every mile. At that time, I was not that hardcore. It was about the journey, and we had heard "hike your own hike" several times. To my knowledge, nobody really knows who coined that phrase, and I've read that people were repeating that mantra on the trail as far back as the 1980s. There are nay-sayers who will bark and gripe about the legitimacy of a thru hike, but I can tell you that I just never had any interest in judging anyone else's thru hike experience.

Milkman was a strong hiker, and he definitely started after us and passed us. So many people passed us. We were comfortable, and I think we were successful with nary an injury because we weren't pushing ourselves too hard. Milkman ended up getting hurt and had to get off the trail, but gosh, he was the nicest guy and fellow hiker.

To this day, I believe Puma could have completed this trail in a lot less time than five months and three weeks. The only hard timeline we had was making it home in time for Thanksgiving, which at this point felt like forever away. We were very fortunate to pick our pace every day. Puma studied *The A.T. Guide* maps and told me when to start and when to stop. She pointed me in the right direction and I was off!

To all hikers who managed to hit every inch of every mile, I lay my backpack and trekking poles at your feet. My hat's off to you for your dedication and perseverance. To all the current and future thru hikers on any trail, "Hike your own hike," as the saying goes. It's such a gift just to be out there.

Sunday, June 9, 2013 – Carrabassett River and Daydreams

Starting Location: Maine Roadhouse, Stratton → Destination: Carrabassett River

Today's Miles: 8.40 – Trip Miles: 187.40

We're getting into the 4,000 footers and the notches now. Came over the North Crocker and the South Crocker mountains; Puma quickly corrected me when I told her we were headed for the South Crotch Notch Mountains.

We had a really nice day of hiking today, and I think we're getting better at the longer climbs. My brain goes on auto pilot, and I think of random memories. Today's random memory was of when I was a child and I could almost go right back to the exact moment of what it felt like being in the seat that was attached to the back of my dad's bicycle. That rhythmic sway back and forth from his pedal pattern put me to sleep in no time. So sweet.

It's funny how our brains can put us in totally different places at totally different times. Climbing straight up for five miles is a good place for that; sometimes, you can even do it in a one-on-one meeting with your boss. (Love ya, Sass.)

*Y'all, we are heading for Sugarloaf Mountain tomorrow, and I day-
dream of that state line into New Hampshire regularly. We want to thank
you for all your support and love that you send. You are the light of our lives.
We'll holler at y'all tomorrow.*

Dreaming of my dog Peejay tonight,

Number 2

*Creating her own line of cleaning products, be sure to look for the amaz-
ing new Pumasol (not available in all stores):*

*This is the day I realized the mental stress of hiking the A.T. You have
to be in the right head space to get it done.*

It's absolutely true; I could be anywhere in the world while hiking
steadily up a mountain. Puma's mind was full of constant calculations
of mileage, while I was a million miles away. I'd make up little movies or
relive fun memories of anything and everything. It was such a privilege
to have that kind of freedom, day-in and day-out. Just knowing that all
I had to do was hike to the next point was so freeing. Just walking. I had
stepped away from a 9 to 5 job to daydream about anything *all day long.*
I never got bored with my daydreams.

Tackling a long-distance hike is physically hard, yes, but the mental
game, in my opinion, played a way bigger role, like Puma said. Taking on
such a feat with so many unknowns was a lot to comprehend and took
a lot of adjustment. We learned how to be loose with our plans which I
think played a major role in turning this dream into a reality.

Monday, June 10, 2013 — Poplar Ridge Lean-to

Starting Location: Carrabassett River → Destination: Poplar Ridge
Lean-to

Today's Miles: 13.10 – Trip Miles: 200.50

Today we started going up, and we also ended going up. Hiked for nine hours straight and the last little bit was puttin' a hurtin' on me mentally. Puma has said this before, but this thing is all mental. I had to put on my headphones to make it up the last stretch to Poplar Ridge. Wouldn't you know Jimmy Buffett's "Tin Cup Chalice" was rooting me on all the way to the top.

Today entailed tough climbs, two successful river fords, and lots of you know what...mud. It was sunny most of the day, and I'm sure glad we got across those rivers before the rain comes in tonight.

Puma and I kick it into high gear when the terrain is "flowy" as we say, and when we do kick it into high gear, we call it "boosting." By the end of the day, all my boosts were exhausted, but I'm so happy to be in this wonderful lean-to tonight.

We had a Lipton Cheddar Broccoli packet for dinner (still sharing at this point), and we also have a sweet peach tea with every dinner (also sharing the tea because neither one of us wants to get up and pee in the middle of the night).

The time has come to crawl into our warm sleeping bags and drift off to the Florida Keys. I wish you ALL a pleasant evening and know that we are thinking of you...yes, you. AND you. Sending big squeezes to all family and friends, and to our friends we don't know, we'll send y'all a koozie or coaster of your choice. Thanks for keeping up with us, really serious about that.

Just like the title of that wonderful books says, "Goodnight Moon."
Love,
Number 2
Puu whaa pitty, pitty pum, pitty Pume:

Number 2 hiked strong and fast today. I even had to run to catch her. There are some large mountains to hike up in the morning. It's probably going to rain.

All I have to say about this journal entry is: Thanks, Puma.

Tuesday, June 11, 2013 – Not So Stealth Tenting on the A.T.

Starting Location: Poplar Ridge Lean-to → Destination: Not So Stealth Tent Site

Today's Miles: 5 – Trip Miles: 205.50

Soooo, today was just not what we had planned, and I think we both realized that's how this whole Appalachian Trail thingy is gonna go from time to time.

We started out thinking today was going be our zero day (meaning no hiking this day) in the shelter because of all the rain we had heard was coming our way. We waited around until about 8:30 a.m. and decided to just push on through and see how far we could get. Only had nine-something miles planned anyway.

Y'all, we hiked up Saddleback Junior and the wind was strong enough to boss me around. The rain was coming down and the temperature had decided to sit at 40 degrees. Then we climbed up The Horn and that's where my extremities started to go numb from being so wet and cold from all the wind and the rain.

Puma and I started scouting out places to put our tent because we'd had enough by this point. We kept looking and hiking and looking and finally decided to just put it up right here on the trail. Yep, our tent is blocking the trail for the night (it's easy to get around; any hiker could do it). It took us both a good four hours to thaw out enough to work the zippers on our sleeping bags and jackets. But now, we are settled in, already had a hot meal of chicken teriyaki and rice, and I can feel my legs again.

Now, we wait. Checked the weather and it's not looking pretty for tomorrow either, but we'll think about that tomorrow. I'll keep y'all posted. Tonight, I'm dreaming of all the awesome family trips to the beach.

Thanks for reading,

Number 2

Hey! Who's that riding side-saddle with the really long skirt? Oh, it's Dr. Puma, medicine woman:

This was a rough day for climbing. It was my first time experiencing wind that strong. That was wild!

Being on top of these mountains in a storm is a recipe for disaster. The rain had chilled me to the bone, and I was having a really hard time fighting hypothermia. We also couldn't see more than 10 feet in front of us, so we found the only flat-ish spot on the trail, which happened to be the actual trail. Our tent sat in a tiny little dip that was covered by tiny little bushes; there's just not much cover when you get above the tree line out there.

I was not in a good space. I wasn't talking, could barely move my hands, and I just tried to stay alert and conscious. I believe Puma blew up my sleeping pad for me, and I struggled trying to change into my dry clothes and sleeping bag. Got real quiet for a few hours. I don't remember thinking too much or having any daydreams. I was just quiet and kept listening to my heartbeat while waiting for my body to warm up.

What we also didn't tell you at the time is that water started to come inside the tent. Puma somehow found the strength to get out of the tent to dig a diverted channel for the water to go around our tent. I'm telling you right now that if the roles were reversed, we might not have made it out of that situation without the need of some serious medical assistance. Hypothermia is nothing to joke about, and I believe that was the closest I ever got to shutting down.

I eventually thawed out enough to talk to Puma, but it took a long time. It was so nasty outside, and I did *not* want to risk losing our way or falling or getting cold and wet again. We spent over 21 hours straight hanging out in our tent during a storm on top of The Horn. It's an intense section of the Appalachian Trail, and I'm thankful we made it through without needing a rescue team.

Wednesday, June 12, 2013 - Rangeley and a Little Help from Our Friends

Starting Location: Not So Stealth Tent Site → Destination: Rangeley

Today's Miles: 6 – Trip Miles: 211.50

We made it to Rangeley! Stayed in our tent for 21 hours straight and never ran out of things to talk about.

This morning, we were up by 4:30 a.m. listening to the rain falling on our rain fly, but we also noticed the wind had slowed way down to "moderate gusts," which made us happy.

By 9:30 a.m., we had enough courage to put on our cold wet clothes and pack up camp. Started hiking by 10 a.m. and immediately went up Saddleback Mountain. The rain was steady all day and that was okay because we cruised into Rangeley by 2:30 p.m. I'm sure Saddleback was beautiful, but we could only see about 10 feet at a time because of the heavy fog.

As soon as we crossed the Maine 4 Highway to the parking lot, we high fived and got out the cell phone to call the shuttle to come pick us up and take us nine miles into the town of Rangeley. There was absolutely zero

cell service. After I told Puma to try standing on one foot in one of the last attempts to snag a cell signal, a lovely woman by the name of Kathy offered us a ride into Rangeley. She and her husband, Keith, who is section hiking the entire A.T., invited us to dinner and we swapped stories of rainy days on the trail.

Y'all listen, I am serious when I say that we have met some truly amazing people out here on this adventure, and these are the highlights of this experience for us.

We'll be in Rangeley again tomorrow drying out our tent, socks, gloves, rain jackets, backpacks, and feet.

Now, I gotta' go to sleep so that I can wake up and have my coffee in the mornin'.

Sleep tight and stay dry, y'all,

Number 2

Don't change it, Puma Bloopers will be right back:

I mentioned this before, but I'm hiking the A.T. to see how many amazing people I can meet out here. Seriously, the staff at the hotel offered to wash our nasty hiker clothes for free. There's not enough mention in the world about the wonderful kindness of strangers.

Once I thawed out and could hold a conversation, Puma and I never ran out of things to talk about. I even confessed one of my deepest darkest secrets in life. When I was in grade school (circa 1991-ish), my friends and I made a choreographed dance to Another Bad Creation's song "Iesha." My brother and I convinced our dad to let us borrow the video camera, and the plan was to submit this masterpiece to the one and only Star Search. I publicly confess, I never mailed the tape. To all the members of that summer dance troupe, I hang my head in shame as the reason for your crushed dreams of fame. It feels good to be free from that heavy burden.

Meanwhile, we had been feeling good about our accomplishment of conquering Saddleback Mountain. But getting to the parking lot for a shuttle to then not have any cell service was putting us a little bit on edge. Puma walked all around the parking lot with her phone held high in the air, trying her best to capture just the right position for the call to go through. We got nothin'.

There was one car in the parking lot with a lady sitting in the driver's seat. It looked like she was reading a good book. Windows up and minding her own business, likely keeping an eye on us moving about the parking lot taking turns raising the cell phone to the heavens as an offering.

I think we finally got enough courage to approach the gray four-door sedan after 20 minutes or so, and Kathy invited us to get in her car. She explained that she was waiting on her husband, Keith, to finish up this section of his A.T. hike for the day.

He arrived and was like, "Honey, who's in the car with you?" We were all very polite and cautious, and they had no problem giving us a lift nine miles into town. It if wasn't for them, we would not have made it into town at all. There was no way we would have hiked those nine miles along that curvy, narrow two-lane highway.

On the way into town, we asked them where they were staying, and then we said we'd just stay there, too. Save them a trip! I am so thankful we had the means to cover our asses like that. It was definitely worth all the aggressive saving we had done in the previous two years.

That evening we all went to this bar in town called Sarge's. We had burgers, beers, and great conversation with Keith and Kathy. It was serendipitous, if you ask me. I believe in that kind of stuff. Got to have dinner with them the following evening, too. They are a lovely adventurous couple who are probably *still* traveling around the world and making friendships along the way.

Thursday, June 13, 2013 – The Red Onion and Keith and Kathy

Starting Location: Rangeley, Maine → Destination: Rangeley, Maine
Today's Miles: 0 – Trip Miles: 211.50

Put Rangeley on your vacation destination list. We had a nice morning walk into town admiring all the New England architecture on our way to Mooseley Bagels for breakfast sandwiches and coffee. After breakfast, we checked out a couple of shops in town, and I swear I mentally bought about 100 cute little homemade trinkets with moose painted on them. You just can't have too many of those, you know it!

After getting a couple more re-supply items at the local grocer, we needed to relax. So, I rested my ham hocks, and Puma and I spent the afternoon watching the U.S. Open. I have to say that watching golf this afternoon really made me think of my Uncle Aubrey. He and my Pawpaw were both great golfers. I, however, am really good at watching golf while eating cheese and crackers.

We got to have dinner with Keith and Kathy one more time at The Red Onion. We just think the world of those two! Meeting them made this stop so fun and easy. We wish them all the best in their next adventures.

I guess that's about it for today. All our gear is dry, our bags are packed, and we are pumped to close in on the state line. We thoroughly enjoyed all the posts we received today, and thanks to everyone for their encouragement and support. Shoot, I'll go ahead and throw in a moose keychain for all of y'all, too. Dang! Koozies, coasters, keychains, bug nets...y'all's goody bags are starting to rival the ones they give to the stars at those fancy award shows.

I really love keeping this journal. Thanks for humoring us. Talk to y'all tomorrow.

Watching television flipping between music videos and fishin' shows.

This is,

Number 2

Puma was once a contestant on MTV's "Remote Control." Puma, can you tell us about that:

Bought some more shoes this afternoon. I'm taking my old pair of shoes to the next town in case these new shoes are a bust. I'm ready to get back on the trail.

I loved stopping in at these wonderful local food joints in town. The Red Onion had eye-catching architecture – it looked like a tomato-red Queen Ann barn. I got a C in my Modern Architecture course in college. Still laugh when anyone says the word "Tudor." Anyhow, this place was just wonderful, and the pizza was even better. There's something in the water up there in the north that makes the bread absolutely irresistible. The Red Onion was around for a long time and had a great atmosphere and menu.

We thoroughly enjoyed getting to know Keith and Kathy and kept up with them for a good while after finishing our A.T. hike. I'm so happy we took the time to hang out with them and thank them for all the support they gave us during that critical point on the trail. I think about the what-ifs of never meeting them and how much love and friendship we would have missed out on. Such a wonderfully fun couple to have the pleasure of meeting along the way, and I'm grateful they became part of this story.

Friday, June 14, 2013 – Laughing on the Trail and Meeting Rabbit

Starting Location: Rangeley → Destination: Bemis Stream

Today's Miles: 14.20 – Trip Miles: 225.7

The first day back on the trail is always a little bit rough for both sets of knees, but hey, I am always so proud of us at the end of the day with what we've accomplished.

Got the pleasure of meeting our first Northbounder (NOBO for short) on the trail today! We met Rabbit, and he was a real cool dude. Even asked us if we were Number 2 and Puma! Said his mom has been keepin' up with our journal, and then he took a picture of the three of us. We'd like to thank Rabbit's mom for following us along in this adventure. That was too cool.

We met another couple of NOBOs who were just as friendly, and I tried my best to cheer them on. I can't imagine walkin' all that way. Just kiddin', I think about it pretty much every day.

What else happened today...Puma told me I had the world's slowest and softest fall, not once but twice. Had a fall earlier in the day that had both of us doubled over from laughing so hard...I had to spit out my water because I kept imagining how funny it must have been for Puma to see me eat dirt like I did. It made us laugh for a good while. The roots and rocks and muddy bogs were doin' their best to hold us down today, but we just kept on laughing and having a good time.

Dinner was good, we're tucked in for the night, and I've got to give a special shout out to Number 1 (my older brother) and Number 3 (my younger sister). All this laughing today made me think of y'all! There's nothing better.

Sending love and laughter to everyone,

Number 2

Hey Puma, tell us a joke:

Saw some more trail maintenance workers today, and talked with them for a while. Had a hard time breaking in my new shoes; but even though my feet ache, they are dry. I can't explain how grateful I am for that.

We crossed Maine Highway 17 this day. There are lots of logging semi-trucks running up and down these two-lane highways, and they are going super-fast. Haulin' ass fast. There is no shoulder to walk on. Askin' for it, if you ask me!

I'm grateful for the shuttles, and *The A.T. Guide* book that gets updated and reprinted every year. If you are going to hike the Appalachian Trail, you need that book. It's chock full of maps, shuttle service info, hostels, tips, and it can even be waterproof if you spring for that version.

Puma has the original version, and what a keepsake. I've considered getting the current year version because I have this little voice inside my head telling me to go hike the 100 Mile Wilderness again...but in July or August.

Meeting our first NOBO thru hiker was wild because he knew who we were. Rabbit was a young fellow with reddish hair, and I could tell he was cranking out some serious miles. I kept thinking about how he was finishing and we were just getting started. He was happy to have taken our picture so he could show his mom, and it was wild picturing how our paths had crossed on the same dotted line on the map.

Saturday, June 15, 2013 – Andover and Emotional Freedom

Starting Location: Bemis Stream → Destination: Andover, Maine
  Today's Miles: 12.20 – Trip Miles: 237.90

This morning, we woke up to rain falling on our tent, had a thunderstorm in the wee hours of the morning, and I remember thinking, "Well, if it ain't one thing, it's your mother."

The rain was over and gone by the time we had camp packed up. Our hike started us out climbing up and then leveled out a little bit; got the chance to meet some more NOBO hikers who were all excited to meet their first SOBOs...that was us! Then, the coolest part of the day was catching up with another SOBO named Zodiac. He's also from Tennessee, which made our day. We spent the afternoon talking about the SEC and Southern food. In my head I have given us the nickname "The Tennessee Three" which I think is VERY cute and appropriate.

The last part of today was tough because we were hiking straight down for three miles over some serious rocks and roots...just another day of hiking in Maine.

I tell y'all what, it's the best feeling in the world when NOBOs tell us how this state is the hardest state they've been through.

Tomorrow, we will be hitting the trail again, but we will be doing a couple of days of "slackpacking" (no Dad, this does not refer to the speed at which I pack my backpack). It'll be really nice to get some miles under our belts without the weight of our backpacks as we hike down and up these next ten miles.

Somebody please remind me to tell you what it's like staying at Pine Ellis in Andover. It just takes too much energy right now to explain how great and unique this place is in the journal.

I'm tired, it's late, and I'm pretty sure I'm gonna get too hot sleeping in my socks tonight but they're too far away for me do anything about it right now...you understand.

Thinking of sitting in my Granny's lap around the campfire at Thanksgiving.

Love y'all,

Number 2

Bump...Set...Puma:

Just about the entire trail in Maine is ankle-busting rocks and roots.

Thinking about those rocks and roots makes my feet ache. I had the shoes with the rock plate, shoes that were light weight, shoes that were waterproof, and it just doesn't matter what kind of shoes you have out there because this terrain will wear you and your shoes down.

For those who are unfamiliar with the term "slackpacking," this is when you can leave your big backpack at the hostel and do a speedy day's worth of hiking without the load of a full bag. The hostels sometimes had smaller daypacks that we could borrow to carry our water and some snacks. Puma and I cruised through some big miles thanks to slackpacking. At the end of the day, someone from the hostel would pick us up at the designated stopping point and bring us back to the hostel. I highly recommend it.

I miss being out on the trail. Diving back into this experience is giving me the itch to get back out there and struggle through some miles. I felt alive and free, and it seemed simple, but I definitely had complicated emotions that I suppressed.

I think if I could do it again, I'd give myself the gift of true emotional freedom. I'm older now, and I've learned a lot about myself and my past. I've made mistakes, and there's a lot of power in taking responsibility for them, learning from them, restoring myself, and moving towards renewal. Walking through the woods for an extended amount of time allows me to clean out the mind, body, and spirit.

The adventure is not over! Hell, we still have 13 more states to discuss; I just want to encourage us to get out there. Go to your local trails and state parks. Take a friend or go alone. Breathe in the trees and see what you can see. It's a lot more rewarding for me to be in nature than to be looking at my computer screen all day. Call me, I'll go with you!

Sunday, June 16, 2013 – Pine Ellis, Crab Cakes, and Zodiac

Starting Location: South Arm Road → Destination: East B Hill Road
   Today's Miles: 10.10 – Trip Miles: 248

It was such a nice break to slackpack this section. Within the first four miles, we had ascended and then immediately descended about 1,700 feet.

The next six miles were "pathy" and "flowy" but really overgrown – so much so that it was like walking through a car wash without any soap (ouch!).

It was like having the best of both worlds today after hiking because we got to come back into Andover, eat a pizza, and then chill for the rest of the evening.

We watched the rest of the U.S. Open with our friends Zodiac and Crab Cakes while enjoying wine and cheese and blueberries. I mean, I did not envision evenings like this when we started. Get this, the gentleman who manages Pine Ellis is of Mayan descent. He brought out three of the most beautiful wooden flutes and played them while I plucked around on the guitar. It really came together when we played "Horse with No Name."

Eventually, we progressed to the blues and he got out his harmonica. Y'all, I definitely had a moment in my head while we were all laughing and feeling the wine run through our legs that I thought to myself, "Is this a dream? Am I really this good at playing the blues on a wooden Mayan flute?"

We just had the best time laughing and enjoying each other's company. This has got to be my favorite part of this whole experience...besides the victory sausages. Thanks for reading, America.

We love you all,

Number 2

And now, a word from our sponsor:

Today's trail is brought to you by the letter "W." That's the exact letter made by these steep hills and mountains.

Thanks to *The A.T. Guide*, we had Pine Ellis manager's contact information and easily set up the shuttle ride. He showed up in this old gray van, helped us put our backpacks in the back, and gave us the most refreshing cups of homemade pink lemonade. The sugar and tang of that pink lemonade felt like a million dollars running through my veins. It was glorious.

I sat in the front seat because I was drawn to him, his energy, and I like talking with characters along the way. He had a great sense of humor. I laughed every time he referred to a random squirrel crossing the road as "traffic."

When we got to Pine Ellis, a lovely house, like your grandma's house, he took us through the basement to show us his homemade merchandise he likes to showcase to all his patrons.

He makes earrings out of moose poop. They don't stink; there is a shellac-like coating on them, with maybe a colorful bead or two. Some had a slightly blue tint to them because of all the blueberries the moose were eating. I wish like hell I had bought some, dammit, but I didn't get my ears pierced again until 2018.

We really did have such a fun evening that night hanging out with him and the two other hikers, Crab Cakes and Zodiac. I can't remember who brought the wine out, but I'm sure glad we had it because it loosened up the room. We laughed so much that night. I remember Crab Cakes laughing pretty hard when I suggested we produce our own set of blueberry poop earrings.

If you haven't seen moose poop in real life or looked it up online, it looks like those peanut butter filled pretzels you can buy at the grocery store. Bite-sized poop. It's very fibrous and consistent in size and shape. Definitely one of my biggest regrets on the trail was not buying some of those earrings.

Crab Cakes and Zodiac were so funny and fun to hang out with that night. Just having a good time hanging out in the tiny living room listening to flute tunes. We finished off a couple bottles of wine and a bunch of blueberries. I remember a moment of suspended silence because we were all catching our breaths between laughing. It was a great night.

Zodiac was a young lad who had just graduated from college. He had long dark hair and a great smile. After Pine Ellis he hiked with us for a short while, then he was gone. We heard through the grapevine that he found his way back to Andover, but we never saw him again. He was hiking alone and in the words of Joni Mitchell, maybe just needed to "Come In from the Cold." Wherever you are, Crab Cakes and Zodiac, it was a pleasure meeting you both at Pine Ellis, and I will never forget all the fun we had that night.

Monday, June 17, 2013 – Chinese Food in Mexico, Maine

Starting Location: Pine Ellis → Destination: Pine Ellis
    Today's Miles: 0 – Trip Miles: 248

Today we let some thunderstorms blow through while we rested our knees. Sure glad we did because there were reports of hail just up on Maine Highway 17 (we've already done that part).

After breakfast, we went into the neighboring town of Rumford for our re-supply, then crossed over the border into the next town of Mexico to stop in at the local Chinese restaurant. I thought everyone was joking about Mexico being the next town, but it was no joke. No wonder they stared at me when I just kept laughing about the name.

This afternoon we rode bikes around the block to get some ice cream. I promise I didn't know we'd be riding bikes to an ice cream parlor at any point on the A.T.

Today was fun, but we're ready for tomorrow. Gonna slackpack 10 something miles up and over Baldpate Mountain in the morning. Then it's Mahoosuc Notch time, y'all!

Thanks for following us on this adventure,

Number 2

Now, put your hands together for one of my favorite country music singers, Puma Tillis:

It's crazy how achy I feel after a rest.

It was a great idea to go eat at this Chinese restaurant in Mexico after getting our re-supply of food for our next jaunt. We didn't have any other plans for the day, so we were just along for the ride after that. I love that kind of pace.

The restaurant wasn't a fancy place, but it was delicious. Chinese food always hits right and especially on a big adventure like this. The waitress came by the booth and listened to us tell a little bit of our story.

We were so grateful to the manager of Pine Ellis for driving us around town. I know he has helped so many of us thru hikers at such a pivotal location on the trail. It was easy hanging out with him, and I thoroughly enjoyed the time we spent together.

Tuesday, June 18, 2013 – Grafton Notch and a Bullet in My Toes

Starting Location: Pine Ellis → Destination: Grafton Notch

Today's Miles: 10.20 – Trip Miles: 258.20

This morning we slackpacked again, but we went north instead of south to conquer Baldpate Mountain. There are two peaks to this beast, but gosh, it was a beautiful day, and one of the best days of hiking we've had on this adventure.

The second peak is totally exposed so it's really not a good idea to climb it in questionable weather. I always keep one eye on the trail, and one eye on the clouds; I hope to relax my internal barometer a little more when we get through these big ass mountains.

We cruised into Grafton Notch by midafternoon where the manager of Pine Ellis was waiting for us with that glorious pink lemonade. We just think the world of Pine Ellis!

Then we spent the rest of the afternoon eating cheddar "combonations" while propping our feet up and catching up with our two new hiker friends, K and Bambi. Boy, they were a hoot! K is from Kentucky and is finishing her northbound hike at Katahdin, and Bambi is from Texas and doing the same thing. These ladies were hilarious and really fun to hang out with at Pine Ellis. I hope our paths cross again.

I've enjoyed meeting all these people on the trail; in addition to my internal barometer, I have a running Christmas card list in my head, and it's filling up fast! I always say it's never too soon to think about your Christmas card list.

Y'all, thank you so much for playing along with us, and we truly hope to keep your attention the whole way to Georgia.

We're hittin' the hay now because we've got the Mahoosuc Arm tomorrow after we make it over Old Speck Mountain. Thinking of all our climbing adventures with friends at King's Bluff in Clarksville, Tennessee. We'll be ready for that as soon as we get back!

Climb on,

Number 2

1 Puma, 2 Pumas, 3 Pumas, 4...If you add another Puma, that's too many Pumas:

Thinking about how awesome it would be to slackpack the entire A.T. A couple more days and we're in New Hampshire.

Hanging out with K and Bambi, I remember it was the end of the day, and we were all staying in the same room. There were four twin beds arranged around the room with an extra roller bed, which happened to be my bed for the evening. It was normal to share space like this at the hostels.

There we were, all laying around in our pajamas just gabbing away about our experiences on the trail so far. I had my backpack sitting on the end of my bed. Can't remember what the conversation was at that time, but the end of my bed collapsed suddenly, and my bag fell.

Well, I noticed that when my bag hit the floor, a bullet also rolled into plain sight of everyone in the room. Without breaking eye contact or conversation, I grabbed the bullet with my toes and slowly pulled it back to me. There was a brief silence with everyone looking around at each other. Puma and I felt like we needed to explain ourselves to the group.

We explained that we didn't actually bring this gun with us, and that we bought it from our fellow hiker to help pay for his plane ticket back home after the 100 Mile Wilderness. Nothing like carrying around an extra pound and a half of weight in my backpack. I don't know how they felt about our story, but we laughed about me trying to hide the bullet with my toes. Easy does it, toes.

Wednesday, June 19, 2013 – Bull Branch Campsite, the Mahoosuc Arm, and Inner Peace

Starting Location: Grafton Notch → Destination: Bull Branch Campsite

Today's Miles: 7.10 – Trip Miles: 265.30

What a great hike today! I'm not even kiddin'. We crushed Old Speck first thing this morning and got some fantastic views. We can see New Hampshire.

Made it down the Mahoosuc Arm with flying colors. It was steep, but y'all prolly heard us pull the Mahoosuc finger when we were done. Ha!

We're camped at this tiny little one tent campsite this evening and it's gorgeous. Got in early enough for Puma to take a little nap before dinner. It's always nice when that happens.

We really enjoyed ourselves today and agree that, weather permitting, it's nice to actually enjoy our hikes instead of pushing through them.

Both of us are pumped about going through the Mahoosuc Notch tomorrow. We've been waiting on this for a month now. So, we're resting up and gonna eat big tonight to carb-load for the big climb out of here. We will be crossing our first state line. Can y'all believe it? We have already decided to have a dance party at every state line, and the song we deemed appropriate is Queen's "Another One Bites the Dust." You know that's a great song.

Thanks so much for cheering us on, you've really helped us get through Maine. It's a rugged beast, but we did it. Hell, we all did it together.

Who wants a victory sausage?

Number 2

Puma's in the tennnnt! (But you gotta' read it like "Puma's in the house!"):

I got my moose picture! Saw another bear crossing a road; that's it, no punchline.

The Mahoosuc Arm is a very steep, long hike down to the Mahoosuc Notch. I remember it being so steep that we grabbed hold of the trees on the side of the trail and swung down to the next tree and so on and so forth.

I really miss being immersed in the rugged landscape of Maine. It is like no other place I have been since then. I love my local trails, but I feel like I've exhausted them and just about everything else within a two hour drive. The itch is real, and the time is near.

I remember Bull Branch Campsite; I felt right at home there. The clothesline, the water bag, the tent, making dinner, and the absolute peace I had come to know out there. I was home for the evening. I didn't mind waking up, packing it all up, and moving on to the next spot either. There was this amazing sense of freedom moving about the country at my own pace. Very minimal, no extras. Just me, my backpack, and nature. The most inner peace I've ever had in my life.

Thursday, June 20, 2013 – Mahoosuc Notch

Starting Location: Bull Branch Campsite → Destination: Carlo Col Shelter

Today's Miles: 7.10 – Trip Miles: 272.40

Hiked seven miles today and it only took us a little over eight hours... what? Yep, we hit the Mahoosuc Notch this morning, and it was so much fun. There was some serious bouldering going on, and Puma and I loved

every minute of it. It did take us two hours to go one mile, but that's the Notch for ya!

After the Notch, we still had a grueling day of serious ups and downs. We are a half mile from the New Hampshire state line. There's a tradition in my family that stems from my mother's dad (my Pappy), and the tradition is to holler out "DOG SHIT" whenever you cross any state line. The original purpose of hollering the infamous phrase was to wake everyone up who might have been sleeping in the back seat on the long family car trips. Anyone who wants to join in on the tradition should holler "DOG SHIT" tomorrow at 7 a.m. Eastern Standard Time.

We are ready to turn in for the evening so we can rest up for the big day. I'm so proud and excited to be crossing Maine off our list; we couldn't have done it without our wonderful trail angels and all your wonderful posts on this trail journal. We love you all. See ya, Maine! I see a dance party in Puma's future.

Love,

Number 2

You thought the Mahoosuc Notch was gnarly, check out the Pahuuma Notch:

Tomorrow's final half mile climbs up and into New Hampshire. What a big accomplishment. Just FYI for other SOBOs, there's more bouldering before the notch done.

The Mahoosuc Notch is the most interesting mile of the entire Appalachian Trail. We packed our poles away, cracked our knuckles, and went for it! There are tunnels that required us to take our packs off in order to pass through them. We pulled our packs through gaps we had just crawled through, we climbed over obstacles, tightroped on vines that had grown on the rocks, and thought we were done, but wait, there's more...

We were going in, around, and between *big* boulders trying to follow the arrows mapping out this crazy mile. At times, it felt like we were in the *Labyrinth* looking for David Bowie. The last half mile out of Maine is a rock scramble that goes straight up...or down, depending on if you are going north or south. It was awesome. I would do it again in a heartbeat.

Friday, June 21, 2013 – Maine and New Hampshire State Line

Starting Location: Carlo Col Shelter → Destination: Trident Campsite

Today's Miles: 10.20 – Trip Miles: 282.60

Oh, New Hampshire, how do we love thee, let me count the ways: one, you have the word "ham" in your name; two, you also have the word "new" in your name and it's been really great hiking in a new environment (still rocks, roots, mud, and mountains...but it's NEW), and three, you're so agreeable at the end of your name (sounds like "Sure!") and we like that.

I tell y'all, Maine did NOT want us to leave her this morning. She wanted us to break a leg, stay, and raise a family. I'm not kiddin', the last half mile was a crazy rock scramble straight up. Maine, you were great, but not enough to hold back Number 2 and Puma.

I am so darn proud of us for making it through, and we send lots of good juju to those who are about to tackle Maine. Keep going!

The first thing we noticed today – New Hampshire has a little bit more topsoil and that is sooooo important. I did find enough cobwebs to hit me across my upper lip that I had a perfect Kung Fu mustache (you know the kind that are real long and flowy).

We can see the White Mountains from here and they look big; we're looking forward to staying in the huts along the way. Maybe the hut crew

will ask me to speak to a large group after dinner about our experiences. Y'all know I would love that.

Just want to say thank you again to all those who participated in the state line tradition this morning, and if you missed it, there will be 13 more chances to holler "DOG SHIT!" We love you very much and will give you all our best starting tomorrow. The dance party was epic!

Love,

Number 2

Puma, come downstairs and say goodnight to your friends (we pretend we have an upstairs in our tent all the time):

There's nothing else I can say since Number 2 just said it all.

Maine was without a doubt the most memorable state for me in this whole Appalachian Trail experience. It was the hardest hiking I had ever done by far. Nothing has compared to it since then. I did get emotional at the state line because I was so proud of our accomplishment.

I'd been pushed harder than ever out there, and I was better for it. The routine physical difficulty of the trail, as a whole, did not stress me out. I was never stressed out about the wildlife. What stressed me out the most was the cold, the lightning, the high-water crossings, and a few sketchy dudes along the way.

By this time, the high-water crossings were over. I felt empowered knowing that I had just walked a couple hundred miles, *and* I did it through Maine!

Maine, you were my favorite state, maybe because you were my first. I have been back to see you a couple of times, but it's never enough. You are more than Vacationland, you are Wonderland.

Chapter Four

New Hampshire, Part One

Saturday, June 22, 2013 – White Mountain's Lodge in Gorham, New Hampshire

Starting Location: Trident Campsite → Destination: White Mountains Lodge

Today's Miles: 6.90 – Trip Miles: 289.50

Howdy folks! We had a great hike this morning. Translation, it kicked our butts. The mountains are steep and they ain't cheap either.

We made it into Gorham, New Hampshire, before the rain hit this afternoon. Can y'all believe that we had four days of no rain? We can't either.

Tonight we are staying at the White Mountains Lodge, which is a beautiful home with flower gardens and cobblestone patios. It's run by husband and wife team, Matt and Mary, and they are really funny and awesome.

As soon as we arrived, Mrs. Mary had us pick out some clean dry "hiker loaner clothes" and put all our stinky clothes into the wash, then we hit the

showers. These are some of the nicest facilities that we've used to date on this adventure. I even put conditioner in my hair!

We just never know exactly how each day is going to turn out, and Puma sure didn't know that David Hasselhoff would be tending to her hydrational needs.

We really are havin' so much fun out here even though it's the toughest hiking we've ever done. It's all part of the adventure.

Wildcat Mountain is our next climb and it's a doozie. Our plan is to tackle it tomorrow, but it all depends on this weather. So, we'll just check it in the morning. These mountains in New Hampshire are no joke, and it's important to respect the forecast with these elevations.

Thanks for comin' along with us all the way to New Hampshire, y'all. We keep you close to our hearts.

Love,

Number 2

Puma's sawing logs with the world's smallest and quietest chainsaw (i.e., super faint snoring more accurately described as breathing):

Shhhh...

Walking out of the woods and into a neighborhood, we could see a sign in the yard of this lovely New England home that read "Welcome SOBOS." I thought we were famous, but it was just a clever little yard sign facing the appropriate direction according to its message.

We walked up to the garage area and Mrs. Mary opened the door before we even knocked. She was expecting us. She was so friendly and helpful, but I could barely understand her because she talked faster than anyone I had ever met. I looked to Puma for translation numerous times, and I think Mary could also see that I was lost. We worked it out.

Mrs. Mary showed us the bins of clean hiker loaner clothes, and I really had fun with these situations when they presented themselves. There was nothing extravagant in the clothes bins, but I think it would be a funny prank to add a tuxedo or a lavish evening gown to the selection just to see if any thru hikers take the bait. Surely, that's been done before.

There were multiple bedrooms in this hostel home, and Puma and I lucked out with the one that had a big cardboard cut-out of Mr. David Hasselhoff advertising an iced coffee. It was right above Puma's bed. So every time I looked her direction, all I could see was David Hasselhoff. He watched over her at night. It was funny and also felt kind of weird...like "Babe Watch" instead of *Baywatch*.

Puma navigated us all the way here using *The A.T. Guide* with its clearly marked maps and helpful information. We pretty much knew when we'd be in town and when we'd be in the tent. When I tell people this trip took five months and three weeks to complete, I think they think we actually stayed in the woods for almost six months. That is incorrect. After the 100 Mile Wilderness, hiking the A.T. is like a bunch of three and five-day backpacking trips with lots of places to stop and re-supply in between. I loved being in town *and* on the trail.

Sunday, June 23, 2013 — Waiting Around for the Weather

Starting Location: White Mountains Lodge → Destination: Same

Today's Miles: 0 — Trip Miles: 289.50

Hiking up Wildcat Mountain did not happen today due to weather conditions, but we were able to eat lots of pizza and watch two soccer games on the television. We're packed and ready to try our luck tomorrow, weather permitting.

There's an internal struggle that happens whenever we take a zero, but we know they've been for the best. We met some more SOBOs and enjoyed our time here at the White Mountains Lodge and Hostel.

There are quite a few people from Tennessee and Georgia hiking south this year, which makes sense to us because we all want to walk home. I can tell right off the bat if we've come across another Southerner because of our accents. Puma's had the upper hand being from the north and has translated a couple of times for me up here in New England.

That's about all I know right now, y'all. We're crossing our fingers for decent weather tomorrow and appreciate anything you can do to help with that.

With a belly full of pizza, I bid y'all a good night.

Love,

Number 2

If Puma was a character in a Fannie Flagg book, her name would be pronounced "Pumer," and someone would call out, "Pumer! Did ya hear the rumor?":

Having to take a zero really stinks when I'm wishing to get out there on the path. But I'd hate to risk an injury. No need to push it with this weather.

Staying at the White Mountains Lodge in Gorham was wonderful and hard at the same time. The owners, Matt and Mary, were fantastic, but waiting around for the weather system was eating away at our courage and momentum.

There were photos on the walls in the dining room of hikers who were in bad situations. Like for real, a framed 8x10 photo of a Wilderness First Responder showing up with a body board and putting straps across a hiker's head...in the rain...on Wildcat Mountain.

The forecast was just days of storms with very strong winds and heavy lightning, and this was no walk in the park. We waited and waited and discussed and got frustrated with the situation. It was time to make a decision. So, we decided to skip the White Mountains and come back to them at a later date in this adventure.

We did not want to jeopardize our safety or chance not being able finishing what we had started. We knew we had the funds to come back when the time was right. Plus, at this point, we were used to the workaround approach; Katahdin had taught us flexibility.

The biggest lesson I learned from this whole A.T. experience was probably how to adjust and be flexible with the present moment. The second lesson I learned was how to be comfortable with the uncomfortable. To quote Daniel Boone, "I was happiest amidst the dangers and inconveniences." It's true, I had really come to love the simple goal of each day, and it was ok if I didn't accomplish it.

The trail experience is alive. It is living and breathing, and it changes, much like a monthly budget. Learning how to go with the flow of the unknown is the best way to fight back and not give up.

Spoiler alert: We do make it back. The White Mountains are spectacular. I'm sure glad we got to see them. Franconia Ridge is the most beautiful hike I have ever been on in my life.

Monday, June 24, 2013 – Still at White Mountain's Lodge

Starting Location: White Mountain's Lodge → Destination: White Mountain's Lodge

Today's Miles: 0 – Trip Miles: 289.50

We made an important decision today. Due to the weather conditions that surround the White Mountains, we have decided to bypass that section and head south in hopes of better weather in the future.

It's important to both of us that we enjoy the Whites, and the forecasts just won't allow us to do so. We'd like to tackle that section within our thru hike and think of it as a "trip within our trip" when we come back.

As the saying goes, "hike your own hike," and that's exactly what we shall do. Puma and I are at peace with this decision (especially when the forecasts repeatedly say "damaging winds at 60 miles per hour and continuous lightning"). We wish the best of luck and safe travels to all those who are pushing through the Whites right now. You are amazing.

In other news, we are packed up and heading south tomorrow. Got our re-supply at the Walmart and quickly caught up on "the news" a.k.a. Kimberly Kardashian had her baby. It's exciting and feels good to be hitting the trail again.

Thank you to everyone who has been supporting us and reading our trail journal. More stories to come!

Love,

Number 2

Now give it up for Puma Spice and everything nice:

Number 2 was the one looking at trashy magazines. My brain is 100 percent focused on how to conquer the White Mountains. It will happen.

This was a hard decision for us to make. We felt like we were letting our fellow thru hikers down and all our trail journal readers, too. But the thing we had to remember was that this was *our* hike, no one else's. And looking back on it, I bet you a hundred bucks that Puma would have been just fine forging ahead. I think she folded to me so that I could keep my peace; I was still a little rattled from our "river run" back up in Maine.

Being out there on the trail could take a very serious turn at a moment's notice, and we just couldn't afford to be careless about anything.

It happened the way that it happened, and there's no way of changing the story. It's still a good story!

I've done a lot of soul searching over the years, and one of my biggest mantras is about letting go and moving on. I love to move on.

Tuesday, June 25, 2013 – Permission to Not Care

Starting Location: White Mountains Lodge → Destination: New Hampshire

Today's Miles: 7.30 – Trip Miles: 296.80

Laying down in my sleeping bag at the moment, I can hear the rain fall on our tent, and I'm thinking to myself, "I am so happy to not be up on top of a mountain right now." I do, however, feel like I've been hit by a Mack truck; my body gets really fussy when we take two days off in a row. Another thing, we started our hike at 12:30 this afternoon, and I've got some kind of mental block about starting that late, but it was our only option.

The terrain in southern New Hampshire is just wonderful compared to good ol' Maine. It makes me and my knees very happy. This old bird isn't made of rubber and magic like all these young men running down these mountains. I call them the "Young Guns" (great movie starring Emilio Esteves). In the words of my dear Aunt Frances, "God love 'em." I don't know how they do it, hiking close to 30 miles a day in this terrain, but they do it. Me and Puma are doing just fine at our pace and we have more toenails than they do.

Y'all, I am so happy to be where we are, and I am still pinching myself from time to time because I'm still impressed that we are hiking home. I love the towns, I love this tent, I love meeting all the people, I LOVE this trail journal. We really love our families and all our friends, especially your wonderful, wonderful posts.

Thanks for keeping up with us, and I hope you have enjoyed reading this journal as much as we have enjoyed writing it.

Stay tuned for more adventures of,

Number 2 and Puma

(Name this tune) Pume Pume, Shooby Pume, Pume Pume, Shooby Pume, Pume Pume, Shooby Pume, Pume Pume, Shooby Wah:

In four days we will cross over into Vermont. I told Number 2 that we will not have a dance party. Number 2 suggested we have a funeral. I thought that was funny.

You wouldn't know it from the journal, but I was ignoring my inner struggle during this time on the trail. We made it through, but I was having a hard time thinking about what other hikers might think of us. That's always been one of my weaknesses, worrying about what other people think. Not caring is easier said than done – and just one of those things in life we overcome with intentional awareness and self-care.

It's easy to get bogged down with all the "woe is me" moments in life: not feeling smart enough, pretty enough, financially stable enough, the competitions, not feeling strong enough, good enough, accepted, and so on. Those thoughts were not off limits out there, but I will say that they didn't stick around long because I quickly remembered that I was free. Free to start and stop, free to think about what I wanted to think about, free to give myself permission to *not* care. Also, I just really love hiking and was entertained by the ever-changing scenery.

This all goes back to the previous discussion of how this trail is largely a mental game. It was worth playing along.

Wednesday, June 26, 2013 – A Tiny Cabin in the Woods

Starting Location: New Hampshire → Destination: New Hampshire

Today's Miles: 12.80 – Trip Miles: 309.60

Hiked all day in the rain. Wore our rain jackets for warmth. That's all they're good for when it rains for days on end. We hiked up and over two mountains and crossed a couple streams and a couple streets. That was about it. Just can't see much when it's raining all day.

When we reached the top of Mount Cube, another 3,000-footer, Puma said "Simply breathtaking," and I knew she was joking because all we could see was a blanket of white. That's what it looks like walking through a cloud.

The place we are staying tonight is an actual cabin with windows and a door. This just doesn't happen, folks. It smells rustic and was so nice to walk up on when we were soaked from the rain. Met quite a few NOBOs today, and every one of them gave us great advice for the upcoming towns. Makes me excited to hear about all the cool stops ahead.

Well, y'all, we are gonna turn in for the night. The sun is shining a little bit right now, and I hope it dries out the trail. If not, then that's fine, too.

This evening my belly is full of beef stroganoff. Thanks for reading.

Love,

Number 2

Puma Puma, bo booma, banana fana fo fooma, me my mo mooma, Puma (FYI: she's allergic to bananas):

My feet were dry for most of the day. Hiked for eight hours. We're hoping our gear airs out in the cabin. Two more days until re-supply.

I remember this little cabin in the woods. It was very tiny, and there were two NOBOs packing up their stuff to head back out as we were heading in. By this time, we were used to sharing tight spaces on the trail with other hikers, and it's really a cool human experiment. In civilization, we are so cautious about our boundaries and protecting what is "mine" and "yours," but out there on the trail, it was about community and survival.

We were still cautious, but we also had no problems sleeping in the tiny cabin with two other dudes. They were just as soggy and tired as we were. I hope we didn't alarm them or scare them away from doing what they needed to do.

It was a lovely little one-room cabin. There was a table and a shelf; can't remember there being a chair, but that's really all I would need to set up shop there for the rest of my life. Surrounded by rugged trails and beautiful scenery every day. Sure, it might get old after days on end, but I think I could spend June through November in a tiny cabin in the woods, and then spend December through May fishing on the coast or on a lake somewhere.

Thursday, June 27, 2013 – Front Porch Ice Cream and Cokes

Starting Location: New Hampshire → Destination: Vermont

Today's Miles: 12.40 – Trip Miles: 322

Another great day of hiking, folks! We climbed up and over a couple more mountains, and it did not rain on us one bit. Pretty sure it'll be raining tonight, but it's all good.

Halfway through our hike, we stopped at this adorable house along the trail that offers free ice cream and cokes! Such a nice treat in the middle of the day. Met some more NOBOs there and enjoyed talking with them about all their adventures.

Puma and I are doing our best to stay hydrated, and with lots of streams and brooks, the opportunity is ample. It's real important to keep on drinking water...makes my joints work better.

Almost to our next town. We're excited and ready for another cheeseburger. I swear all I think about out here is cheeseburgers...and my family and friends.

Y'all, keep us in your thoughts and prayers, and we'll just keep on truckin'! Thanks for reading.

Love,

Number 2

Puma's watching television and eating Hot Pockets, if only in her dreams:

Had an awesome hike today. The path isn't the same as it was in Maine. We're hiking closer to three miles per hour now. I found a new blister, but I'm happy with my new shoes. Can't stand having wet feet.

I tell you what, I would not mind living in that quaint little house right off the Appalachian Trail. There was no one home, but they had supplied a bunch of ice cream and Coca-Colas for hikers to help themselves. I mean, the pure joy this brings to hikers is immense. We started seeing the colorfully painted ice cream signs and had been hearing about this particular trail magic before we arrived. It was just as magical as I had hoped it would be; my only complaint is that the owners were not around for us to meet and thank them.

The house was soooo cute with its perfectly placed rocking chairs, books, lamps, and blankets. The furniture was functional, and I seem to recall there were flyfishing pictures on the wall and L.L. Bean duck boots in the corner by the door. I couldn't have dreamed it up any more perfectly. I was looking through the window into the coziest scene of my life, but I couldn't stay.

I'd lose my focus with all those creature comforts like a rocking chair, books, an adorable tea kettle and a porch. To the owners of that lovely home, thank you for all the ice cream you supplied to the hungry hikers. We will never forget your generous hospitality.

Chapter Five

Vermont

Friday, June 28, 2013 – Walking Through Dartmouth

Starting Location: Vermont → Destination: Vermont

Today's Miles: 11 – Trip Miles: 333

There was a storm finishing up when we woke up this morning. I could feel the wind and rain blowing inside the shelter, and we both decided to sleep for another hour to give it time to cool its jets. It was a good move.

We wore all the clothes we have in our bags and stayed warm as we hiked 11 miles into town. I was actually comfortable in the wind and the rain this time and sure was glad we brought our extra layers.

The trail brought us down the sidewalk into the heart of town, and I waited with our backpacks as Puma purchased two sandwiches, chips, and a cherry Coke from Subway. The folks in town were looking at me covered in mud up to my knees, so I simply sat on the public bench with my legs crossed and tried to clean the dirt out of my nails. I got to watch a guy parallel park his boat-sized vintage car between two smart cars; I told him how impressed I was when he finished.

The last four days have been full of good hiking, but our feet need to dry out a bit. They start to get itchy and red after days of water and mud. Got to take care of those feet!

The next week is calling for more rain...it just wouldn't be the same without it.

Drying out, this is,

Number 2

Look, Days of Blisters, I mean Days of Thunder is on television, Puma:

That wind was wild. Everybody in town keeps saying this weather is not typical. All we can do is keep moving forward or use a day to air out gear. We're hiking strong by our standards. Reached our goal by lunchtime.

We emerged from the trail in the trees to this open collegiate softball field. There were some people getting ready to play; it did not look like an official game or anything. They definitely looked at us, and I definitely waved at them. It was strange for both parties to encounter each other like this, and I loved it.

When we got to town I found out that it was one of the softball fields at Dartmouth College. I was so impressed and had vivid daydreams imagining walking out of the woods, catching a fly ball, and everyone cheering.

What if we had seen Mindy Kaling while we were there? When did she graduate? It doesn't matter. It was a beautiful campus and town with all of its charm and stone architecture. Even the Subway felt fancy. I had a good time being the outcast on the public bench while Puma was getting our lunch. The people walking by were looking at me with expressions of "ew" or "who or what is that?" I guess the mud, my backpack, and glasses were confusing.

I didn't feel the need to prove myself to anyone. Covered in mud with everything I owned strapped to my back, I felt great.

Saturday, June 29, 2013 – Chugging Beer and Scaring Babies

Starting Location: Vermont → Destination: Norwich, Vermont

Today's Miles: 0 – Trip Miles: 333

Slept in until 6:55 a.m. and it...was...awesome. Caught up on some Sports Center and took a nap shortly after breakfast. Whenever we stop in a town, all I want to do is sleep and eat, so that's what we did.

Puma dried out all our gear this morning, and we made a list of things for our re-supply. Took a cab into a neighboring town, had a lovely time perusing the shops, and ate some real good pasta.

We called a cab to come pick us up when we finished our errands, and they said, "We'll be there at a quarter til." So, Puma suggested we go grab a beer until the cab arrived; well, we walked into this bar, ordered a couple local micro-brews, and munched on the free popcorn. Puma's phone rang as soon as I poured my beer. She said, "Chug! The cab's outside."

Anybody who knows me knows that I'm a terrible drinker. My eyes were watering, I got the shakes just like when I eat yellow squash, and then I burped and scared a baby in a booth behind me. BUT we both finished our beers in less than 30 seconds. That too...was...awesome. Now, we're chillin' out and ready to hit the hay so we can start hiking again in the morning.

Thanks for reading,

Number 2

Anheuser Puma, Missouri?

That's my fastest time ever finishing a beer. I had fun today.

Seriously, though, burped so loud I scared a baby in a booth. Scared myself, too.

Saw my first L.L. Bean store during this stop in town. My love affair with L.L. Bean started way back in high school, and it hasn't waned since. Even though we had to wear school uniforms, there were three things that brought me great joy: the enormous L.L. Bean backpack with the reflective stripe across the front pocket, the ever-popular L.L. Bean pullover jacket with front zipper pocket, and of course the beloved duck boots. We were overly prepared in the halls of my high school.

I was not able to spend more than a minute inside that L.L. Bean, but I just had to walk in there to say that I'd been there. I have yet to make it back to an L.L. Bean, but something tells me it won't be long now.

Another thing about L.L. Bean up there in New England, it is everywhere! We met this guy who worked as a ridgerunner on the A.T. His main duties were to educate hikers and maintain a specific section of the trail (i.e., pick up trash and keep the privy functioning). He had this amazing set-up in the middle of the woods, complete with a big white tent set up with sturdy metal poles, I reckon to withstand the weather, and he had everything he needed: water supply, a desk, a lantern, some books. It looked very cozy. He was all decked out in *the best* L.L. Bean apparel, and had a great attitude even in the cold, wet rain. I was inspired by his set-up, his attitude, his outfit, and his job. To this day, I think about how rewarding it would be to work a season as a ridgerunner. It's a paid position to live in the woods. What more could I ask for?

Sunday, June 30, 2013 – Just Puke and Keep Hiking

Starting Location: Norwich → Destination: Vermont
   Today's Miles: 14.60 – Trip Miles: 347.60

We made it! Started hiking at 7:00 a.m. and made it through a bunch of towns in Vermont. The houses and yards were just as I imagined they would be – storybook cute.

Today was the first time we actually hiked through multiple towns; we ate at this tiny little deli called the Full Belly Deli and it was delightful. I had the chicken tenders and Puma had a sandwich with turkey and cheese and apple slices...she would.

The second half of our hike had us walking through some tall grass (taller than me) and it went on for a while. The hills were steep, but the trail had hardly any roots or rocks to trip us up.

Tonight, we're sharing a shelter with more NOBOs than we ever have before. Nice guys. I'm looking forward to hitting the trail again tomorrow. As always, thanks for reading.

Falling asleep to chitter chatter and the smell of a campfire...I like it,
Number 2

Puma puked today because she drank too much water (it was just a little bit of puke, but she handled it waaaay better than I would have):

I was sweating so much and couldn't drink enough water. It was sloshing around in my stomach. That's when I puked. Number 2 recommended we take a timeout. I just puke and keep hiking.

I never puked on the trail, not once. Puma puked a couple of times, but it didn't slow her down one bit. She experienced blisters, puking, getting stung, almost drowning, and a few other things during this experience. I didn't get any blisters, I never puked, and I didn't get stung. If *I* had experienced those things instead of Puma, it would have been a different story.

My main challenges were not having enough food and getting too cold. Looking back, I could have done a better job in my food selections and clothing selections, but now we know for next time.

Puma was tough. She *is* tough. I've said it before and I'll say it again right now, I'm grateful to have shared the journey with her.

Monday, July 1, 2013 – Somewhere in Vermont

Starting Location: Vermont → Destination: Vermont

Today's Miles: 11.60 – Trip Miles: 359.2

All in all, Vermont is just lovely so far. Granted, there is quite a bit of mud, but that's nothing new.

Today's hiking was kind of like riding a rollercoaster because of all the ups and downs in a row. We also had more experiences of hiking through the overgrown fields. Every time we do this I get Sting's version of "Fields of Gold" in my head; I try to sing it just like he does. Sounds awful.

The rain fell on us steadily after our quick little lunch break. It was raining hard, and I never got cold. That made me very happy. I guess we are getting closer to the warmer temperatures and my body is handling it better than the cold.

What else, what else, we are still having fun out here, and I still day-dream about the beach and my puppy back home.

Dinner was a delicious pack of chili mac with beef...we eat everything with tortillas and wash it all down with sweet peach tea. Man, that stuff is good! That's really all I know right now, y'all.

We'd like to send our families great big hugs. Thanks for reading!

Love y'all,

Number 2

Are you kiddin' me, Puma's socks always smell like lilacs:

Even using inserts does not stop my blisters. Oh well. Forded a river this morning. Put my camp shoes on to try to work around having wet hiking shoes. I don't understand how all this water doesn't bother Number 2's feet.

You might have noticed that we stopped being so specific about our locations. Let me explain –

We felt like we were being followed. Someone made ugly comments on our trail journal threatening to harm us out on the trail. This person recommended that we be careful because gay people have been murdered out on the Appalachian Trail.

We decided not to acknowledge this person's comments, and our faithful readers were fussing with this person enough through the guestbook. I wanted to move past this negativity because the trail journal had become such an important piece of this journey for all of us.

To make matters worse, we were in areas with really bad cell service. We'd be offline for a while and our family and friends were getting pretty worried about what was going on out there on the trail. Everyone kept asking for updates and requesting that we give some kind of signal that we were alive. They all thought the worst.

We delayed the trail entries by a few days rather than giving our exact locations and posting every day. I think my dad even had one of his buddies in the police department do some investigation on who this person was or where they were. To my knowledge, we never saw this person.

I had some disturbing mental warfare out on the trail in Vermont, too. I can't remember where we were, but I could feel the negative energy surrounding this one shelter. Someone's fully loaded backpack was inside the shelter leaning up against a far wall. That was not too alarming at first; but when no one ever came for it, that bothered me. And this was all around the same time that our "favorite reader" was harassing us. It put me on edge.

I remember trying to fall asleep in the super dark night, already knowing that it was not going to go well. I'll try to describe what I saw in my dream –

A dark image aggressively zoomed towards my eyes and forehead. I knew I needed to wake up, I mean I remember trying to yell at myself in my dream to, "*Wake Up!*" I awoke with my whole body on pins and needles. I sat straight up and realized I slipped off my sleeping pad. Couldn't see anything, but whatever was coming for me knew I was awake. I never heard anything, never saw anything, but everything in my being was begging me to stay alert. So, I stayed up. I don't know if Puma ever woke up, but I stayed on guard until the sun came up.

I was so ready to get the hell out of that shelter and away from that backpack.

Tuesday, July 2, 2013 – Boudreaux's Butt Paste on Her Feet

Starting Location: Vermont → Destination: Vermont

Today's Miles: 9.90 – Trip Miles: 369

Well, when we signed off last night, the rain came down harder than ever before! Man, I'm telling you it was absolutely pounding the shelter and everything else all through the night. That seems to be the pattern lately: rain starts in the early afternoon and continues until morning. That's why we like to get an early start AND an early finish.

We forded a couple of creeks that weren't anything to write home about, but the last one was high enough that we went downstream a bit to find us a better crossing, and we found it a-okay.

We've already had our victory sausages, our clothes are hanging on the line, I texted my sister, and now we're resting our feet and thinking about dinner.

I think I have my first blister of the hike...at least I think I do. I try not to make a fuss about it since, you know, Puma's had such a time of it.

I can't believe it's already July, y'all! I hope you have a fantastic Fourth of July with lots of cheeseburgers, tater tots, crinkle fries with chili, water balloon launchers, fruit salad, super soakers, homemade pies, and sparklers! (Makes me think of all my family parties...we don't ever need an excuse to have sparklers.)

Love to you all,

Number 2

I just shot Puma out of canon holding a banner that says "Lee Greenwood for Mayor!":

I smeared Boudreaux's Butt Paste on my feet today. I thought it would work but it didn't.

She tried everything to keep the blisters away. She held a flame to the needle, doctored herself, buttered 'em up, put second skin on top, tied a bandana over 'em, and duct taped 'em. Still, the blisters came. Don't make this religious! The journey of a thousand blisters begins with a single step. I said don't!

Wednesday, July 3, 2013 – The Inn at Long Trail and Darn Tough Socks

Starting Location: Stony Brook Shelter → Destination: The Inn at Long Trail

Today's Miles: 8.10 – Trip Miles: 377.20

Woke up to a puddle inside the tent – thankfully, it was on Puma's side. The rain came down hard again last night, but it's all good because we walked into town today.

The place we're staying is called The Inn at Long Trail. It's got this old-fashioned country feel to it, including an Irish pub with lots of furniture made of logs and a huge stone fireplace. I bet it's hoppin' during the winter months. Puma and I went in there for some potato skins covered in Vermont cheddar cheese. We also had two chicken sandwiches, two pints of Guinness, and two vodkas and diets. Don't worry, there weren't any babies around for me to scare.

We did catch up with our good friend, Emily, this afternoon via telephone, and she filled me in on all the world's current events. Sent some more texts to friends, and planned our next days of the trip. I'm looking forward to hiking up and over Killington Mountain.

My friends, this is a whole lot of fun out here. Even with the rain and the mud, we are still finding ourselves laughing and having a good time. I'm thinking about heading back down to the pub for a snack. They might let me try to play the Irish drum with the stick that's laying over in the corner of the stage. I wanna try to play "Wipe Out." Thanks to everyone who has been following our journal.

That's all folks,

Number 2

Oh dear, Puma's using her lounge singer voice to order more appetizers:

Number 2 would be on the other side away from the puddle. We hiked past a local outfitter and got us some more Darn Tough socks. Number 2 had a hole in one of her socks, so she got a free pair. After leaving the outfitter, this guy in a truck pulls alongside us and asks if need a lift. He happened to be the retired captain of the Killington Fire Department. Showed us all around town. How about that for some trail magic.

I must confess about my Darn Tough socks. Darn Tough socks are the absolute toughest socks out there. Proudly made in the great state of Vermont. Y'all, when we walked past this outdoor store right on the trail, I lied and said I had gotten a hole in my sock by natural wear and tear. The policy with Darn Tough socks basically says that if you ever have a natural defect with the sock, they will give you a free replacement pair.

I had been wearing the same pair of Darn Tough socks since the start of the trail, through the mud, the rain, the cold, the sweat, and the miles. Nothing would break these socks. I had a small hole in the toe area from when I accidentally caught my sock on fire trying to dry it out. It was totally my fault. Not the sock's fault.

I got a free pair of socks. I still feel some kind of way about this situation. I mean, I'm no saint, and I've done way worse, but I still feel some kind of way about it.

Thursday, July 4, 2013 – Rutland Re-supply and Celebrating Our Independence

Starting Location: The Inn at Long Trail → Destination: Same great place

Today's Miles: 0 – Trip Miles: 377

Happy Fourth of July, everybody! This morning we had a fantastic complimentary breakfast that mimicked something out of a food and culture magazine. Puma had an omelet with mushrooms and cheddar, and I had a fried egg sandwich with more of that delicious Vermont cheddar cheese. Dang, that stuff is so good!

After breakfast, we caught the two-dollar bus ride into the neighboring town of Rutland, which was about nine miles down the road. Rutland has a population of about 63,000 people and it's adorable. Lots of beautiful

houses, old stone churches, a few bars, some delis, a Wendy's (we hit that hard as soon as we got off the bus), and it's all tucked away in between these big beautiful, tree-covered mountains. Oh, and we learned that the wonderful inventor, Mr. John Deere, was born in the town of Rutland. Isn't that something! We got the rest of our re-supply items in town and enjoyed walking around for a bit before catching the bus back into Killington.

On our bus ride back, I was taking in the scenery – lots of little American flags lined the sidewalks – and I found myself thinking about all of those who came before us (insert patriotic flute and drum roll).

As we got closer to our stop, Puma and I were lookin' out the window to see where we pick up the trail again in the morning; we identified it easily because two folks were just coming off the trail vigorously waving for the bus to stop!

This couple had been hiking south, and we exchanged names and discussed how muddy the trail is right now, yadda yadda, right. Well, the lady asked Puma where our backpacks were, and Puma explained that we had gone into town for our re-supply, yadda yadda, you know. Here's the funny part – I picked up on this lady's British accent, but Puma did not. So, as soon as Puma finishes talking about the trail she says, "We're just out here getting our re-supply and celebrating our independence!"

The lady rolled her eyes in a hilarious sort of way, and her American hiking beau quickly followed with, "Ha! Yeah, independence from HER!" while lovingly pointing his finger and laughing. The bus stopped, and Puma and I curtsied just before we hopped off. I slapped my knee because I was laughing so hard. These are the moments that I love.

We hit the trail early tomorrow morning, and I do hope you'll be following us along in this crazy journal.

Love to you all,

Number 2

Spelling her entire message out with a sparkler in cursive, here's Puma:

I was happy to be watching the storm from inside the Irish pub. I couldn't tell which way the wind and rain were blowing. Stopped by a discount clothing store in Rutland and bought some different clothes to hike in; all for less than 20 dollars.

I have told this story about Puma and the British lady so many times, and it never gets old. I wish I could have taken a video of the whole conversation in real time. The boyfriend and I found it all to be quite funny; and he pointed his finger at his girlfriend so fast when he said, *"Yeah, independence from her!"* I loved it.

Friday, July 5, 2013 – Where the A.T. and Long Trail Meet

Starting Location: Inn at Long Trail → Destination: Governor Clement Shelter

Today's Miles: 10.60 – Trip Miles: 387.80

And they're off! That's right, folks, we hit the trail this morning after another hearty breakfast at the inn. Puma had the omelet and home fries again while I had the pancakes and sausage.

The hike started out real foggy this morning, and at times in these thick trees, it was dark enough for our headlamps.

Once we got to the top of Killington Mountain, we were above the clouds and saw the sun for JUST a moment. It does exist; I saw it.

Oh, and on the way up the mountain, we saw another bear. He must have had his headphones in because he did not hear us coming until we were about 20 feet away. I stopped as soon as I saw him, and he just scampered off. Y'all know we started singing again after that.

This evening we are sharing a shelter with six other folks who are all hiking the Long Trail. Really great people. The shelter is quite impressive because it's all stone and has apparently been here since the 1920s – before the A.T.

And don't you know there's a storm moving in right now, right as I type this. I'm so happy to meet all these people, hear their stories, and take these moments with me.

Wishing you all happiness and health.

Love,

Number 2

Practicing for her public library debut, welcome to Puma's story time hour:

I was reminded of Maine at certain points of today. Roots and mud, same as Maine. I've adjusted our plan, and my feet are dry today. It's a good day.

Two trails exist on the same path in Vermont. The Appalachian Trail and the Long Trail share the same path for about 100 miles. The Long Trail runs the length of Vermont all the way up to Canada. The shelters were accordingly bigger than the ones we had been accustomed to at this point. Made sense to me.

I remember sitting around with other hikers waiting for our water to boil so we could pour it into our dehydrated dinners. We had a nice time sharing stories and experiences, but I was tired and not up for playing "hostess with the mostest." I packed up my food bag and my camp stove, then said, "Well, I'm gonna go watch some television." Their eyes got so big and jealousy was oozing from their faces until I said I was kidding and was just going to lay down.

This was before we all watched movies and television shows on our phones. This was before Facebook and Instagram were really popular.

Our phones were used in the same way as when cell phones first came out, only for emergencies and my nightly journal routine.

I recall my father giving me my first cell phone and telling me to, "Never use it!" We were truly unplugged back then and out there on the trail. It was like the good ol' days of grade school entertainment when we'd enter the word "BOOBS" on our calculators for a good laugh. 80085.

Saturday, July 6, 2013 – That Level of Tired

Starting Location: Governor Clement Shelter → Destination: Greenwall Shelter

Today's Miles: 14.50 – Trip Miles: 402.3

The trail sure is busy on a Saturday! We crossed paths with many groups, families, section hikers, and individuals. The rule is that the person going uphill has the right of way, and a lot of people already knew that rule. I seem to always get it backwards, but it's not a huge, huge deal.

Today's hike was good; we took some extra breaks and a nice guy gave us both an oatmeal cream pie. Some steep hills again today, but we just keep our heads down and keep on moving. We're getting into some bigger miles up ahead. For some reason, no matter the mileage, my feet are toast by the end of the day.

Also with these longer days, we've started comin' up with what I like to call "Excellent Questions" in our conversations. Here's an example: Does Nelly still wear a bandage under his eye? And in order for it to count, we both have to be stumped by the question. There have been other Excellent Questions, but I can't remember any of them at this present moment.

Thanks for reading the journal.

I'm pooped,

Number 2

And now, I give you the inspiration for Excellent Questions, Countess Pumala:

Out on the trail today, we ran across someone we met way back in Monson who was a friend of the lady who owns Shaw's. This friend is out here on the Long Trail. Number 2 believes she gets a point for seeing someone she "knows."

I remember being so tired. That level of tired after hiking an average length of a half marathon day after day felt amazing, but I was exhausted. My backpack had become a part of my body. I was to the point of not wanting to take it off even if I needed something inside because I was too tired to fuss with it.

I was so tired that if I propped one of my trekking poles up against a tree and it fell to the ground, I would truly debate whether or not I should bend over to pick it up or just leave it. Anything extra was out of the question...or was at the very least questioned. My brain had gone irrational, "I don't really need that trekking pole on the ground, I'll buy another one once we get to town." You know how it was as a kid when you'd fall asleep on the living room floor or couch and were too fussy and tired to move to your bedroom? I was that kid.

It was too hot to utilize the lovely stone chimney at Greenwall Shelter, and I was, of course, way too tired to gather firewood. I remember picturing how lovely a little fire might have been on a cool day in New England, but then I fell asleep.

Nothing ever dries out on the trail. We were trying to air things out on the bench, but I'm here to tell you that everything stays damp and stinky until washed. Even then, after a wash, the funk is never really gone. I liked having one shirt at a time. It made for efficient decision-making.

Sunday, July 7, 2013 – A Bridge in Vermont

Starting Location: Greenwall Shelter → Destination: Peru Pond Shelter

Today's Miles: 14.50 – Trip Miles: 416

Good hiking today! We got an early start, which was nice, and the weather was just perfect this morning. Ran into quite a few folks who are hiking the Long Trail and also a few more NOBOs.

Puma and I really enjoy meeting all these different folks along the way, and we try to encourage all those who are out here.

Not too much to tell today. The trail is really muddy at times and flat at different points, too. We absolutely fly through the flat parts! The mud is thick enough to walk on in places, and also thick enough to make some stellar mud pies, if you're into that.

There's this bird that has been following us since southern Maine; I'm pretty sure it's a Hermit Thrush. Somebody go look this bird up online, turn your computer speakers waaaay up, and play back the song of this particular bird. That's what goes off every morning at 5:30 a.m., unless Puma has installed an alarm on my watch and didn't tell me about it.

We've passed many streams and brooks so far (all had a bridge AND a handrail), and I think about my mom's fly fishing club every time. Those ladies are just the coolest; Puma and I are just guppies right now, but one day we'll be full-fledged members.

Thanks to all who keep on reading this journal of ours. We appreciate your words of encouragement. It's time for me to go to bed.

With old country tunes running through my head,

I bid y'all a good night,

Number 2

Please welcome the anonymous fourth member of The Judds, Puma Judd:

Hiking southbound on the A.T. has us expecting hard conditions. Whenever we hear water, we assume we're getting wet. When we come to the base of a mountain, we assume we are climbing to the very top. But that's not what's happening out here anymore. They have bridges down here.

The trail had gotten "kinder" in the ways of bridges and summits. We had grown accustomed to up and over, but down around this section of the trail, we would get close to the top then skirt around the edge of these mountains and hills.

The bridges were a lovely sight, and we would actually stop and discuss our appreciation for their handywork. We were recognizing our gratitude pretty hard at this point on the trail because Maine had done a number on us.

I'm so happy we decided to hike the A.T. southbound. In all honesty, I don't think we had a choice in the matter, psychologically speaking, but it was unique and hard and I really had no idea what we were getting ourselves into. It's the more popular choice. Both directions are difficult in their own right. Finishing on top of Katahdin would be epic, and I know a few people who have had that experience, but we wanted our families and friends to join us at the finish line. Whether we read about it or experience it first-hand, either way can ignite a sense of adventure that changes us forever.

Monday, July 8, 2013 — Mickey D's Coma

Starting Location: Peru Pond Shelter → Destination: Green Mountain House

Today's Miles: 10 – Trip Miles: 426.80

Bumped into a fellow Nashvillian today. He was headed north up the mountain as we were coming down, and he asked what we were listening to

on our iPods. I told him country and he said, "That's my neck of the woods, I'm from Nashville!" Then we said, "We're from Nashville, too!" Immediately we started trying to figure out if we had any mutual acquaintances – and we did! After discussing our pre-trail life for about three and half minutes, we discovered that we both knew the same guy from Mt. Juliet, Tennessee.

We made it into Manchester City this afternoon and are staying at the Green Mountain House. Every hiker gets a free pint of Ben & Jerry's ice cream!

We also found our way to our first pig-out at McDonald's on this adventure. Thanks for keeping up with us, and we'll talk to everyone tomorrow.

Feeling the Mickey D's coma, this was,

Number 2

In my best Ed McMahon imitation, Heeeeeere's Puma:

The hiker hunger hit today. The plan was to keep moving past Manchester Center, but I had to stop. Both of us ate all our food in our food bags. It's a fun weight loss plan.

How'd we get into town? I'll tell you. We hitchhiked! My first time with that, and it felt...odd. Getting picked up was not as odd a feeling as actually sticking my thumb out in the wind.

We were hiking along with another hiker, and he made the decision to hitchhike into town first; and since we had eaten all of our food, we thought it was good idea to follow his lead. As a novice, I made the mistake of getting up on the road a ways down from our fellow hiker and realized that was not going to work. Who was going to pick up two separate parties of hitchhikers? No one.

So, I got down off the road, and we hid in the tree line until he got picked up, which I'm sure he appreciated. Sorry, dude. This was a lonely road winding through the mountains, and it took a good while for someone to stop for him. I wondered if the people from the nearest town had grown to expect hikers on the side of the road.

Finally, it was my turn. Puma stayed on the shoulder with the backpacks while I made myself presentable. I walked up to the side of the road with nervous giggles, sharpened my thumb, and flung it out there with a smile. We wanted to make it known that this was a "twofer" situation – both riders were a part of the deal or no deal. No, I did not show any skin! I was covered in mud stains and had crazy hair sticking out the top of my Buff.

The first couple of cars went by, and I couldn't make eye contact with them. The shame and discomfort was obvious, my thumb might have been bent or something, too. I had to give myself a talking to because we really needed to get into town. So, I tried again, and this time with more confidence. I gave "honest eyes" to all those who passed me by. It was hard not to take it personally. Then it happened! Wouldn't you know it, a Subaru stopped within a short running distance, and Puma did all the talking. Inside were a couple of fellas headed to the golf course, and they were nice as could be. We were grateful for the ride, and they enjoyed our stories as we rode into town. They asked where to drop us off, and as soon as we saw the "golden arches," it was on! I ate like a linebacker.

Tuesday, July 9, 2013 – The Green Mountain House Hostel and Pat Summitt

Starting Location: Green Mountain House Hostel → Destination: Same lovely place

Today's Miles: 0 – Trip Miles: 426.8

What a great stop! The Green Mountain House is definitely worth checking out if you're ever in Manchester City, Vermont. The owner does a great job!

Now, one of the main reasons we stopped here in Manchester City is because Puma has been dealing with some numbness for about a month. She didn't tell y'all about it because she's a real puma. We were able to get her an appointment with a local chiropractor who worked out all her kinks. Thank goodness!

We spent the afternoon resting, soaking our feet in Epsom salt, and eating Ben & Jerry's ice cream. Oh, and I finished off an entire bag of Cheese Puffs.

More NOBOs came in this evening, and we all sat around the kitchen table talking about all the different hostels to stay at along the trail. We also ate dinner together, and it was a very nice evening shared with fellow hikers.

The other main reason we stayed today was that we knew ESPN was going to air a film about Pat Summitt. Puma and I both sat on the couch with tears rolling down our faces as we watched her colleagues, former players, her son, and many others tell heartwarming stories about how much Pat had influenced and elevated their lives. It was scary, too, because there was a good bit about the Pat Summitt stare. You know that look that can scare the crap out of you even through the television. We just have the utmost respect for Pat Summitt, and it was really great to be watching a program all about Tennessee women's basketball all the way up here in Vermont.

Y'all keep the prayers and encouragement coming, and we'll keep heading down south! Thanks for reading.

Love,

Number 2

And now, someone who saw Pat Summitt many times in Knoxville, please welcome, Puma:

I was at a college sporting event when I first saw her. It was a powerful moment for me. I'm glad I went to the chiropractor during this little break. I needed it. For any SOBOs reading this journal, if you plan to stay at this hostel, call ahead of time. This place gets booked up quickly.

A little bit more about the Green Mountain House Hostel; this place was nice! I remember it being a two-story home with lovely forest green siding and white trim. There was a detached garage that was equally storybook quaint, and that's where the owner lived. The main house was for us hikers. Very homey and very Vermont – earthy, rugged, outdoorsy, and organized.

We walked into the kitchen, which had everything we needed if we wanted to cook a family-style meal, and then it opened up into a very welcoming living room. The lightly colored carpet still showed the vacuum lines, and the big sectional couch looked fresh and plush. There were floor to ceiling bookshelves full of books and DVDs of different topics, all organized by author and genre.

The upstairs was divided into two bedrooms (maybe three, can't remember exactly), and there were two or three twin beds in each room. Each bed had its own little section of the room, and the bed sheets were tucked high and tight. Down comforter included! There was a window unit that ran all the time and lullabied me into a cool, deep sleep.

Puma and I got cleaned up, put on the hiker loaner clothes, grabbed our ice cream, and wrapped up in our own blankets on the couch to watch the ESPN special about Pat Summitt. I'm glad we caught the show, and I felt inspired. Everybody knows, "Defense wins championships."

I remember feeling like an intruder, like I had broken into this nice family's home, and the kids were going to be coming home from school soon and find me, this dirty hiker trash, rummaging through their belongings. I kept waiting to find the smoke in the mirrors, the trap door to the underworld, or a dead fly on the windowsill. Nothing! This place was spotless. We had the place all to ourselves. It was a lovely trap of comfort and amenities. This was a nice retreat, but it was time to suit up and get back out there.

Wednesday, July 10, 2013 – Is it a Bear or a Labrador?

Starting Location: Green Mountain House Hostel → Destination: Stratton Pond Shelter

Today's Miles: 10.50 – Trip Miles: 437.30

We got to the trail by 9 a.m. and as soon as we started to cross the street, Puma yelled, "STOP!" Just then a good sized black bear ran across the street. In my brain, when I saw it, I thought, "Oh look, that's a big Labrador crossing the...wait, that's a bear." We gave the bear some time to get ahead of us.

The hike today was still pretty muddy, but we managed to get into the shelter before the rain started to fall. I love when that happens.

We met some more fun folks in the shelter this evening. Puma and I make friends with people for a day, then both parties move on. It's all good.

And now, it's that time when I get ready to close my eyes and dream of those beef and cheese stick combos that are usually sold at the checkout line in every grocery.

Goodnight America.

Love,

Number 2

Fun Fact: Puma wears ear plugs in her nose when the stench of hikers gets overwhelming in the shelter.

Puma, now back to you:

It makes me so happy when we dodge the evening thunderstorms. It's been raining for the last seven days, and we only got rained on once. I got close to snapping a picture of that black bear today, but a car came around the corner too fast and it ran off.

A guestbook entry that made me laugh:

Hahah....I was reading your July 10th entry about seeing a bear that looks like a Lab! That made me think of the time my dad took us kids on a vacation camping in the mountains. His goal was to see a bear and he'd been looking everywhere for one all week. Well, we were driving down the road and all of a sudden, Dad shouts, "BEAR!!!!!!!!!!!!" He speeds up and when we get close, there was a BIG, HUGE, GINORMOUS...BLACK LAB! Yeah, we never let him live that one down! Anyway, still loving reading your stories.

TJ, Saturday, July 20, 2013

By this point, we had seen a few big black bears in their natural habitats, and they really did remind me of large black Labs. Matter of fact, I even turned a corner and found myself within an arm's reach of a bear. I remember stopping and just staring at it like Walter Sobchak stares at Donny in the *Big Lebowski* (blink, blink). I turned to Puma and said, "He must have had his ear buds in and didn't hear us coming." Honest mistake on the bear's part; there was no drama. Not even once did we have any trouble with bears. That's a good bear.

Thursday, July 11, 2013 – A Smelly Shelter with Good Company

Starting Location: Stratton Pond Shelter → Destination: Kid Gore Shelter

Today's Miles: 15 – Trip Miles: 452.30

Ooo wee, what a good day! We slept in until about 6:30 a.m. and were on the trail by 7:30 a.m. Today's terrain had a lot of rolling hills and mud and rocks and roots. We went up and over Stratton Mountain this morning and did not get a view from the fire tower up there because one, we didn't climb up the tower, and two, there was a thick blanket of white all around us. Thank you, clouds.

Got into camp this evening and there it was...finally, a view...from the shelter. The sky has been kind to us today dropping zero rain; today was just a really nice day.

There's some cool folks coming into the shelters in the evenings, and everybody lately has a really great sense of humor. I just love it!

Thinking of all those back home.

Love to you all,

Number 2

Making more friends than she can count; she is Puma:

"Vermud" is the muddy nickname for Vermont. I was exhausted and starving, but once I finished my lunch, I was good to go again.

The view from Kid Gore Shelter was lovely, but this shelter had a stink like old smelly, warm ketchup packets. Barf. I'm not complaining, I'm describing. We still slept in the shelter that night and had a wonderful evening with fellow hikers. Blue Bird was the name of the lady who also stayed at that shelter that evening; she had a great sense of humor. She gasped when I identified the call of the Hermit Thrush bird and looked at me like I was the most impressive bird watcher she'd ever met. I laughed out loud and explained that the Hermit Thrush was the only one I knew because it was extremely common in the dense forest areas, *and* it happens to be the state bird of Vermont. I assured her that I was not at all her birding hero. We all laughed about her reaction pretty hard.

I don't recall why we stayed in the shelter that night, maybe it was because we enjoyed the company so much. I loved being in the tent with my sleeping pad, my sleeping bag, and my backpack. I loved all my gear, and I spent a solid two years researching the absolute best gear for this adventure. For key pieces, like my sleeping bag and sleeping pad, we sprang for the best of the best products at the time. They were well worth the money for the exchange of quality, warmth, and weight.

I have included a list of all the gear that we used for the trail at the end of the book. Remember this was over 11 years ago now, so I'm sure there's better stuff on the market, but I still love my backpack and my sleeping bag. Just can't part with these things, ever.

Why did that shelter smell like warm ketchup packets? I still can't totally figure that one out, but I will say it's important to practice Leave No Trace camping methods. It doesn't take much for these shelters to get trashed, and not all shelters can be lucky enough to have a constant caretaker. I just follow one of my cardinal rules: leave it better than you found it. This is a practical recommendation for communal living and common areas, even in the workplace.

Friday, July 12, 2013 – The Healing Powers of Chips and Salsa

Starting Location: Kid Gore Shelter → Destination: Melville Shelter
Today's Miles: 12.80 – Trip Miles: 465.10

Hands down, today was the nicest weather we've had on the trail so far! There were times that I had to remind myself that I wasn't hiking in Tennessee with fall weather conditions.

We came across another fire tower in our hike earlier this morning and decided to climb up to the top for a look at Vermont. It was so beautiful! These clear days really make the hiking experience so different.

After a few hours we stopped for lunch on a rock; the lunch menu consisted of two packages of gummy snacks, two Clif bars, and a bunch of summer sausage.

We passed a guy heading north on the trail and asked him about recommendations for our next town. He told us a good place to stay and added that there was an awesome Mexican restaurant right across the street. Puma and I spent the rest of the day discussing the healing powers of chips and salsa. This coming from the person who thinks "Pilates" is the Spanish word for "please."

We're comin' up on Massachusetts pretty quickly now! I hope you'll stay tuned for more journal entries.

Shout out again to Numbers 1 and 3. I think about y'all all the time out here.

Love yew,

Number 2

A tribute to Los Tres Amigos restaurant in Nashville, Tennessee: We love your sweet tea and cheese dip. Puma has confirmed that she will be back for more in the near future:

We took ten hours to hike 13 miles in Maine one time. On this day, we finished in six hours. Glad to be heading south.

Vermont was beautifully green. The thing I noticed most about the overlooks in Vermont was all the space. No malls, no office buildings, no condos, just a bunch of hills and trees and sky. Absolutely beautiful.

I live across the street from a busy parkway, a mall, and the Grand Ole Opry. I am awakened by the cacophonous sounds of "crotch rocket" motorcycles at all hours of the day or night. The bright lights of the mall pollute any chance of seeing a starry night. I do not want my A.T. adventure to be as good as it gets for me. I want to see those certified "dark sky viewing" national parks. I need to sleep out under the stars with nature's symphony. I think maybe I've been in a bad mood for the last year and half, and the only way I can make it better is to shake things up, make some changes, explore for eight hours a day, write about it, and then experience the healing powers of chips and salsa.

Saturday, July 13, 2013 – Giving It My All for an Audience of Two

Starting Location: Melville Shelter → Destination: Almost to the border
  Today's Miles: 15.40 – Trip Miles: 480.50

Laying down on a full belly of my backwoods mashed potato burritos right now thinking about how good that Mexican restaurant is gonna be tomorrow.

We pushed past our planned destination today so that we could maximize our stop in town tomorrow; only got four miles and some change before walking into town. It's prolly gonna rain tonight, too, so we'll need to dry out the tent.

It feels really great to be close to our next state line. Y'all know what to do: just take a moment to reflect and then holler "DOG SHIT!" It's liberating!

We thoroughly enjoyed hiking through Vermont. The Green Mountain Forest sure is worth a trip if you ever get up this way. Wishing you all a great evening.

Fat and full,

Number 2

Channel Pume News, working for you:

So long, Vermont. Number 2 and I decided Maine was muddier...for us anyway. We hiked up on a second bear yesterday. We were standing in a clearing under the powerlines, and the bear never heard Number 2 singing Nelly's solo in Florida Georgia Line's song "Cruise."

Damn, I wish she hadn't said that...so, yeah, I remember standing on this rock in the big powerline clearing and singing Nelly's part of that song. Standing there, I felt like I was the headliner at the old Starwood Amphitheatre in Murfreesboro, Tennessee, or better yet Bonnaroo. No, that song was not on my iPod, it must have been playing in the Mexican restaurant (doubtful).

The music on my iPod was only for emergencies, and I used it only a few times. That's pretty good considering we were out there for almost six months. My head was full of tunes all the time like an around-the-clock disc jockey, but in that clearing, I was a star! Giving it my all on a full stage for an audience of two; the bear never looked up, never spun around in his chair. Maybe it would have gone differently if I had chosen a different song? Perhaps something from the Gloria Estefan collection? We will never know, and that's okay; just means I haven't found my higher calling yet.

Chapter Six

Massachusetts

Sunday, July 14, 2013 – Massachusetts State Lane and Desperados

Starting Location: Almost to the border → Destination: Williamstown
  Today's Miles: 4 – Trip Miles: 484.50

Held our state line dance party and hollered real loud this morning as we crossed the border into Massachusetts. Got into Williamstown early, called the folks who run the Williamstown Motel and they came and picked us up within five minutes. Perfect timing!

I scarfed down two donuts, two glasses of orange juice, a bagel with cream cheese, and a bowl of cereal while Puma was getting us checked in. They had a breakfast buffet, what was I supposed to do?

We dried out all our gear, cleaned up, and took naps while pretending to watch television. After that order of business was completed, Puma planned our next few days. We've got Greylock Mountain in the morning, and I've been staring at it all afternoon. Looks good, looks real good.

This evening we went to dinner at the Mexican restaurant across the street, and the waitress said, "Are you hikers?" I guess our little sandwich bags for wallets gave us away. The name of the restaurant is Desperados, and they have FREE entree items for hikers! It was a great deal! We ate tacos, chips and salsa, and yes, cheese dip; it was all very good and worth the stop. I'm so full right now.

Looking forward to getting back on the trail in the morning. We'll see what else Massachusetts has to offer. Thanks for keeping up with us, y'all!

We love ya,

Number 2

At dinner, Puma had a glass shaped like a cactus full of sangria that required both hands to hold it. Now, what have you got to say for yourself:

We crossed another state line today. I'm focusing on getting us rerouted to the White Mountains. Almost have it all figured out.

I believe it was here when we ran into another hiker who had lost his wallet. I saw him in the lobby area with his backpack and a panicked look on his face. He reminded me of an old co-worker of mine, and I felt sorry for him. I think we asked him if there was anything we could do, but he graciously declined.

I can't imagine how it would feel to lose a wallet while hiking a long-distance trail. Like where the hell do you start looking for that? The concept of "retracing your steps" just feels way too much to think about. If I were him in that situation, I would have started my new life right then and there. Congratulations to Williamstown on their newest resident! Because she lost her wallet, she is now going to be a contributing member of this community.

I mean it's one thing to open up to a stranger on a flight but being in a new town with no ID...and no idea where to go and no way to pay for it...something had to give. I'm sure it worked out in the end; I mean there is no way that young man is still standing around in that lobby. Probably just failed to close his tab at the Mexican restaurant across the street – aptly named Desperados.

Monday, July 15, 2013 – Mount Greylock and Sister Mary So-and-so

Starting Location: Williamstown → Destination: Cheshire

Today's Miles: 15.40 – Trip Miles: 499.9

Y'all would not believe who we ran into this morning as we were hiking up Greylock. Remember the British lady and her American hiking boyfriend that Puma impressed on July 4th?

Yep! It was those two again! She recognized us right at the same time that I recognized them, and we both reacted like we'd been best friends for twelve years or something crazy. After Killington, which is where we first saw them, they headed down towards the bottom of Massachusetts and started heading north.

I asked Puma if she caught the accent this time, and she did. I'm sure both parties were snickering as we walked our separate ways. That was just too funny.

Once we got to the top of Greylock, there was a huge war memorial tower that was just beautiful, and there were also a lot of people. Puma and I looked out of place as we stepped over the guardrail and into civilization. It takes us a minute to get our wits about us and with everybody staring at us, it seems to take a lot longer than just a minute. I think it's hilarious.

The best part of being at the top of Greylock (the highest point in Massachusetts) is the lodge that serves food and ice cream. I had the bar-b-q sandwich, and Puma had the grilled cheese sandwich. They each came with a side order of potato salad and coleslaw, which were really good.

We ran into some fellow SOBOs as we were eating, two guys by the names of Fifth Meal and Meal House, and they said they'd been trying to catch us for a looong time. We all caught up on the news from the trail, they informed us about how crazy the weather was in the Whites when they went through, and how awesome it is to be done with Maine. It was really great catching up with them.

We hiked past our planned destination again today and into the next town of Cheshire to stay at the local Catholic Church, St. Mary's of the Assumption. Slept on the floor of one of the Sunday school classrooms. We had our own bathroom and a water fountain! The little things mean so much. Brought back lots of memories of my parochial school days (including in-school suspension memories – remember kids, spit balls are not ceiling decorations).

Oh me, it's been a great day, and I'm looking forward to tomorrow. We're still having fun out here.

Love y'all,

Number 2

Playing ragtime on the organ in the gymnasium, give it up for, Sister Mary Puma:

Working on our plan for the White Mountains. It's all happening.

Puma was planning, and I was remembering. Puma is a master of logistics. She worked really hard planning our return to the Whites – looking at the maps, calculating the miles, and coordinating our rides. I had no part in the planning, but I knew it was happening. This was nothing for her, though. She spent several years working as a professional in logistics. Think about how many semi trucks are making deliveries to our local grocers all over the country every day. Somebody had to think about that while I was napping.

If I had a nickel for all the times I hung out on the floor of a Catholic school classroom...It was a common pastime during my youth and adolescent years, from kindergarten all the way through high school, to spend a good bit of time on the floor. The reasons ranged from required naptimes and play periods to chilling in the hallways or gymnasiums during breaks or Confession.

Being in that empty classroom was flooding my head with memories. I'm particularly proud of the time I snuck out of the gym to go buy some Krystal hamburgers for me and my friends. True story. I think I was in fifth grade; we were all hanging out on the gym floor during play practice for The Wizard of Oz. I was part of the Lollipop Guild (a small but mighty role) and had ample time to execute my plan. It was simple.

I collected whatever pocket change we could scrounge while chewing a piece of gum (another highly illegal piece of contraband). I easily faked needing to use the restroom, shut the door behind me, ran over to the exit doors and stuck my gum and wrapper on the door catch. This prevented the door from closing all the way and locking me out. I bolted across the back parking lot and playground like a fox, scaled the eight foot chain link fence with ease in my uniform jumper and saddle oxfords, climbed up the embankment and over the guardrail into the Krystal's parking lot. I waved to the patrons staring at me in the drive-thru line and made my way inside.

I waited in line like every other adult until it was my turn to put my bag of change on the counter. Asked the pretty lady for as many Krystals and small orders of fries I could get with my lot, then poof! I was gone again, hopped the guardrail out of sight! Down the embankment, up and over the eight foot fence; I was like the neighborhood cat darting across the playground and parking lot, maybe seen but never caught.

We hid our Krystals in the bellies of our jackets. Laughing to ourselves as we'd work a French fry slowly up through the opening of the collar of our jackets and into our mouths. The smell of fast food filled the gymnasium, and if you knew, you knew. I like to think Sister Mary

So-and-so would have laughed about this now, but I'm grateful I lived to tell the story.

Tuesday, July 16, 2013 – Trail Towns Along the Way

Starting Location: Cheshire→ Destination: Key Wood Shelter

Today's Miles: 13.20 – Trip Miles: 513.10

Got a lot of miles done before lunch today. It's really nice walking through towns so much more frequently now. For lunch, we stopped by Angelina's Sub Shop and it was delicious! I highly recommend that place.

Getting back on the trail after lunch was slow going because I was so full, the heat was beating off the pavement, and I think I ate my Italian sub too fast.

We had a couple more hills to hike up this afternoon, but the temperatures drop a good bit in the shade of all the trees. Got bigger miles to do tomorrow, which will put us in the next town of Lee. I tell y'all what, I might be putting some of this weight back on as we keep walking through towns.

We're very excited about our pending trip back to the Whites! It's great to be able to go back and cross those off our list. Thanks for all your encouragement, America!

Turning in for the night,

Number 2

Gnomes and William Shatner call HER for travel advice, and you know her as, Puma:

I think I'm going to get different backpack. The one I have now has little to no air flow in the back. I'm hoping to give it a test run in the White Mountains.

There are two locations for Angelina's Sub Shop, one in Adams and the other in North Adams, Massachusetts. It's a fine little spot with big, satisfying sandwiches and wraps. I liked how quaint the towns were up there. Felt like we could get everything we needed within walking distance whether it was a new pair of shoes, a sub sandwich, or a place to stay. It was easy. Never had to think about where to park.

Sidewalks everywhere with modest trees, small homes on spacious lots with manicured lawns, and zero traffic; all of this was nice to see and, in a way, made for easy transitions from trail to town and town to trail. Like I always do on vacation, I picture myself settling in the area and look at the town through a new resident lens. Not sure what my job would be, but I think I could be happy making sub sandwiches and hiking around while figuring out my next career move. The Berkshires in Western Massachusetts are beautiful, artsy fartsy, and outdoorsy. Year-round or just for the summer, I'd like that.

Trail towns along the A.T. are essential assets for all hikers providing food, gear, and entertainment. Further south in Virginia is the town of Damascus, known as "Trail Town, USA." These communities make re-supplying along the way a lot easier, and walking down their sidewalks, I felt a sense of belonging. I'll claim every one of them as my own.

Wednesday, July 17, 2013 – Singing to My Mac-n-cheese

Starting Location: Key Wood Shelter → Destination: Lee

Today's Miles: 16 – Trip Miles: 529.10

Moved pretty quickly down the trail today, and my feet are a little sore. It always feels good to have another good day of miles behind us. The best part about today is ending in this air-conditioned room at the lodge just off the trail.

After a little while – a very short while – we got real hungry. The nice folks running the Berkshire Lodge gave us a bunch of recommendations for food. We ended up with pizza, chicken wings, and cheese bread for dinner. It was gone within 15 minutes.

I hope y'all don't get bored reading about what we're having for dinner all the time; it's just such a big part of our lives. I mean, we found ourselves singing to our Velveeta shells and cheese yesterday because, in the words of Ms. Sinead O'Conner, "NothING ComPARES 2 You."

Now I'm gonna let Puma fill y'all in on our upcoming plans. Thanks for reading our journal, everybody.

Love to all,

Number 2

The person not responsible for Bret Michael's new RV show, please welcome, Puma:

We are ready to return to the White Mountains. Heading out Monday! Many thanks to my buddy Don who is driving long distance to help us coordinate this plan. This wouldn't be possible without you, Don.

I remember singing to our macaroni and cheese that afternoon. We were sitting on some old picnic table having our mac and cheese lunch, which is not the best for a quick post-meal cleanup. But it was *the best* lunch on the trail. How many rounds of that Sinead O'Conner song did we sing? So many rounds.

What a simple moment. Hiking or not hiking, I like singing to my food. It's about appreciation of what's before me, and boy, out there, it was appreciated. We were eating all the time, and my body was not telling me, "That's enough." We were burning enough calories that we could eat whatever we came across because it was going to be burned up shortly thereafter. These days, I'm full after eating a medium-sized apple and a small bag of Cheez-its.

Our only job was to walk every day – and to survive. I love going on walks and hikes, always have, but to be able to have the freedom to do it day after day was incredible. I hope to get back to that point in my life again. I hope we all get a chance to step away and take a good long walk.

Thursday, July 18, 2013 – Beartown National Forest and Free Beer and Pizza

Starting Location: Lee → Destination: Beartown National Forest

Today's Miles: 17.40 – Trip Miles: 546.50

Even though the mountainous part of the trail has slowed down a bit, the hills are still proving to be very steep. That, combined with the heat, is kicking our "bootanices," as my dad would say. Today was a long day of hiking, but it felt great to get to our final destination, Beartown National Forest.

Currently, we are in the tent listening to a torrential downpour while watching the water rise higher and higher all around us. Puma is telling me that we might need to move our tent right now because we could float away.

In other news, we did score some popcorn and a couple of beers from this other hiker who was kind enough to share his good fortune. That was a really nice way to end the day.

Tomorrow we hike 10 more miles into Great Barrington to meet our friend Don. I'm ready for a little R&R before we head up to the Whites on Monday.

I am being forced to cut this one short because we're laying in six inches of water. Thanks for reading.

I gotta' get movin',

Number 2

Puma ALWAYS has a plan:

I swam in the lake just before a thunderstorm. We had free beer, pop-corn, and pizza for dinner. What a great finish to long day out here on the trail. Started out this day with some trail magic from Bee Hive's parents. They had a bunch of vegetables and fruits and cookies. It was such a nice treat to get some rare trail magic.

Puma did take a swim, and I did not. It has to be in the mid to upper 90s for me to consider going swimming. I love to swim, but I am a huge baby when it comes to cold water. She's got that Northerner blood, and I'm wearing a hoodie at the beach if it's not above 85 degrees.

I remember the beer, pizza, and popcorn being amazing. It wasn't like we didn't have food in our food bags, but it wasn't like we had beer and pizza either, know what I mean? We had the usual dehydrated meals for dinner (which are tasty), and then we had Goldfish crackers, Slim Jims, fruit snacks, and tuna packets. Anything outside of that was a golden gift from the gods, especially if it was just given to us.

Sometimes re-supplying in these little trail towns didn't give us many options outside of a gas station. Pizza flavored Combos, beef jerky, granola bars, maybe a banana…it was a bunch of processed foods that we burned through quickly. I never had any problems with the daily menu, and I've been told that I put weird food combinations together even at home. So, I was easy to please on this front, and receiving free beer and free pizza was most excellent.

Chapter Seven

New Hampshire, Part Two: The White Mountains (Wobanadenok)

Friday, July 19, 2013 – High Carb, Fatty, Comfort Food, Feeding Frenzy

Starting Location: Beartown National Forest → Destination: Don's house

Today's Miles: 9 – Trip Miles: 555.50

Besides hiking through really aggressive patches of mosquitos, today was just beautiful. Plus, it's always a little bit sweeter when we know that there's fast food and relaxation in our near future.

Don picked us up early this afternoon and stopped by the nearest Mc-Donald's so we could get our fix. I had a double quarter pounder with cheese, a large order of fries, a 10-piece order of chicken nuggets, and two large cupfuls of Dr. Pepper. Puma had her own smorgasbord, and then we

split an ice cream thingy with Oreo cookies. That held us over for the next couple of hours.

Don's house, family, and hospitality are just tremendous. His wife, Denise, brought home five pizzas and filled us up with more brown carbonated goodness (also known as Pepsi). We sat around the kitchen table telling stories and laughing for the rest of the evening, and it was just so much fun. Thanks, Don and Denise, for being wonderful hosts! We can't thank y'all enough.

Our sights are set on the White Mountains. Puma has worked diligently to get the logistics together for this "trip within our trip." It's finally here. I hope y'all will stay with us through the Whites. We have a couple surprises up our sleeves, so keep a close eye on us! I'm gonna finish my coffee now.

Love y'all to pieces,

Number 2

Talking about competitive bird watching (one of her greatest passions in life), give it up for, Puma:

We got up early this morning knowing that our friend Don was coming to meet us on the trail. I think this was my best day in the woods. We hiked past a bunch of big boulders and discussed how we would climb to the top of each one.

I remember stuffing my face at McDonald's in front of Don. Don is big guy. I mean, I wouldn't want to pick a fight with this guy; his arms were as big as my body. He's also a wonderful human being, a good sport, a sailor, and a badass drummer. Don and Puma worked together in the logistics industry for a few years.

I remember sitting with him at the McDonald's and talking in between bites of food that I couldn't shove into my mouth fast enough. This was a high carb, fatty, comfort food feeding frenzy. I think we either embarrassed him or impressed him with how much we ate. I'd like a reason to eat like that again.

I know I said it in the actual journal entry, but I really need to stress how integral Don and Denise were to our success in getting back to the White Mountains in New Hampshire. We wouldn't have made it back without the love and support of those two wonderful human beings. They housed us, fed us, encouraged us, supported us, and drove many miles to pick us up and drop us off; they truly opened their home to us and it felt like we were part of the family *and their couch*. I could feel their parental care and vibrations the whole time. Thank you for everything.

Saturday, July 20, 2013 – Don's Couch and George Washington Wigs

Starting Location: Don's house → Destination: Don's house

Today's Miles: 0 – Trip Miles: 555.50

Don's got this sectional couch that has swallowed me up these past couple days. Seriously, it chews me up and spits me back out; I can't do anything with that couch around.

After the lovely breakfast that Denise made for us this morning, we went into town, and I found some lightweight pants that I wanted for when we are sleeping in the White Mountains. Not too much to report after that.

We laid around most of the afternoon until dinner, which was at this awesome hibachi restaurant. We were so full and brought back all of our leftovers. I know Denise is gonna turn those into something delicious.

Had a little red wine this evening and watched a little television. The wine put me right to sleep. I'm actually sleeping right now.

Love,

Number 2

Also, totally asleep right now, Puma:

Got the rental car today, and it was super weird driving it around.

This was the night we made our wigs. We had this idea to make George Washington wigs for our big summit of Mount Washington in the White Mountains. We'd been hearing about the treachery of Mount Washington through other hikers' journals, and this was one way to combat the nervousness with excitement. One video I saw online showed this dude inside the observatory on top of Mount Washington prepping his bowl of cereal and saying he was going to try to eat his breakfast outside. As soon as he gets out the door, he and his cereal are obliterated by the 100 mile per hour winds. The more pumped we could get, the better. We spent this day gathering supplies such as shower caps, a bag of cotton balls, some quilt batting, and some ribbon. Don and Denise had the bowling ball that we used as our makeshift head to get these wigs just right.

My mom still loves to tell the story about calling all the main points along the Appalachian Trail to get patches for the vests she made for us to wear at the big finale at Springer Mountain, Georgia. She recalls asking the person on the phone at the observatory on top of Mount Washington if they remembered us. She said the staff person was like, "Lady, we have hundreds of hikers come through here every year." Then my mom mentioned that we were the ones with the George Washington wigs, and the person on the phone actually remembered us.

Sunday, July 21, 2013 – We Got a Rental Car

Starting Location: Don's house → Destination: White Mountains Lodge

Today's Miles: 0 – Trip Miles: 555.50

Road trip! We loaded up and hit the road for our four hour car ride back to New Hampshire to conquer the Whites. Puma was a little "touch and go" on the mechanics of driving as we backed out of Don's driveway, but it all came back to her pretty quickly.

We're excited! The weather has improved quite a bit since the last time we were up that way (about a month ago to be exact).

Thanks for all your support!

Love y'all,

Number 2

Making thank you cards with macaroni art for everyone. I give you, Puma:

We walked close to 300 miles in about a month, and it took us four hours to drive that far. I'm proud of us for getting this far.

Yes, we rented a car to drive back to New Hampshire. This was a necessity for our adventure. There was no way we were going to miss the White Mountains. It's a bit unorthodox for a thru hike, but that's usually how my life goes.

It was an indigo blue sedan with a twin-turbocharged V6 engine, sunroof, power everything, and super quiet windshield wipers. I remember being in the passenger seat looking at all the buttons and the big screen in the dash feeling like a time traveler. Everything about the car felt fancy, ridiculous, and fun. I don't know why, but I felt like some adult authority figure was going to put a stop to all this at any moment, but it never happened. We were in charge, and cranked up the 90s music the whole way back to the White Mountains.

I was excited and nervous at the same time. We made it down the highway and all the way to a parking lot that felt safe enough to leave our rental for the duration of our hike. There was nothing left in the car, all our valuables were on our backs, and besides, this was an elite hiking area. Nobody wanted anything we had because they likely had better stuff anyway.

It was finally here, time to tackle the White Mountains, and I will declare this section of the A.T. as my second favorite of the entire trail. If you ever get the chance to go hike these mountains, it's an absolute must! This was the most beautiful scenery I have ever seen in my entire life. It was some hard hiking that paid off in fantastic views.

Monday, July 22, 2013 – Madison Spring Hut

Starting Location: Pinkham Notch → Destination: Madison Spring Hut

Today's Miles: 7.80 – Trip Miles: 563.30

Up, up and away! That's what it felt like hiking up Mount Madison today. Started out in the trees, then we entered the "alpine zone" and the trees got smaller and smaller until there was nothing left but lots and lots of jagged rock.

Once we hit the alpine zone, we put our trekking poles away and were using our hands to pull ourselves up and over a lot of these boulders, but Puma and I like rock climbing, so it was more fun than difficult.

When we were coming down Madison and were about 100 yards from the hut, we ran into a couple of NOBOs who we had crossed paths with in Vermont at Peru Peak Shelter. They recognized us and said, "Hey! You guys weren't kiddin' about coming back to the Whites! Way to go!" It made us feel pretty cool.

After chit chattin' with them for a minute, it started to sprinkle just a little bit. I was so thankful all day for the wonderful weather we had during the hike up. Thank you, thank you, thank YOU.

Here's the part I wasn't gonna tell y'all, but Puma insisted:

As we were hurrying down to the hut before the rain could pick up, I got too excited and started to run a little – against my better judgement. It was about three steps of awkward running, and I face planted right in front of the large windows directly facing the porch. The rain stopped as soon as I fell down. I really wish I could have seen that from one of the large windows. I didn't even have time to laugh or cuss or make up any excuses as to why I fell.

After dinner, we listened to a woman named Alice, a Volunteer Naturalist for the Appalachian Mountain Club; she told the history of Lucy Crawford and her husband, Ethan Allan, and how they settled in the Crawford Notch area of the White Mountains in the early 1800s. Their story was so tragic, and so romanticized – perfect folkloric essence. I am definitely going to read more books about the history of the area (after we finish the trail). Y'all know I just eat that stuff up.

Today was awesome. Now, we wait for tomorrow. Turning off my night light. Sleep tight.

Love,

Number 2

Puma got captured by the sunset this evening. How does that make you feeeel:

I felt great out there on the trail again. The White Mountains have been my focus ever since we left Katahdin.

Well, it was definitely important to us that we get back to conquer this stretch of the A.T. I believe it was important to our readers, too. That climb up to the top of Mount Madison to start the "presidential range" was a beast. I recall it as being one of the hardest climbs of the entire trail, for me anyway. I remember stopping for a "breather" during one of my unlimited timeouts and looking around at my surroundings. This section was *steep* and *long*. Imagine tons and tons of rocks piled to the sky. It was as if the mountains were the printout of my EKG reading.

The White Mountains are really beautiful and magnificent. There are these huts dispersed throughout the mountain range, and they are staffed by young college students known as the "croo" who will cook for, clean up after, and entertain all the guests. It's a summer camp kind of feel similar to the staff in the movie *Dirty Dancing*. You *know* they are hooking up, making fun of the guests, and having a ball. I believe there is some kind of rule to treat thru hikers like dirt, though.

I mean, we were thru hikers who happened to be paying customers for a bunk and a meal, but there was still this judgy feeling from this one particular blue-eyed bombshell fellow. I could tell this was not his first summer on staff, and he must have been the leader of all the croos. I mean the kid's confidence (a.k.a. haughtiness) was outrageous.

I saw him tell some other thru hikers that they could sleep in the basement crawl space bunks. Wet and cold, it was not a problem for them to stay in the underbelly of the hut in these majestic mountains. If the weather was bad, and it was, then I reckon this was a gift from the Lord of the Hut.

The college kids reminded me of the Von Trapp family. They'd perform a little skit introducing themselves and then say what they were majoring in and what college they were attending. *Back, turn, and swing!*

Now, please understand that I am just trying to paint a picture here. These kids were impressive. I bet they went up and down these mountains multiple times a day, and they did it like it was nothing. They had these wooden framed crates they'd strap to their backs to carry the supplies up and down the mountains. I want to say I saw one girl with six extra-large cans of green beans stacked on her back heading to a hut to prep for that night's dinner.

There were locals and travelers from afar all over these trails, and the shuttle system was a well-oiled machine. I would love to get back to the White Mountains again. I'm grateful I can say "again." Oh, and one of my most cherished souvenirs from the Appalachian Trail is a green fleece pullover from Madison Spring Hut in the Whites. I still have it.

Tuesday, July 23, 2013 – Crawford Notch and a Shot of Adventure

Starting Location: Madison Spring Hut → Destination: Crawford Notch

Today's Miles: 3.80 – Trip Miles: 567.10

I wanna know who brought the thunderstorms with them to the White Mountains? Who was it? Prolly me.

Our chance for Mount Washington just wasn't in the cards today, so we made our plan of attack with better chances of a clear summit later this week.

With all that said, we hiked down the mountain and got a ride with our friend, Alice (Volunteer Naturalist for Appalachian Mountain Club) down to Crawford Notch in an attempt to come at Washington from the other direction. We shall see if it works out for us. It's been really rainy and cloudy today but our spirits are high with rumors of better weather in the next day or so. Keeping our fingers crossed.

My name is,

Number 2

Puma is crossing her arms, crossing her legs, crossing her eyes, and crossing just about everybody she meets (yikes!):

The rain just keeps following us. We're gonna reach the summit of Mount Washington if it's the last thing I do. I have more than five plans prepared.

Puma was not going to have a bad picture of the summit on Mount Washington. She was in her element with all the logistics of these shuttles and summits and huts. I was just hiking and following directions. No problem with any of the plan, just going along.

My hats off to her for all her navigation and figuring on this adventure, not just for the White Mountains, but for the whole damn trail. We had very different experiences out there. That's the thing about having one of these adventures – nobody knows what it's like until they get out there and walk through it. It's different for everyone; it's part of the individual's journey. For me, this was a shot of carefree adventure, and frankly, I just can't behave for too long in an office setting.

Wednesday, July 24, 2013 – Lake of the Clouds Hut

Starting Location: Crawford Notch → Destination: Lake of the Clouds Hut

Today's Miles: 6.80 – Trip Miles: 573.90

That's right, folks, we have seen the weather forecasts for today and tomorrow and the words "mostly sunny and clear" have come up! I can't believe it either.

Another thing that happened this morning that I couldn't believe was watching a big black bear walk right up to the patio of the dining hall at the Highland Center hut. In the words of our friend Alice, if we'd been on a ship at sea, we would have tipped that thing over from everybody running to the windows. That bear probably smelled the bacon from miles away and couldn't help himself. I know exactly how he feels.

Today's hike brought us back up the mountain, albeit through the wind, rain, and cloud cover, but at least now we are one and half miles from the summit of Mount Washington. I cannot wait to get that picture.

Another really cool part about comin' back up here to this section is bumping into our NOBO hiker friends that we met in Vermont. We sat around all evening talking and laughing about great A.T. stories. We also met another couple that did their thru hike of the A.T. back in 1990. Their trail name is the Holy Smokes. They were a hoot and really fun to spend the evening with. I felt like we were at home sitting around the kitchen table laughing all night. That's a good night. I hope our paths cross again someday.

Soooo, we summit Mount Washington tomorrow morning. (Insert heavenly trumpet songs and an Aretha Franklin solo here.) It's gonna be Awesome (pronounced Awe-seem)! Thanks for keeping up with us, y'all. We love you days and nights and nights and days.

Forever,

Number 2

Wishing she had learned more about mountain mammals this evening; you know her as Puma:

Man! That was a huge black bear! The clouds were so thick today, and I couldn't see any views. Looking forward to tomorrow.

We had so much fun on this particular night. We found some other thru hikers we met back at Green Mountain House in Vermont, and it was just magical to see each other again. The Holy Smokes of 1990 ended up being some of our lifelong friends from this adventure.

The dining hall is full of long tables, and of course, everything is served family style; it was just like camp after dinner that evening sitting around with 10 of our very best friends. There wasn't even any wine to share, but we still had the best time visiting and laughing on top of the mountain.

There was this buzz about the next day's clear weather that had everybody acting like it was Christmas Eve.

Thursday, July 25, 2013 – The Summit of Mount Washington (Agiocochook)

Starting Location: Lake of The Clouds Hut → Destination: Greenleaf Hut

Today's Miles: 5.50 – Trip Miles: 579.40

Hair's to you, George Washington! Today's weather had us hiking up in winds at five miles per hour with sunny and clear skies. I mean did y'all ever think that would happen? Like this? I still can't believe it.

We'll be hiking over Franconia Ridge and down to the car tomorrow to head back to Don's in Connecticut. Time to really start moving SOUTH!

What, What!

Number 2

Turning in the paperwork for our George Washington wig patent (really think they ought to sell these in the gift shop on top of Mount Washington), please rise for the stately Ms. Puma Washington (no relation):

I got a little emotional after hearing the weather announced after breakfast. So many other people cried, too. This is a huge deal. I just can't believe it.

I can't help but smile when I remember the young female croo member getting up in front of all of the hikers in the dining hall that morning. She read some poem that I could not place, but then she read the forecast which included "100 miles of visibility."

The whole room erupted! I'm talkin' people were hugging and crying and laughing, and that blue-eyed bombshell dude ripped off his shirt, ran out the door, and jumped into the Lake of the Clouds. That water must have been frigid, but I almost wanted to join him.

Everyone basically ran to their bunks, gathered their belongings, and started heading out for the trail to the top of Mount Washington.

Puma and I had been keeping our wigs a secret, and it was just too fun putting them on and hiking through the crowd. People laughed and cheered us on all the way to the top. I will also let you know that hiking in a shower cap is not the most comfortable thing in the world. But the show must go on!

We passed a warning sign on the way to the top of Mount Washington, and it reads: STOP. THE AREA AHEAD HAS THE WORST WEATHER IN AMERICA. MANY HAVE DIED THERE FROM EXPOSURE, EVEN IN THE SUMMER. TURN BACK NOW IF THE WEATHER IS BAD. – WHITE MOUNTAINS NATIONAL FOREST.

It was smooth sailin'.

Friday, July 26, 2013 – Franconia Ridge to Don's House

Starting Location: Greenleaf Hut → Destination: Don's house

Today's Miles: 8.80 – Trip Miles: 588.20

The clouds stayed at 5,000 feet today, which gave us a beautiful view of Franconia Ridge. We absolutely loved this hike, and I can think of a bunch of people that we'd love to bring back here to experience it with us again someday.

As we were hiking down to the car Puma said, "What am I gonna think about for the rest of the trip now that we are done with the Whites?"

I immediately said, "Cheeseburgers, RVs, bicycles, tater tots, or the Ford Raptor." None of those were what she had in mind.

One thing's for sure, we are headed south for the hike, and that makes both of us very happy. Just like my dad says, "It's time to get the show on the road!" I couldn't agree more, Daddy-O! My mom's been sending us pictures of all the fish she's been catching without us and that's enough motivation to make me run the rest of this thing. We all know that's not a good idea, though.

Thank you to all our friends and family for your support. We can't do this without y'all.

Heading to Don's,

Number 2

Hey Puma, here's some more things you can think about – popcorn, world peace, hot sauce recipes, or biscuits. Just pick one and let me know, okay:

I've mentioned this before, but I can't believe how this all came together. I'm so glad we didn't miss the views of Franconia Ridge because of the weather. We actually got to enjoy the experience up there in New Hampshire.

I am so happy I got to actually *see* that spectacular mountain range. I haven't seen anything as beautiful since then, so that would have been a *big* whiff in my book. Swing and miss, but naw, we actually got to *see* the ridges *and* the edges of these mountains.

I was really impressed and envious of the locals I met out there in the White Mountains. I mean, to have those mountains in one's backyard and easily spend weekends or summers exploring them would be amazing. I remember meeting a lady and her daughters at Lake of the Clouds Hut who had been out there for four days, and they were wearing their rain pants and jackets with big smiles on their faces. No hoods on their jackets, just wet hair stuck to their faces and happy as could be.

Saturday, July 27, 2013 – Don's House to Don's Couch

Starting Location: Don's House → Destination: Don's Couch

Today's Miles: 0– Trip Miles: 588.20

Don's super comfy couch finally spit me out at 7:00 a.m. so I could get a cup of coffee. Denise made us breakfast and Puma started planning out the next month on the trail. We did some laundry, returned the rental car, and swung by a local sporting goods store for some odds and ends.

I'm pretty sure I ate every two hours today with my second breakfast, second lunch, and second dinner. Time to get hiking again so I can stay ahead of this magical metabolism. Denise cooks all day, which totally reminds me of my mom, and I can't wait for some of the homemade blueberry pie that's sitting on the counter. We had a lot of fun tonight sitting around the dinner table. Don and Denise are exceptional folks who have made us feel so welcome in this short time together.

Puma and I have our plan of action, our stuff packed, and we're ready to go. One more night on this super comfy, ridiculous couch and we're outta here! (Secretly, we'd like to bring Don and Denise AND their couch with us.)

Y'all be looking for more.

Love,

Number 2

Taking full advantage of the super comfy, ridiculous couch, everybody stare at Puma:

You can't beat a homemade meal. Dehydrated noodles in a bag just don't cut it.

Mountain House dehydrated meals are delicious. They really are. I have tried every single entrée, and none of them are bad. The water amounts vary per meal, and sometimes when it calls for two cups of water, a cup and half works better. Also, the cheese from the cheesy meal entrées is going to turn into cement on your spoon. It's really not an issue though, because getting it off the spoon is a fun and delicious way to pass the time. Make sure to get a long-handled spoon. It will help you get every little morsel of food instead of putting your knuckles down in the bag.

I remember loving the tiny square potatoes in the beef stew and feeling a little fancy when we ate the turkey tetrazzini. We started out sharing these meals in Maine, but I also remember wanting to turn my bag inside out so I could get the sauce that was stuck in the corners.

Eat, sleep, hike, eat, sleep, hike; that was it, and it was a marvelous life to live for almost six months. I've even had friends over for dehydrated dinners around the campfire. Try it for your next dinner party; it's fun and an easy clean up!

Chapter Eight

Connecticut

Sunday, July 28, 2013 – Rural Connecticut and Glen Brook Campsite

Starting Location: Don's house → Destination: Glen Brook Campsite

Today's Miles: 3.50 – Trip Miles: 591.70

Homemade blueberry pie for breakfast. It...was...really good. Denise gave us coffee and orange juice and cheesy eggs in addition to blueberry pie, and I seriously considered adopting her and Don but we settled for havin' them visit Nashville next year.

They brought us back to the trail today after one more quick stop at McDonald's. We appreciate Don and Denise so much for taking good care of us. We're gonna miss those two!

I have to say it felt good to be "Back in the Saddle Again" and hiking up these hills. We got beautiful views even in the rain this afternoon. Puma and I set up camp and actually made our first campfire on the trail (our good buddy Lieutenant made all the campfires back in the 100 Mile Wilderness). Smelling the smoke made me think about sittin' around the fire pit on my parents' back patio, and it also made me think of the upcoming 30th Annual Thanksgiving Camping Trip. There's nothin' better than eatin' a plate of potato salad under a blanket of stars, I don't care who ya are.

Well, I guess that's about it for today. We'll be in Salisbury, Connecticut, tomorrow and I heard Ms. Meryl Streep lives there. I'm sure I'll be thinking about what to say to her if we run into each other at the grocery. You never know, it could happen. I'll see if Puma can snap a photo of that if it comes to pass. Alright, this has gone on long enough.

Love,

Number 2

Tougher than a zip tie, y'all know who it is, everybody's favorite Puma:

Soon we'll be crossing into the fifth state. I think these upcoming states will go a little quicker than the previous ones. I've been following a fellow hiker's journal who is a part of the Wounded Warrior Project. Wishing all of them the best.

I'll never forget the look on Denise's face when they dropped us off at this dirt path in the middle of nowhere Connecticut. I could tell her motherly instincts were turned all the way up to eleven. They kept asking us if this was the right spot. This deserted stretch of highway where the trail picked back up was making both Don and Denise a little nervous. We got out of the car, Don popped the trunk, we strapped our backpacks on, and hugged them. Like the parents they are, they stayed in the car and watched us until we were out of sight. I remember looking back and waving at Denise, and she had the biggest eyes with the most nervous half smile I had ever seen while she was watching us hike up to the ridge and out of sight.

It must have been hard or at least bizarre for them to drop us off like that. We'd just spent four or so days as their adopted daughters, and now we were walking away waving like kindergarteners heading off for our first day on the Appalachian Trail. Poor Denise, I just wanted to give her another hug and tell her everything was gonna be alright.

Glen Brook Campsite was our only platform tent site during the whole time out there on the A.T. I remember it well because I was having the period from hell. I think the first couple of months out on the trail shocked my system so much that I actually skipped my period, but then it came back with a vengeance. I was lying in the tent having the usual bloating, constipation, irritability, and discomfort. It was awful. Of course, it would time itself to be active while I was out on the trail and not in town. My period has always been a surprise for me. Even after 30 years, I'm always surprised.

I've been asked this question a few times, how was it having your period out on the trail? It was gross. Had to pack all that mess in a baggie and carry it until I found a trash can. I will admit that I did fling one tampon into the woods somewhere in Connecticut. Just one time. Helicopter'd that thing and got a good release. Biodegradable or not, it's still not a good idea, and I'm ashamed of myself. It should be gone by now.

Monday, July 29, 2013 – Bearded Woods Hostel

Starting Location: Glen Brook Campsite → Destination: Bearded Woods Hostel

Today's Miles: 13.50 – Trip Miles: 605.20

Good day! We had a great day of hiking up and over the Taconic Range, which includes Mount Everett, Mount Race, Bear Mountain (tallest point in Connecticut), and Mount Lion. Such a beautiful hike with lots of great views of Massachusetts and Connecticut. We had our state line dance party tradition into our fifth state right after Mount Race.

We're staying at Bearded Woods Hostel this evening, and I told Puma that I felt like we were staying in the nicest chalet in Gatlinburg. Anybody who gets the chance to stay here has got to do it. My belly is full of bar-b-q chicken, roasted corn, potato salad, and cornbread.

Holy Mackerel,

Number 2

Our special guest tonight, the world's greatest toilet paper connoisseur, Puma:

Only 11 more states lines. We just keep moving and making our way. Bear Mountain was a good climb today.

Bearded Woods Hostel brought the wilderness inside and competed with the nicest cabin in Gatlinburg. I noticed every little detail, from the cairns lining the driveway to the massive photo of the owner sitting on a mountainside that hung in the living room. Pretty sure it was him sitting on Katahdin.

He had little display cases full of animal skulls and skeletons, all labeled according to their biological families. He had vintage camping gear, Katahdin memorabilia, survival equipment; I mean this guy was an outdoor enthusiast to the max.

His wife was the sweetest lady and an excellent cook. She was also an excellent shuttle driver, laundry assistant, secretary, and anything else. She was the one who picked us up from the trail and brought us back to their hostel. I think there were six of us at the dinner table that night. We talked about our experiences thus far and listened to the owner tell stories of his grand adventures along the A.T. I found him to be very intelligent and prepared, and I like that. Thank you both for your hospitality and a seat at your table.

Tuesday, July 30, 2013 — 17 Miles, Meryl Streep, and an Organic Grocery

Starting Location: Bearded Woods Hostel → Destination: Salisbury, Connecticut

Today's Miles: 17.50 — Trip Miles: 622.70

Hiked through some beautiful hills today and got a couple of fantastic views.

We covered a lot of ground thanks to the slackpack shuttle provided by the owner of Bearded Woods, and had a lovely lunch of summer sausage, crackers, and fruit snacks.

We did a small bit of shopping for our re-supply in the town of Salisbury. I kept my eyes peeled for Ms. Meryl Streep but had no such luck.

We head south tomorrow; I tell y'all what, I am lovin' this terrain down here. Puma and I both still feel as though we are under Maine's spell because we assume we're going to the very top of every mountain or hill. That's prolly a good thing.

Thanks again for keeping up with us. Waiting for my Swiss mushroom burger to finish cooking.

Love,

Number 2

Please welcome the star of the new Deet perfume commercial airing on E! next fall, Puma:

Y'all might not believe this, but Number 2 hiked 17 miles in just under six hours. She was boosting.

We were flying through those 17 miles. Even the owner of Bearded Woods was impressed, and his words of affirmation made me feel so good. Slackpacking made a world of difference.

After completing our miles, we got to check out the town for a little bit. I popped in the local organic grocery store that was dripping with the coolest granola organic bohemian patchouli vibe ever. I was in heaven. I was also seriously looking for Meryl Streep. She must have been on set somewhere. Figures.

Found our way to this fly-fishing shop, too, and I felt very out of place. Not just stinky and dirty, but out of place like I wasn't rich enough to be in there, not even close. It was awesome.

Salisbury is picturesque and delicious. I could have spent the rest of our savings in that tiny organic grocery store, and I bet Meryl knows exactly which grocery store I'm talking about. I wanted to buy all the fancy olives, expensive mustards, and a shot of wheatgrass. But I would have had to dump them all in my macaroni and cheese that night and thought better of it.

Wednesday, July 31, 2013 – Preparing to Order a Sandwich in New York

Starting Location: West Cornwall → Destination: Mt. Algo Shelter

Today's Miles: 15.90 – Trip Miles: 638.60

Started hiking at 8:00 a.m. The first five miles were steep hills, then the second set of five miles were absolutely flat. I'm talkin' flatter than my momma's hair in the seventies, flatter than a flat iron skillet, flatter than that lady who sings off key in church. It was so flat. We walked parallel to a river the whole time and it was beautiful. Made us think about fly fishing on the Caney Fork in Tennessee.

The third and last 5.9 miles – those were tough. It got hilly again, and at times, I thought I was back in Maine. My dogs are still barking at me.

We just finished our dinner – chicken and rice, peach tea, and some sea salt and cracked pepper chips. Oh, and a pack of Tom and Jerry fruit snacks. Puma asked, "Which one is Tom?" And I said, "Tom's the cat." I do think Wayne would be a funnier name for a cat. But it'd never fly as a cartoon show, "Wayne and Jerry." Not happenin'.

Oh y'all, I'm just having fun. We walk into New York tomorrow! That's the start of our sixth state! Whaaaaaat!

It's gonna be fun stopping in at a real New York Deli. And since we all know it's gonna be a disaster for me to try to order a "samwich," Puma may be doing all the talking. We'll see. Could make for a funny story.

Okay, okay, I love y'all.

See ya in New York!

Number 2

Totally scared that I'm gonna ask the guys at the deli to cut my sandwich into triangles; I give you Puma:

In three short days, we are done with Connecticut. We actually crossed the state line three times.

Have you ever felt embarrassed for someone else? I hate that uneasy feeling. I have always marched to the beat of a different drum, and I think Puma was a little nervous about me interacting with the local New Yorkers. We weren't anywhere near Manhattan, but it was still New York. Such a silly mindset to be nervous about New Yorkers; I blame old Pace Picante commercials.

I wasn't going to put on a show or anything, just order a sandwich. It got to my head, though. I was nervous, and for some reason I ordered my sandwich in a softer volume than normal. Why? I don't know. Nerves.

Even in college in Chattanooga, I'd get nervous ordering my favorite sandwich from the New York Deli. A total transplant from New York came to Chattanooga, opened a deli, and even then, made me nervous.

I didn't want to waste anybody's time, so I ordered the same damn sandwich for four years.

Chapter Nine

New York

Thursday, August 1, 2013 – My First New York Deli

Starting Location: Mt. Algo Shelter → Destination: Wingdale

Today's Miles: 14 – Trip Miles: 652.60

Holy moly, I am pooped. We hiked into New York at 9:30 this morning, and the trail was dry most of the day until about 1:00 p.m.

We made it to our first deli around 2:30 this afternoon, and I'm telling y'all I had the best sandwich I have ever had in my life (except for any time I get to have a fried bologna sandwich).

This sandwich had thinly sliced turkey, bacon, melted provolone, fresh lettuce and tomato, CREAM CHEESE, and a tangy honey mustard on a perfectly chewy, toasty roll. It...was...divine. Puma had a ham sandwich and stole my sandwich after I ate the first half.

We had a great day despite the rain, and I'm looking forward to tomorrow. Another great part about today was talking to the folks in the deli. We had a lot of fun answering their questions. I know I've said it before, but meeting all these great people during this adventure is one of my favorite parts of the whole thing.

Can't wait until the next deli,

Number 2

One fried bologna sandwich with crushed potato chips and lots of mayonnaise for pick up at the windoooooow! Thank yew!

Puma, I think your order is ready:

Crossed into New York this afternoon and saw a sign at the top of a hill that read 1,000 feet of elevation. Also listed were the remaining miles left to Georgia – 1,453. We know that doesn't include Maine or New Hampshire, so we're good. The deli gave us a bag full of buttery rolls. Score!

Everybody talks so fast up there in the north. I love talking to people, but I don't like asking them to repeat themselves so that I can understand what they are saying. It makes me feel weak, and I'm afraid I might offend them or something. To the people of New England and the Mid-Atlantic areas, I am desperate to hear what you have to say, and I'm sure glad I had Puma to translate.

I want to say it was Virginia when I started to understand what folks were saying to me. People were friendly and we had such a good time talking with all of them. I just needed a translator. Speaking speeds are different in different regions of the country. We all know that. Just like there are different southern accents. A Georgia accent is different than a Tennessee accent, and it's all in the drawl, but the speeds are relatively similar. Talking to these fine folks in that New York deli was like trying to listen to a tape in fast forward.

I'll tell you one thing, though. That was the absolute most delicious bread I have ever had in my life. The water really does make a difference in bread baking up there, and I would love to have that sandwich again.

Friday, August 2, 2013 – Bear Baggin' in Beautiful New York

Starting Location: Wingdale → Destination: North of Stormville

Today's Miles: 14.30 – Trip Miles: 666.90

Felt like we floated through the miles today. Before I knew it, it was time for lunch! The nice lady behind the counter from yesterday's deli gave us about six of these big buttery rolls, and Puma had the bright idea of putting our tuna salad on them! It was delicious.

After lunch, we floated through about seven more miles and found ourselves a nice little tent spot right by a stream. For dinner, we had turkey tetrazzini. Never had it before, shoot, I'd never even heard of it before. It had asparagus, turkey, spaghetti noodles, and carrots in a flavorful sauce similar to a chicken and dumplings sauce. I swear, all I do is talk about food.

It's August, y'all! Puma and I are looking forward to catching some SEC football when we can. This marks the beginning of my favorite time of year.

Wishing y'all all the best from the trail.

Walking home,

Number 2

Once ranked the number one quarterback in the SEC, and now slingin' her bear bag like a champ. Y'all make some noise for Puma Manning:

My lower half was already sore, and now my upper half is sore from tossing the bear bag. Makes me appreciate bear boxes when they are available.

Slinging a bear bag is just one of those things that became one of our daily jobs or "chores." Puma made the process a little easier by tying a small zipper pouch to a long strand of paracord. She'd put a couple of palm-sized rocks in the pouch, zip it up, and toss it over the designated tree branch. Once up and over the branch, we'd tie the paracord to the food bag and hoist it up into the air to then tie it off around the tree.

The hard part was finding the right branch. Sometimes it took several tries, and a lot of times we'd laugh about that situation. Other times, Puma might get frustrated with how many times it took to get it right. Puma is very athletic, so don't go thinking she weenie-armed it up there; she could throw!

We'd take turns trying to heave this little bag of rocks up and over those branches. Here we are 11 years later, and I see people using bear canisters now. Just set it on the ground at the base of a tree 75 yards away from the tent or something like that. I can't help but picture the bear picking up the canister and walking off with it.

Saturday, August 3, 2013 — I Spy a Saw Blade and a Train Station

Starting Location: North of Stormville → Destination: Sunken Mine Road

Today's Miles: 14.70 – Trip Miles: 681.60

The trail here in New York is a real workout. It's rockier here than I expected, and the hills are steep. No matter how many miles we've already hiked, they are still steep.

We had good weather today and a nice breeze followed us. Passed a few more NOBOs; they usually tell us what number SOBOs we are because they've been counting us along the way.

There's a handful of guys ahead of us, but Puma said, "If this were the LPGA Tour, we'd still be bringing home a buttload of cash!" I thought that was hilarious and told her it was going down in the journal entry for today.

We get asked all the time why we are hiking the A.T. and I seem to always come up with a better answer about ten minutes after we've hiked past that conversation. Puma's out here to see that there are still really good people in the world; I just like to hike and camp and this gives me the opportunity to do it a bunch of times in a row. (See! I'll think of something better in about 10 minutes.)

We are still havin' lots of fun out here, and I'm getting more and more excited for that Mason-Dixon line. It's actually marked out here on the trail.

I hope all is well back home. We love y'all more than ever, and I can't stop thinking about my momma's homegrown tomatoes.

Love,

Number 2

Puma can live on two things in this world – homemade dill pickles and plum jelly. Fascinating combo, Puma:

A NOBO asked, "Why is no one talking about the rockiness of New York?" Pennsylvania is known for the rocks. It's coming up.

Inside the hillsides of New York, there wasn't too much to get excited about. I saw an antique saw blade leaning up against a rock. It was a big saw blade, like one of those that requires two people to push and pull it back and forth. Wonder what the story was there?

To pass the time, Puma and I would play silly games like "I Spy" which was hard to play with everything falling into two color categories (green or brown). We still played along; had nothing but time.

Then we saw the one of the coolest things I have *ever* seen! The Appalachian Trail train station is a commuter rail stop on the Metro-North Railroad's Harlem line. It is the only railroad station located *directly* on the Appalachian Trail. Tiny little thing. It's a built up wooden platform with a couple of steps and a wooden bench. There's a metal sign that stretches out above the bench that says "Appalachian Trail."

I remember walking up onto the train station and wishing we had enough time to take it into town. I've never been on a train or been to New York City before, and that would have been a feather in my cap. Still feels like I could show off a tiny feather in my cap just for seeing the train station.

Sunday, August 4, 2013 – Sensory Overload on the Hudson River

Starting Location: Sunken Mine Road → Destination: Fort Montgomery

Today's Miles: 18 – Trip Miles: 699.60

Since leaving Don's place we have hiked almost 115 miles, and frankly, I needed a shower. Coming into town, we hiked in the rain for a little bit, which was actually refreshing and made me hike a little bit faster than normal.

The rain stopped as we got to Bear Mountain Bridge over the Hudson River. There was so much going on: folks riding a stand-up jet ski, the train rolling by, cars racing through the toll, and a great big sneaky barge was passing right below us. Sensory overload.

We got some bar-b-q and an ice cold beer in town. There's nothing better than a cold beer after hiking all day. Well, actually, all I wanna do is lay down.

Looking forward to a little relaxation and some clean laundry tomorrow.

Watching the Hall of Fame football game this evening. Third string quarterbacks have all the fun.

Good night, y'all,

Number 2

Glued to the outcome of this football game (i.e., falling in and out of sleep), that's Puma:

Today we had lunch inside the Appalachian Deli. That sandwich helped us to hike to a Holiday Inn.

The Appalachian Trail goes right down the sidewalk of the Bear Mountain Bridge. It was wild walking through such a fast-paced environment. I felt a little anxious walking along the bridge with all the vehicles whizzing by and blowing their drafts in my face. I couldn't help but think about how much we had slowed our pace of life compared to how we used to be back home. And even now, I am conscious of how fast-paced my life can be and how hard I have to work to slow it down.

These days, I'd like to hit the brakes and regroup, not only to find a more simplified pace but a different direction. I want to find a way to make ends meet by talking about what I want to talk about (camping, hiking, biking, climbing, fishing, and kayaking adventures). I want to capture the magic of the wilderness and write about it. Hiking the A.T. revealed to me that I am a mystical adventurer who has a bold openness to traversing the world around me. Whoopdeedoodaaday.

Monday, August 5, 2013 – Keep Doing the Things that Make Us Happy

Starting Location: Fort Montgomery → Destination: Holiday Inn

Today's Miles: 0 – Trip Miles: 699.60

Continental breakfast, a heated indoor swimming pool, a queen size bed, and a coffee pot brought me back to life today. Plus, I got to spend the

day watching a bit of television to catch up on all the drama with Johnny Manziel and Alex Rodriguez, so that was productive.

We did laundry and ate some chicken wings while watching the movie "The Client" starring Susan Sarandon and Tommy Lee Jones. What a great movie!

Puma has our plan for the next stretch, and we are sneaking up on New Jersey. But first, we get to hike through the zoo. Seriously, the trail goes through the local zoo and it's like we're a part of the exhibit. This ought to be good.

I wanna thank all of y'all for keeping up with us, and please continue to send us your messages of encouragement.

We LOVE hearing from you!

Roar!

Number 2

Nailing down her best Hermit Thrush impression, been practicing since 8 a.m., Puma the Insatiable:

We are nearing 700 miles on this adventure, and I'm going swimming in a hotel pool. I love it. I need to stay active.

We were in our early 30s on this adventure, and I think about how much my activity level has slowed 11 years later. I didn't think much about working out; I just wanted to have fun, and working out is not much fun for me. I can't jump real good, I'm definitely not a fast runner, the group classes give me anxiety, but I *can* ride my bicycle up steep hills really fast. I love a good climb, whether hiking, biking, or climbing.

I've got some nerve damage behind my left knee that came out of nowhere in college. The nerve damage atrophied my left calf and foot muscles. It didn't stop me from hitting the climbing gym, but it took some adjustment. A dear friend said it's what gives me my pirate powers.

Doc said I shouldn't drive a stick shift anymore, but that's all I've been driving for the last 20 years. A lost art in today's society, if you ask me.

I refuse to surrender! I will keep doing the things that make me happy, and I plan to be the odd little old lady on the auto-belay in your local gym on Tuesday and Thursday mornings.

Tuesday, August 6, 2013 – Walking Through the Zoo in New York

Starting Location: Fort Montgomery → Destination: William Brian Shelter

Today's Miles: 10.10 – Trip Miles: 709.70

Well y'all, we got to the zoo at 10:01 this morning and had the whole place to ourselves (I sure was hoping for long lines and buses but no dice). The A.T. goes right through there, but the bear exhibit wasn't quite open yet. A zoo worker was filling up their play pool. Cute but no touchy!

We did see a fox and a coyote (both had been previously injured by cars so that's why they were in the zoo), and the coyote made me think about my baby dog, Peejay. He looked just like him.

The rest of the day was beautiful; we had great fall-ish weather and got to see the New York City skyline far off in the distance once we reached the top of Bear Mountain.

Looking forward to tomorrow. Per The A.T. Guide, we are supposed to pass a vending machine! You'd think I'd just won the lottery when I get something out of the vending machine these days. Hopefully that will change after this adventure.

There's more rock climbing terrain ahead of us here in New York, and we are ready for it. I can pretty much see New Jersey from our campsite tonight.

Thanks for reading, y'all. We'll holler at y'all tomorrow.

K, bye!

Number 2

And now, for Puma's next trick, she shall rollerblade the rest of New York and New Jersey (AND Pennsylvania):

We passed the lowest point of elevation at 124 feet. It's only uphill from here. I'm disappointed the bears were busy during our zoo hike. There was a porcupine, but I haven't seen one on the trail yet.

I mean with the A.T. actually trekking *through* the zoo, it sounds like it should have been a good story, but it was like walking through a closed amusement park or an abandoned flea market. Nobody was around, there was nothing to see, and all the booths were empty.

We'd been seeing bears, foxes, and coyotes this whole time out on the trail, and I can say it's much more interesting to see them in their natural habitat than in a zoo. But hey, if this is the only chance these animals have for survival, then by all means, let's break out the kiddie pool and spoil these fur babies rotten.

Wednesday, August 7, 2013 – Creeks Run Dry and Trail Angels Fly

Starting Location: William Brian Shelter → Destination: Mombasha Road

Today's Miles: 12.50 – Trip Miles: 722.20

What a day. We'd been stressed about running out of water because the streams are pretty dry up here, but we came across gallon jugs of water multiple times on the trail.

The best stop was just across a road where we met a gentleman named Jim, and he had a cooler full of cold apples, oranges, nectarines, and Capri

Suns! Puma and I both inhaled our first Capri Sun (and I had half a mind to throw it down like a shot glass on the counter but that would have been too much).

After talkin' with Jim, with my mouth full of apple, we learned that he is looking to relocate down to Maryville, Tennessee. Soooo, like good Southerners, we started talking about gardening and tomatoes. Well y'all, he went over to his truck and brought back two homegrown tomatoes and a couple cherry tomatoes for us to try. Puma's been listening to me talk about my momma's tomatoes for at least a couple of states now. They were delicious! Sweet, tangy, and ripe. Man, I love homegrown tomatoes. Enough about that.

The trail was hilly and rocky. Puma and I both gassed our legs going up and down these steep blips, but I can tell our lung capacity is much better than when we started in Maine.

Tomorrow, we pass a Subway! Don't even get me started. We love Subway.

Love,

Number 2

Hey Puma, do you want another bag of dehydrated buffalo chicken flavored rice, or a footlong meatball sub with extra cheese? Those are your only two options:

We decided to skip the vending machine today because of a large hill. I did find a couple of a quarters while hiking that will go in the pot for next time. Jim's trail magic was awesome, and it's rare SOBOs see that. We can't thank the trail angels enough.

The streams were running dry, and we definitely stretched the water supply a little thin through this part of the trail. It's early August and the Mid-Atlantic heat had dried up all the creeks. Y'all read that we would share a peach tea with most dinners. The peach tea comes in those little packets that go into the water bottle, shake it up, and poof! You've got the most delicious peach tea.

We would sit across from each other watching one another take sips of the peach tea. It was hard to not down the whole thing. I know we both could have used our own peach tea, but since the water was getting scarce, we had to ration what we had for the next day's hike. There were definitely some sly eyes and extra sips that were taken, but all in all, we shared because we needed each other to make it through this thing.

We'd sit there for prolly 15 minutes after finishing the peach tea and discuss how refreshing and delicious it tasted. I wish we had a recording of some of those conversations. Like SNL's skit "Delicious Dish," our show would have a similar vibe, but would have been called "Delicious Wish."

Seeing all those water jugs out on the trail truly felt magical. Trail magic is very real, and I can't say thank you enough to those who are dedicated to the cause. The trail angels are the ones who leave the trail magic, and a lot of the times, no one was there for us to thank. So, I tell you now, to all the trail angels out there, your efforts year after year are helping all the hikers press on with their missions.

Thursday, August 8, 2013 – Helloooo Chicken Enchilada

Starting Location: Mombasha Road → Destination: Greenwood Lake
   Today's Miles: 9.10 – Trip Miles: 731.30
   Someone told us to not be surprised by southern New York. I have to say that it is beautiful and rocky and fun to climb up and down and squeeze through the terrain.

We had been looking forward to the Lemon Squeeze, a very narrow path through some tall boulders that also leans a little and makes the trek a bit more challenging, and the Fitzgerald Falls, a beautiful waterfall trickling down jagged rocks.

We are about to enter New Jersey, but before we do, we're gonna let this thunderstorm roll through. Making a stop at this nice little waterfront motel overlooking lots of pontoon boats and vacation homes.

There's a Mexican restaurant in town that is calling my name. Helloooo Chicken Enchilada! (It sounds more exciting if you say it really loudly.)

Love y'all a great big ol' bunch,

Number 2

Introducing, el mejor caminante en el mundo, Supa Puma:

Ate another Subway sandwich today. Got our re-supply at a CVS. I like that we can re-supply in any store.

A word about the waterfront motel – I checked and this place is permanently closed. We arrived and as advertised it was on a lake (Greenwood Lake) and there were some boats. That part was cool and fine, but there was something eerie about the place. The lady at the front desk was dressed like my mother's hairdresser (who I adore) complete with her leopard print smock. Just something I noticed right away. Still fine with the situation.

We get checked in, and I'm noticing that there is no one else around. That's cool, right? We were used to that already. The gentleman who showed us to our room was wearing a weathered green polo shirt, some faded jean shorts, and boat shoes, like the kind with leather shoelaces that never actually get tied together. His outfit was fine, and something I would wear. His vibe was a little bit on the "creeper" side though. What I'm trying to say here is that he lingered, and I was not ok with that.

Once he left, we were able to do all the things we needed to do, like go through our bags, throw away the trash, clean out the tent, put some laundry together, and change out of our nasty hiker clothes. *That's* when it happened!

Yep, as soon as we were in the middle of changing, dude tried to come into our room. Like uninvited with the chain and deadbolt locked, and he was using his key to come *inside!* We were shocked and started hollering at him to get the f*ck out, and it took him a minute before he stopped, which felt like an eternity. I remember being very firm in letting him know that we did *not* need any other services. I think we rigged the desk chair in front of the door for a little more peace of mind.

Other things to mention, there was broken glass all over the bathroom floor. I thought the jacuzzi tub would feel nice on my muscles, but it made me feel weird – like I was on the set of an 80s drama movie. I don't regret staying there because it's part of the story, but I can say that I felt safer and cleaner when we got back on the trail.

Friday, August 9, 2013 – So Long New York

Starting Location: Greenwood Lake → Destination: Greenwood Lake
  Today's Miles: 0 – Trip Miles: 731.30

Whew wee, the rain came pouring down this afternoon, and thankfully, we were not in that mess. I love when we dodge the rain.

Puma and I went to the Mexican restaurant today. They were playing oldies on the radio, and we couldn't help but sing along to every song. I told Puma, "See, back then they used their hands to make the clapping sound in a song instead of hitting a button on a keyboard." It was fun to sit and listen to all those great songs. I tend to sing the backup singers' parts, you know all the doo whops and bum bums and ding-a-dong-dings, while Puma sticks with the lead vocals. We were the only two people in the restaurant.

Hitting the trail again tomorrow!

So long New York, hello New Jersey!

Y'all keep the posts coming, and we'll keep the journal rolling.

Thinking of family and friends all the time.

Love,

Number 2

Making a mental note of all new karaoke songs on a master level, pass the mic to Puma:

I realize it's not possible to skip the rain every time, but it worked this time.

That's the thing, it always works out. It's the story! I've been reading these journal entries just like you, and I can't change the story. Don't want to. It is what it is. On the trail, I was cool as a cucumber. I wasn't stressed about the miles; I had no worries at all. Just ready for whatever was coming next, and I lived in the moment. Why is it a constant struggle for me to get back to that state of mind in my present day?

I'll tell you why. Because it's time to make a change.

Chapter Ten

New Jersey

Saturday, August 10, 2013 – Rattlesnacks, I Mean Rattlesnakes

Starting Location: Greenwood Lake → Destination: Glenwood

Today's Miles: 14.20 – Trip Miles: 745.50

There I was face to face with a rattlesnake. Let me start from the beginning. We got a late start from Greenwood, New York, this morning, but the blueberry muffin was delicious. Finally reached the New York/New Jersey border, took our picture, and hiked another 10 miles. Took a break at a road crossing for some fruit snacks and a Clif bar. That gave us the energy we needed to climb down to the town of Vernon, New Jersey.

Just at the top of the ridge, I took maybe two steps more on the trail then my brain signaled WHOA! to my feet, and I stopped right in my tracks. There was a three and half foot long rattlesnake shaking his rattle to give me some warning before I got too close. He was just to the right of the trail, and after I stopped, we backed up about 10 feet and watched it slither to the other side and further on down.

It was amazing to actually see this snake in its natural habitat; what an incredible creature. I will continue to respect the wildlife, back up, stay calm, and try to not to pee myself.

We decided to hike past our original destination today and made it to the next town of Glenwood. Staying at a lovely bed and breakfast that gives their guests free wine, tapas appetizers, and fluffy white robes! We didn't save money for two years for nuthin, y'all!

Hitting the trail again in the morning and cranking out these miles to get to Pennsylvania. I love hiking this trail. More to tell tomorrow.

Love y'all,

Number 2

And now, the person who prefers snakes over spiders any day (seriously, she can't even watch or read Charlotte's Web), Puma:

That rattlesnake was cool; I took a great picture of it. Let's not forget that we crossed another state line today. That means we have seven more.

Never have I walked up on a rattlesnake before this moment. I was just hiking along and heard the rattle – then my brain told my eyes what I was looking at – and I think I did yell "Whoa!" and turned around to face Puma. The snake was curled up in a big pile with the rattle sticking straight up in the air.

I remember Puma grabbed my shoulders and walked me away from the snake. I was frozen. I felt like a sweet little bunny rabbit, like Thumper, just gabbing and bee-boppin' along, until I was frozen by the warning sound of this big rattler. Then to see it move across the trail and stretch out as if to show off its baseball bat physique was chilling. Puma snapped a great picture, and I missed a good chance of being snake bait.

I take full responsibility for disturbing the snake in its own habitat. I mean we said it over and over again, we are walking through the wildlife's living room. Can you imagine if someone just walked through your living room? I'd at least scoff and look around.

While up on that ridge in the woods, the closer we got to civilization, the louder the music. It sounded like a music festival was going on, and we were starting to get excited about this. The music was booming, but I didn't recognize any of it. I want to say it was electronica or techno, but the only song in those genres I can peg is "Sandstorm," and it wasn't that.

We finally got down off the ridge and walked onto an open field that looked like it was ready for the crowds, but there was no one around. The music was pumping and the PA system was workin', but there was not a soul around for us to ask what the heck was going on. I wanted so badly for there to be a bunch of hoppin' food truck vendors.

I kept searching and looking for some kind of sign or signal that we had stumbled onto the coolest music festival, but it was just us. Very odd. I tried to search the internet for any music festivals in Glenwood, New Jersey, in early August, but there's not much coming up. Maybe it has something to do with the rattlesnacks, I mean rattlesnakes.

Sunday, August 11, 2013 – A Rustic Farmhouse Romantic Comedy

Starting Location: Glenwood → Destination: New Jersey Route 23
    Today's Miles: 16.80 – Trip Miles: 762.30

I kept my eyes peeled for more rattlesnakes today but I never saw another one; Puma did tell me about this event down in Texas called the Rattlesnake Roundup where they catch'em, cook'em, and eat'em. Made me so hungry, I could go for a snake sandwich with some snake fries and a strawberry milksnake.

We got started around 11:00 a.m. today because we had to take advantage of the gourmet breakfast at the Apple Valley Inn. So so good!

All day long, I thought we were only hiking 14 miles, but Puma informed me that we did almost 17 miles. I thought my feet were a little achy for a 14 mile day. She prolly does that on purpose. I just don't do numbers, never have.

Now, I gotta' go to bed so I can kick some more miles tomorrow.

Love y'all,

Number 2

And now a message from the person who is constantly calculating numbers in her head (I was a C student, so...), give it up for, Puma:

That's correct. I am constantly crunching numbers in my head all day long. We got to walk through a wildlife preserve this afternoon, and it was super flat. Felt like it went on and on.

The Apple Valley Inn was this amazing bed and breakfast. I felt like I had wandered (literally) into a beautiful, rustic farmhouse romantic comedy. We arrived and the owners were entertaining a couple of their friends at this long wooden table with a gorgeous charcuterie board, bottles of wine, wooden bowls full of perfect apples, and warm conversation.

They even invited us to join them for a bit, and I was trying so hard not to reach across the table at everything like Animal from The Muppet Show. The wine went howling through my veins, and I didn't even have a full glass. I think my body was like, "Heyyyyy wherrrrre's the parrrrrrtaay," but my brain was like a stuffy librarian giving my body that over the top of the glasses glare.

They showed us to our room, which had a high ceiling, lots of dark mahogany, a fireplace, big windows with flowing white curtains, our own bathroom, and a very comfortable four poster bed. I was lights out in a third of a second, which is my fastest time.

Oh, and the robes! Yes, the fluffy white robes were magnificent. That was my first time staying at a place that provided a white robe, and I wore it like I lived in that house. It was absolutely the nicest place we stayed on the Appalachian Trail. The owners were generous, fun, and made me want to stick around for a few more glasses of wine and a charcuterie board the length of that table.

Monday, August 12, 2013 – This Trail is Unpredictable

Starting Location: New Jersey Route 23 → Destination: Branchville

Today's Miles: 16 – Trip Miles: 778.30

I have to start out by thanking the owners of the Apple Valley Inn Bed and Breakfast in New Jersey for their incredible hospitality and gourmet breakfast. We thoroughly enjoyed our stay, and I highly recommend their cozy abode to anyone looking for a fantastic bed and breakfast experience.

The hike today was full of rocks, and we're expecting more rocks the closer we get to Pennsylvania. Our feet were communicating to us that it was about time to call it quits for the day after about eight hours on the rocky path, so we planned to stay at a tent site at the local state park that, according to our guidebook, was just a stone's throw from the trail.

Well, about two and half miles later, we flagged down this family in a minivan and asked if they knew how much further the tent sites were, and they told us, "Maybe another mile down the road." Look here, we knew that wasn't gonna happen. We had already hiked about 16 miles and another mile was the last straw. Puma was pissed. I was pooped.

We plopped down in front of the park office, used the restroom, and started to devise another plan for the evening. That's when this really nice guy, Ryan, came up to us and started asking us questions about our hike. He ended up letting us pitch our tent behind his cabin, and offered us pizza and a ride back to the trail in the morning! It just goes to show that there are some great people in this world.

I took a shower at the restroom facility and only had half a Sham Wow towel to dry off with, which gave me a flashback to when I was about six years old at "Slip-n-Slide Day" at my daycare. My mother sent me with an olive-green washcloth while all the other kids had these never-ending flowy, colorful beach towels. Even the daycare workers were like, "Damn kid, that's rough," while they stood back and sprayed everyone with the water hose.

This day turned out great! We got a big day tomorrow.

I hope y'all will continue to read our journal and leave us posts. Thanks for reading.

Love,

Number 2

Puma's internal timer went off about two miles before we were done hiking today; I'm sure she has a comment for this evening:

I was feeling frustrated and then had tears of joy. A message for Lieutenant, if you catch this, you wouldn't believe the hold my feet had on the rocks here. One slip and it could be trouble.

There we were sitting on the steps of the restrooms, and I remember this minivan stopping and the driver eating his banana while telling us the tent sites were another mile or so down this big hill. We were immediately defeated. Just tired. You know.

Right as Puma started switching into planning mode, this guy pulls up and starts asking us about our adventure. He seemed cool, and he offered to let us pitch our tent behind the cabin that he rented for himself and his partner and her daughter for the weekend.

He stopped at a gas station on the way, and that's how we got the pizza. Gas station pizza was one of my favorites. His partner's daughter (who was probably about eight years old) was so amazed that we were going to sleep in our tent *outside*. She kept asking if the bears were going to get us, and we were like, "Noooo, the bears are really chill or run off as soon as they see us." It didn't ease her worry, and I appreciated her concern.

I think taking a shower in a restroom facility is great. Free water. I do not like tiny towels, though. A washcloth is not a towel. But this trail is unpredictable, and it goes back to what I've already said are some of my biggest lessons from this experience – getting comfortable with the uncomfortable and figuring out a solution. It's just not feasible to bring a lovely towel on a thru hike.

Whenever we accepted a ride from anyone, I rode in the front seat, and Puma sat behind the driver. I think it gave us the edge if things got hairy. Thankfully, Ryan was a nice guy. We slept through the night just fine behind their cabin, and he dropped us off at the trail in the morning.

Tuesday, August 13, 2013 – Beautiful New Jersey

Starting Location: Branchville → Destination: Mohican Outdoor Center

Today's Miles: 17.80 – Trip Miles: 796.10

Hiked almost 18 miles today, and my brain and my feet were getting real fussy during the last couple miles. It all blows over once I get some food, though.

The first four hours of hiking were in the rain. It wasn't so bad, just enough to get everything soaked. The next four hours were great. We came

out on top of this ridge and could see for 100 miles, farmland, farmhouses, farm hands, you know, lots of farm charm. Beautiful countryside.

The rocks are definitely becoming more and more prevalent. Puma's prolly gonna have to get some new shoes by the time we reach Pennsylvania. We're only 10 and half miles from crossing the New Jersey/Pennsylvania border. Y'all know what that means! The state line dance party is still going strong. We haven't given up on that, and I imagine it'll only get stronger as we get closer and closer to home.

For dinner tonight, we had Goldfish crackers and fruit snacks. I'm getting a steak tomorrow.

We love y'all. Keep sending us messages.

Love,

Number 2

Falling asleep before completing her part of the journal...oh, wait! She just woke up:

I am absolutely getting another pair of shoes. This pair has been through almost 600 miles. I saw an adorable baby rabbit today. It saw me, too, and wasn't scared at all.

It was one of our longest days of hiking for the entire trail. Ultimately, we topped out at 18.5 miles as the most we would ever do in a day. It was long enough. The Mohican Outdoor Center reminded me of my good ol' summer camp days with the same cabin style buildings with screens stapled directly onto the window frames.

We did get to take a shower in the tiny utility closet, and I was thrilled! Had a lovely tent site that was surrounded by wild blueberry bushes, and I can't really remember much else from that day besides being really proud of ourselves for hiking almost 18 miles. For my fellow Nashvillians, that's like walking from Centennial Park to Mount Juliet. No thanks.

Chapter Eleven

Pennsylvania

Wednesday, August 14, 2013 – The Steak Dinner in Pennsylvania

Starting Location: Mohican Outdoor Center → Destination: Delaware Water Gap

Today's Miles: 11.60 – Trip Miles: 807.70

Woke up to a breezy 57 degrees this morning with beautiful blue skies. Such a perfect day for hiking and there were lots of folks out on the trail.

This afternoon we coasted into Pennsylvania walking over the Delaware River. That was a very long walk over the bridge that also doubles as a four-lane highway. I could feel the bridge bounce a little when big semi-trucks zoomed past us. One driver gave us a friendly honk and a wave, and that was something!

We saw a sign at this adorable little ice cream shop that said "Two Franks and a Drink for $3." It reminded me so much of my college job as the assistant manager of an ice cream shop in Chattanooga, Tennessee. I had a root beer float with my hot dogs and tapped my foot to the big band music playing over the speakers...I could have spent a lot of time with a notepad and a pen in that place.

This evening we treated ourselves to a nice steak dinner and it was a little slice of heaven. I absolutely cleaned my plate and thought long and hard about some dessert, but I passed. I didn't have anywhere to put it.

We have another long day ahead of us; the halfway mark is coming up real soon, and I hope y'all will stay tuned for the second half!

Sending lots of love to family, friends, hikers everywhere,

Number 2

Puma's getting sleepy again. Quick! Say something before it turns into sleepy nonsense:

Everything about today was just right. The hike, the weather, the rocks, and it was mostly downhill. I also bought another pair of shoes. I'm ready for my next round of blisters.

I just couldn't believe it. I will never forget the flyer I saw hanging in the window of that restaurant. I've been waiting to tell this part of the story, waiting for the entry about the steak dinner in Pennsylvania.

My belly was so full, and all I wanted to do was lay down. Making our way out the door, Puma noticed a flyer with the words "Missing Hiker." I looked at the picture of the woman, and thought to myself, "Gosh, she looks so familiar to me." Then as soon as I read her trail name, it all came back to me and then some. I'd like to dedicate this entry to her.

Somewhere in Vermont around the latter part of June (that's my best guess) was when I had the pleasure of crossing the path with this fellow hiker.

I always hiked in front, and I remember seeing a couple of NOBOs coming towards us on the trail. The first lady was not in the best of moods, so we just nodded and kept it moving, respectfully. The second lady had a big grin and was wearing a hat that said "Nashville Marathon" across it.

As soon as I could make out what her hat said, I stretched my arms across the trail as a signal that we needed a chat. We introduced ourselves with trail names only, and then we talked a little about Atlanta and then Nashville. Nothing too involved, just a short little "Hey! Look at us out here doin' it!" kind of moment.

Things I noticed about her: she had impressive calf muscles, she had excellent gear, her glasses were very becoming, and she was so happy. I was hugely impressed by her all the way around, and we wished each other well, and that was it.

Now, going "Back to the Future" to that steak dinner in Pennsylvania:

Holding on to the flyer, it took me a few minutes to rummage through my mental filing cabinet to remember why this missing hiker looked so familiar to me, and then it hit me. It was actually more like a sucker punch to the gut because her real name also sounded very familiar. Then it all came together, and I just sat down on the bench outside, buried my head in my hands, and cried. I had to put it all together before I could explain it to Puma.

She was not only a fellow hiker, but the mother of a girl who was a year or two ahead of me in high school. I knew of her family. It absolutely blew my mind, and I wanted so badly for this to not be true.

Puma and I were both pretty disturbed by this story, and I still just can't believe how it all ended. I'm glad I missed out on all the news and media stories, and I can't imagine how that must have been for the family.

For those who don't know the story, this hiker lost track of the trail in a very dense and remote area of Maine, and her body was found two years later. That's all I can say about that.

What I can confirm is that she was really very happy when we spoke to each other on the trail, and her positivity has stayed with me ever since.

It's been over 11 years since I had the pleasure of meeting her, and I think about my experiences out on the A.T. every single day. I'm grateful she is a part of my story.

Remember I am retelling this story because I was trying to protect my mother from all the scary things in the first version of the online trail journal. I sent a subliminal signing off salutation that evening of August 14, "Sending lots of love to family, friends, and hikers everywhere." To that fellow hiker, thanks for the chat; you inspire me every day.

Thursday, August 15, 2013 – The Backyard of The Beer Stein

Starting Location: Delaware Water Gap → Destination: Wind Gap
　Today's Miles: 15.80 – Trip Miles: 823.50

Had a great hike on our first Pennsylvania rocky ridge. They ain't kiddin' about these rocks, y'all!

We took our time and took breaks, but my feet are still a little achy. We passed some day-hikers and a couple of NOBOs. The NOBO "hiker bubble" has really thinned out though; I think they are in the finishing stretches of Maine. Got a couple of posts from some NOBO friends who let us know they summited Katahdin. Congrats to all!

We hiked into Wind Gap this evening and headed straight for this place called The Beer Stein that everyone had been telling us about. We started off with two large beers and some hot wings. It just doesn't get any better than that; but wait, we also both had big cheeseburgers and fries and another big beer. The food was amazing, and the beer hit the spot. Love those moments.

We are pitching our tent in the backyard of The Beer Stein. Don't worry, it's allowed, and we got permission. We should have had more beers since we weren't going far but my belly just didn't have anywhere to put it. What a great way to end the day!

We love y'all,

Number 2

Pitching a tent in the backyard of The Beer Stein reminds Puma of her younger years. Welcome to another edition of Heartfelt Memories with Puma:

We covered about 16 miles on the rocks today. Happy to say I have no extra blisters. These shoes are Number 2's colors from high school. Go Irish!

The Beer Stein was a great little dive bar inside a small white cinder-block building that stood alone on a no frills road in Wind Gap, Pennsylvania; it had all the required accoutrements including a drop ceiling, neon-lit beer signs, and a large collection of beer steins. I think we would have had more tales to tell if I hadn't been so worn out from the day's hike. I mean, I remember sitting at the bar feeling like a sleepy toddler in a highchair. Plus, eating a huge meal after a long day's hike is the perfect recipe for the greatest sleep of one's life, no matter if it is in a gravel parking lot.

Friday, August 16, 2013 – Wilson Phillips, The Clash, and J.J. Cale

Starting Location: Wind Gap → Destination: Danielsville

Today's Miles: 17 – Trip Miles: 840.50

Okay, this is a pitch to the Travel Channel (seriously, you never know, it could happen): Hiking the Appalachian Trail one bed and breakfast stay at a time. Real people, real towns, real stories, and REAL reviews. I promise it'd be entertaining!

Well folks, we are in fact at another bed and breakfast this evening. Puma planned out the rest of Pennsylvania, plus a couple rendezvous with some friends along the way. Looking forward to the halfway point!

We watched the movie Bridesmaids this evening. Damn good movie if you ask me.

Reliving the days of the Wilson Phillips hit "Hold On." What is the message of that song anyway? I think The Clash said it better with "Should I Stay, or Should I Go?"

Missing the 80s and the 90s,

Number 2

Blaming "creaky floors" for the suspiciously familiar sounds of farting, the person who always makes me laugh, it's time to hear from Puma:

I loved growing up in the 90s. Salt-N-Pepa was my very first concert. R. Kelly was the opener.

Reading this entry brings back that uncomfortable feeling of watching old home videos. Nothing much to go off here. Nothing about the Apple Inn, but I do remember the ghostly general store that was attached to it. It was closed. Lights were off. I remember wondering if the owners ever flip the lights on and crank up the old timey music? Did they sell a bunch of homemade candles or make their own taffy or chocolate bars? And certainly, did the cashier wear those sleeve garters and a vest?

This place was full of knickknacks and antiques, but nothing I really needed at the time. I don't like a lot of clutter, and I'm trying to live a life where I'm not owned by my possessions, within reason. That's one thing about having everything I needed in one backpack, I got used to the simplicity and the freedom. Like one of my favorite artists, Mr. J.J. Cale, sang, "Travelin' Light" really *is* the best and also the only way to hike.

Saturday, August 17, 2013 – Rocky Pennsylvania

Starting Location: Danielsville → Destination: Blue Mountain Summit
Bed and Breakfast

Today's Miles: 13.50 – Trip Miles: 854

*Hit the trail by 9 a.m. and had beautiful weather. Made it over Bake
Oven Knob and the Knife's Edge today; both were fun to hike/climb. There
were lots of weekend hikers out today and it's always fun to talk with them
about our travels.*

*This evening, we hiked to PA 309 and are staying at the Blue Mountain
Summit Bed and Breakfast. This place has the best food we've had since the
start of this adventure. I'm not even kiddin, y'all!*

*These rocks in Pennsylvania are starting to thin out a bit, but I'm not
holding my breath for tomorrow's hike.*

*My belly is full and my feet are tired; just another day on the trail...and
I love it.*

*Watching the Golf Channel wishing Puma would take up golf profes-
sionally. I'm just sayin'.*

Love,

Number 2

*Introducing the golfer who thinks the 4/5 hybrid is the cutest club, as
always, Puma:*

*There's enough rocks here that we could build a bridge over every body
of water on the A.T.*

Oh, the rocks of Pennsylvania...just thinking about them makes my
feet ache. That innocent little blaze on the tree was just the messenger,
and we all know we can't be mad at the messenger.

Prepping for a thru hike on the A.T., we trained on the Fiery Gizzard
Trail in Tracy City, Tennessee. Just do the section from the Grundy

trailhead up to Raven's Point a bunch of times in a row; I believe that section is called the "Fruit Bowl" (or is it Fruit Salad?) because of all the rocks and boulders. Makes for a great trail name. That particular stretch of the Fiery Gizzard will give you a small idea of what it's like hiking through Pennsylvania.

I personally love the Fiery Gizzard Trail and recommend doing the whole thing. You're guaranteed a diverse hiking experience. Just know that it is *not* a loop trail, and don't forget the car keys. I made that mistake, not once but twice! That's right.

Puma and I were hiking that trail with some buddies, and I left the car keys in the vehicle at the starting point of the trail. Can you imagine how Puma must have felt? Made it to the other end of the Fiery Gizzard Trail, thinking about beer and pizza, to then realize that we had to go back the way we came. Puma was preparing herself to run a half marathon down US 41A back to the car when a park ranger pulled into the parking lot and gave us a ride back to the other end. The other time I forgot the keys, my mom drove all the way from Nashville and brought us back to our vehicle. What a sport! Both times were accidental, and I may be the only one who laughed about it. It still makes me laugh. I had to hold my giggles the whole hour drive back home, and let me tell ya, *that* was rough.

I'm trying to remember the Blue Mountain Summit Bed and Breakfast. I have these memories of a small bed and breakfast we stayed in around this time, but I'm not sure if this was this place. The one I'm thinking of was run by one woman who seemed to be doing it all by herself. I'm talking the shuttles, the cooking, and the cleaning. Her place was not a big operation, and I seem to recall it was us and maybe two other people staying there for the night. Our room was full of dark antique furniture with brightly painted yellowish walls. There were long black lace curtains over the windows, a creepy one-eyed porcelain doll that I tried not to look at (the eye wasn't missing, just wasn't open), and a small old television sitting on top of a VCR on the dresser. I laid in the bed watching the movie *The Great Outdoors* starring one of my heroes, Mr. John Candy. I kept one eye on that damn one-eyed doll all night.

Sunday, August 18, 2013 – Seriously Big Spiders

Starting Location: Blue Mountain Summit Bed and Breakfast → Destination: Eckville Shelter

Today's Miles: 11.50 – Trip Miles: 865.50

Let me tell y'all something about these rocks here in Pennsylvania...I can't even daydream, even just a little bit, because I have to concentrate on every step; otherwise I'd be bouncing around like those folks on the big red balls in that show "Wipeout."

There was a light drizzle that came down most of the day, which dampened the rocks just enough to make them slippery. Gladly, no falls to report, but I did accidentally try to move one of the boulders with my knee.

We made it to Eckville Shelter in the early afternoon. Puma and I unpacked everything, made up our beds on the bunks, and went to go check out the advertised "flushing toilet." Love them things.

When we came back to the shelter, I was putzin' around fumbling with my raincoat or something when I heard Puma say, "Oh my Gawd." I looked at her; her pupils got real small and I turned my head to see what it was she was staring at on the upper part of the bunkbed post. It was the largest spider I think either of us have ever seen in our lives.

Puma doesn't do spiders. Period.

I knew right then that she was either gonna throw up or scream. Neither one happened, thank goodness. She went outside and I packed up our stuff

so we could set up our tent across the street. She handled the situation waaay better than both of us thought she would have since we hadn't hardly seen any scary spiders since the start of this adventure. Way to go, Puma.

For dinner we had fried spider legs. No we DID NOT!

For dinner, we had broccoli and cheddar rice, peach tea, some Goldfish crackers, one beef-n-cheese, and some chocolate filled rolled up cookies that looked like Black & Mild cigars. Don't tell my mom, but those aren't bad with chocolate milk.

Listen here, we are definitely still having fun and looking forward to every day. I hope y'all continue to post on our journal and keep this thing going.

I have to give a special birthday shout out to my Granny and my Aunt Ruth! I love y'all VERY much!

By the way, everyone gets a free flyswatter in Puma's honor tonight!

Love y'all,

Number 2

Certain to never be a guest on Andrew Zimmern's "Bizarre Foods America" spider eating episode, Puma "Pesticide" Pumacin:

It's true, I do not like spiders. We haven't had any problems with spiders until today. Back home I would just stare at a spider in the house until the cats or Number 2 took care of it. The spider I saw in this shelter was bigger than my hand. Even Number 2 was scared. Glad we have the tent.

I got a "D" in biology, but I *can* confirm that these were seriously big spiders. You know the kind of spiders that have big furry butts, like the kind in those nature shows? That's the kind of spiders we're talkin' about here, folks. I do remember seeing a lot more of them while I was packing up our stuff inside Eckville Shelter. It was like a hostel for spiders.

Now, I'm sure we slept near a spider or two in the previous states, but none of them were as big as these grandaddies. Which now has me wondering if I used to say "grandaddy long-legs" or just "daddy long-legs?" We'll need to check the genealogy on that, but for now, just believe me when I tell you those spiders in that shelter had some girth to them. Just one stroke of the pen on that shelter sign could say it all – "Eekville Shelter." Eek!

Monday, August 19, 2013 – Are We at Opryland Hotel?

Starting Location: Eckville Shelter → Destination: Pine Grove

Today's Miles: 16.30 – Trip Miles: 881.80

Today there were moments on the trail that made me think I was walking around the Cascades of the Opryland Hotel in Nashville. The vegetation was super lush with the sound of a trickling stream just to our right that flowed over rocks and little wooden footbridges. If there had been an Oak Ridge Boys laser light show, I'd have felt right at home! If there had been a Dippin' Dots vendor, I'd really have thought we were traveling back in time and hanging out at Opryland theme park.

Also came across a four foot black snake on the trail. That was prolly the longest snake I've ever met in person. He was cool, just slithered on by, but I still don't want to curl up with one on the couch and watch a movie or nothing. Know what I mean?

Got off the trail this afternoon and ate at our first Taco Bell of the trip. I ate three crunchy tacos with extra Fire Sauce in about 90 seconds flat. That was just a snack.

We ended our day at the Hampton Inn in Pine Grove where they serve dinner, as well as a nice continental breakfast. That's known as a "twofer" where I come from!

Puma's working hard on coordinating our next points where we will meet up with Don and Denise (our good friends from Connecticut), and alls I'm doing is watching Tennessee play in the Little League World Series. I actually love the Little League World Series. Okay folks, thanks again for keeping up with us.

We'll holler at y'all tomorrow,

Number 2

Make welcome the person who's been trying to teach me the crow hop throw for a long time now, the never frustrated, Puma:

The animals and insects of Pennsylvania are so big they remind me of the movie Jumanji. The rocks are slowing down a bit now. This makes me happy.

Pennsylvania was more than I expected. It was rugged and wild. Prior to the A.T., I never once considered Pennsylvania as an adventurous getaway, but I wanted to grab my flyrod at least 100 times or more. And gorgeous, I mean the streams were clearer than any unspoken rule, and the Delaware River winds its way through the Poconos Mountains showcasing breathtaking view after breathtaking view. I felt a sense of home in those mountains. Maybe because the streams really did transport me back to walking around the Opryland Hotel.

I have lived across the street from Opryland almost my entire life; it was my babysitter when I was growing up. We could hear the roar of the Screamin' Delta Demon rollercoaster from our backyard, and many a time it fooled me thinking it was thundering outside on a clear summer's day.

Walking around in the hotel has been a favorite pastime of mine, at least around the holidays. It's changed a lot over the years, but I will never forget the magical feelings I had walking through the lush rainforest atmosphere of the Cascades area. It had a sprawling jungle of large plants, secluded waterfalls, a meandering riverboat, tiny plastic winking trolls, and antique mechanical families dressed up for Sunday dinner intermittently turning towards each other to greet and sing the chorus of the carols. I pictured that scene so many times while hiking through Pennsylvania. I could feel the end of summer in the air and see the start of fall in the trees. Truly, it was a perfect setting for observing the changing of the seasons.

Tuesday, August 20, 2013 – We Just Needed a Day

Starting Location: Pine Grove → Destination: Pine Grove

Today's Miles: 0 – Trip Miles: 881.80

When it came down to it, we just needed a day to get some things done:

• My folks are coming to meet us in Shenandoah National Park in Virginia, which we are very excited about. So, we put together a list of things for them to bring, and you better believe homegrown tomatoes are on the list.

• I got a haircut.

• We got a little bit more re-supply.

• The plan for meeting Don and Denise is in place.

• Oh, and we did laundry.

Those were the things we did today instead of hiking, and it was a good day. We'll get some good rest tonight and head out in the morning – after I eat the entire continental breakfast.

We are literally gearing up for the second half of this adventure, and I'm so happy we're headed south!

Thanks for tuning in, y'all.

Love,

Number 2

Puma missed her calling as a barber. She gave me an awesome haircut with a pair of kindergarten rounded-tip scissors. Get in line for Puma's up-do's:

My appetite is not what I expected. I get really hungry but can't eat too much in one sitting. Had a six inch sandwich and a small milkshake, and I felt like I was going to throw up. Glad we took the day off.

Reflecting on the hiker hunger then and now, my hiker hunger was very different from Puma's. I could eat and eat and eat, and then an hour later, eat again. I was eating extra-large portions in town and then sticking to my rationed amounts out on the trail for three to five days at a time. It was hard for me to not eat everything in my food bag every night, and I found my metabolism to be working in overdrive around the clock. I think the scientific word for it is ectomorph, meaning I can eat like a pig and stay like a twig, especially while hiking long distances.

Now in my 40s, I'm noticing things are slowing down a bit, and my hand strength isn't what it used to be. I find myself squinting more, being done for the day by 6 p.m., and routinely getting up before 5 a.m. without an alarm clock. I like for things to be in order, can't stand clutter, and errands count as going out.

The phrase "I just needed a day" still rings true then and now. Whether we need a day to get things done or to just step away, both are valid in my book.

Wednesday, August 21, 2013 – A Walk Across the Street to Dairy Queen

Starting Location: Pine Grove → Destination: Pine Grove
  Today's Miles: 0 – Trip Miles: 881.80

Well, y'all, another fun-filled day on this adventure. After breakfast, we walked to Arby's (it was a couple hours after breakfast, it wasn't like RIGHT after breakfast). Then, we watched a marathon of that show Mountain Men on the History Channel. I was hooked! Saw lots of images of the Blue Ridge Parkway in North Carolina, and I am so excited to get down that way.

Not much else to report except that we ate Subway for dinner. Now I gotta' settle in and watch a new episode of Mountain Men. I am HOOKED on this SHOW.

Thanks for reading about our incredibly interesting day. I'm thinking about a 4x4 dune buggy for when we get back home.

Love y'all,

Number 2

Resting up for our walk across the street to Dairy Queen tomorrow, the ever talented, Puma:

I needed this extra time off. Preparing for all the fun with upcoming visitors.

Extended rest for a dessert quest. It makes me laugh thinking about how different my pace of life was on this adventure. I mean the only thing on my to-do list was to walk across the street to a Dairy Queen and rest. Seems silly and unproductive, frivolous and petty, irresponsible and irrational, oh the guilt I can create and carry is scary. To this day, I have feeeelings about my guilty A.T. hiking conscience; but I'm a Gemini Sun, so I can choose to feel guilty OR be proud of my accomplishment. Both sides ring true, and that's the beauty of it all. I was lucky enough to step away from a full-time job in Nashville, Tennessee, to hike across the street to a Dairy Queen way up in Pine Grove, Pennsylvania.

Thursday, August 22, 2013 - Gravitational Pull of Crockpot Spaghetti

Starting Location: Pine Grove → Destination: Pine Grove

Today's Miles: 0 – Trip Miles: 881.80

Got it all planned out (tentatively). Virginia, the Smokies, and all the way to Georgia! This adventure is definitely one of a lifetime, and at different times it seems to fly by and then take forever. I'm just happy to be here.

It's been amazing reading all of the posts on our journal from family, friends, and people we don't even know. We are totally humbled by your comments of encouragement and support.

We are also very excited for this second half, not just because we're back in familiar territory, but because of the time of year. The leaves are changing, somebody's grilling out, football season is starting, the smell of campfires is in the air, and I get to start brainstorming our Halloween costume ideas (yes, I usually start thinking about that now). I've already got a couple of really great ideas – just depends on if Puma will approve.

This is truly an amazing time in our lives, and I feel blessed to be right here, right now. Y'all better keep on following this journal because we are about to turn it up a notch and have even more fun. Lots more laughs ahead.

Thanks for reading, America!

Livin' the dream,

Number 2

Making less noise than a fly landing on a bed sheet, give it up for Puma:

I get more and more sore with each passing zero day. Soon, we will be leaving and hitting the trail.

We stayed in that hotel room for four days! It was like the movie *Groundhog Day* starring Bill Murray. I remember us looking at each other every morning wondering if we were going to hit the trail or stay in the cozy beds one more day. It happened four times in a row! Those pillows and sheets at the Hampton Inn were real nice and powerful.

This was hard for me, mentally, because I was basking in our accomplishment but also feeling guilty for taking so many "zeros" in a row. The guilt was eating at both of us, so we gave ourselves a good pep talk and made it out of there.

I will mention that the free dinner was a crockpot of spaghetti. Like something you might find at the Ladies of Charity free lunch hour, and I was thrilled! There was something very nostalgic about it for me. It made me think about so many things from my past. Funny how small things can bring back a rush of memories. Crockpot spaghetti will get me there every time; makes me want to sit at the kitchen table and work on my Christmas card list. It was time to break free from the gravitational pull of that crockpot spaghetti.

Friday, August 23, 2013 - Camping by the Train Tracks in Duncannon

Starting Location: Pine Grove → Destination: Duncannon

Today's Miles: 0 – Trip Miles: 881.80

Got in a lot of good people watching at the Pilot/Subway/Dairy Queen complex today. I love when two or more franchises come together under one roof. We saw a Taco Bell/Long John Silver's the other day, and I knew we were getting closer to the South. Pure brilliance.

We got a shuttle from a lovely trail angel, and she told us about other SOBOs she shuttled earlier in the day. This lady has a wonderful story of

how she came to the Appalachian Trail family, and I admire her tenacity.
I could tell she loves helping hikers along the A.T.

This evening, we are staying at a campground in Duncannon, which is
right smack between the Susquehanna River and the train tracks. About
every 30 minutes there's a train roaring by. Doesn't bother me one bit
(prolly because my parents used to run the vacuum cleaner under my crib
just to get me to sleep when I was a little).

Tomorrow we get the honor of checking out The Doyle Hotel, which is a
MUST on this experience. We've heard many, many different stories about
this hotel and restaurant. I'll give y'all a full write up tomorrow.

I hope you're hungry for more, America!

See y'all soon.

Love,

Number 2

Making a belt and sash out of all the pennies she's flattened on the tracks,
please welcome the original bohemian, Puma:

Apparently, I get car sick easily. I take it as a signal that it's best to hike.
We meet up with Don and Denise tomorrow afternoon. It will be fun seeing
them again.

Camping out behind the restrooms at this campground, I remember
the camp host telling us the specific area that we could pitch our tent and
thinking to myself, "We've seen worse." The river was maybe 20 yards to
our right and the train tracks were maybe 20 feet to our left. This was
not one of those campgrounds with restrictions against old model RVs
or campers. This place was full of hard-working people who just wanted
to have a fun weekend. Bring your fishing pole, crack a few beers, and
enjoy a fire...in a barrel. I felt right at home!

The train was very timely, felt like every 30 minutes one was roaring
by. No problems there either. The tent blocked out all the worries in my

mind, and the earplugs worked nicely, too. I just couldn't wait to check out The Doyle!

Saturday, August 24, 2013 – The Doyle, Horse Tracks, and Casino

Starting Location: Duncannon → Destination: Horse Track and Casino

Today's Miles: 1 – Trip Miles: 882.80

We saw it from far away – the sign said "Welcome Hikers" and we knew that it had to be the Doyle Hotel. We'd been hearing about this place since Andover, Maine, and the moment had finally come for us to walk through those doors.

The bartender said, "What'll ya have?" as soon as we stepped inside. I was noticing all the alien trinkets and dolls decorating the huge wooden bar as Puma was keeping an eye out for spiders. We bellied up to the bar and rubbed elbows with a few more big guys in the joint.

Many great stories and tall tales are told in that place, and honestly, I could have spent all day in there. We spent a couple of hours trying the local brews and chewing the fat with this guy named Tricks, and he confessed that he wanted to hike the rest of the trail with us because we had such a great time together. Great guy. Good luck to him in the future.

Don and Denise showed up and we ate lunch at The Doyle. Good food, great company. We left there and went into the town of Harrisburg, Pennsylvania. That's where we found the horse races and the casino...

Listen here y'all, I am just as surprised as you are about where we ended up today. But Puma was hot on those numbers and won at the horse track AND at the craps table. I don't have a clue what's going on in either event, but I do know the horses were pretty and the flashy lights were very bright.

I hate to tell y'all this, but we are having so much fun out here! Don and Denise are two of the greatest people in the world. Denise even brought us a slice of her homemade blueberry pie. I am so thankful for their thoughtfulness and generosity.

What a crazy awesome day! It's time to hit the hay.

Love,

Number 2

Running things, Puma:

Don't worry, we were just having a good time. Nothing lost, nothing gained. They gave Number 2 a special lanyard so the staff would quit asking for her ID. It was funny.

Oh, The Doyle...it was small and packed inside, but we were lucky enough to find a seat at the bar. I had a blast chatting it up with everybody in there. I felt as though I had found my crowd, a bunch of awkwardly funny and nerdy outdoorsy hikers. Excellent conversation and the burger was delicious.

As for the hotel part, I'm glad we stayed in our tent. Other hikers were telling stories of their room accommodations having holes in the ceilings and floors. One guy was talking about how he could see that someone was taking a shower through the cracks in the ceiling. There was talk of spiders that were referred to as "roommates." Made Eckville Shelter sound like the Hampton Inn.

We sure did go to a horse track and casino. Puma can hold her own at the casino. I respect that. I remember one time she gave me a $20 bill to gamble with, and an hour later, she asked me how I did, and I still had the $20. I'm fascinated with the whole scene, but I don't have a clue about what's going on. I'm too distracted trying to watch everything. I'm happy as can be with a good snack bar.

Sunday, August 25, 2013 – Orange Pack Covers for a Reason

Starting Location: Horse Track and Casino → Destination: Darlington Shelter

Today's Miles: 11 – Trip Miles: 893.80

Guess what we saw today? A Bass Pro Shop with boats and everything! Yep, this morning we made a quick stop through there and got ourselves some fancy new hunter orange pack covers and let me tell you, they are just beautiful.

It's a good thing we did because as soon as we got back on the trail, we could hear and see some folks having target practice getting ready for the upcoming hunting season. Made me think about the times we went skeet shootin' with my cousins out in Dickson, Tennessee. We love y'all! Good times.

Pennsylvania has been real good to us, and I'm looking forward to tomorrow. We've seen lots of beautiful corn fields along this thin dirt path we all call the A.T., and well, we're still having fun.

We are just a few days away from that old Mason-Dixon line, and y'all better believe we're gonna have a bonafide dance party! We will definitely record it, and Puma's gonna figure out how to get on the journal (I have high hopes that it works). Y'all have GOT to see our moves...well, our good moves. I have a couple okay moves and one good move, but Puma's got a bunch of good moves.

This has been a great day!

Thank you so much for keeping up with us and posting such wonderful messages on our journal. We read all of them and just love it. Okay, we'll holler at y'all tomorrow.

Love,

Number 2

Puma loved the grunge bands Nirvana and Sponge while I was listening to Dolly Parton and Jerry Reed (now, this should paint a nice picture of our state line dance parties...awkward and AWESOME, but mostly awkward):

Don and Denise are two of the best friends ever. The very next best friends are Bill and Melody. We will see them shortly. It's been a fun midway point.

Glad we got those bright orange pack covers. Now, I could be wrong about the hunting seasons in Pennsylvania, but I read that the earliest hunting opportunity is September 1 when people can use their falcons to hunt squirrels, grouse, and cottontail rabbits. If you miss that, then you have to wait until the end of September to use your bow. After that, you're looking at mid-October with a muzzleloader and late October for the first legal gunshot. All that said, we heard a good bit of gunfire out on the trail in Pennsylvania in late August. Must be nice to own your own land. We weren't nervous about it, just wanted to make sure we were seen. I imagine if I ever tried to hunt with a falcon, it'd be like letting go of a balloon.

This entry reminded me about all the hearsay about grouse on the A.T. If a rooster and a dove had a baby, that's what a grouse looks like. We heard about these territorial birds chasing hikers down the trail. I hiked in tall gaiters from day one. Just gave me a little extra confidence and peace of mind for whatever was coming next. I can say we never got chased by them, but we definitely saw them and heard them. They sound like helicopters – no kiddin'! I'd be hiking along and hear what sounded like whirling helicopter rotors "juff, juff, juff, juff, juff." I'd look up at the sky to then realize it was a grouse down below – and it was close.

Monday, August 26, 2013 – A Mid-century Modern Apocalypse

Starting Location: Darlington Shelter → Destination: Boiling Springs

Today's Miles: 14 – Trip Miles: 907.80

Today, we had a lovely hike through corn fields, climbed up and over little ladders on fences dividing cow pastures, came across quite a few footbridges over dried up creeks, and crossed a handful of gravel roads.

The weather was just beautiful, and I hope we're as lucky tomorrow. Puma and I walked into town and found the local pizzeria. I grabbed two bags of bar-b-q chips before we ordered. I just love grabbing stuff and adding it to the bill later. Another example of this behavior would be grabbing a Snapple out of the little refrigerators at Target and drinking it while I shop, then paying for the empty bottle when it's all said and done. Life's simple pleasures, those are the things I absolutely love out here (this list also includes flushable toilets).

We have been so flattered by your posts on our journal. Y'all make us feel like the greatest show on dirt! Thanks so much.

Love,

Number 2

Coupons or cute ponds, I can't distinguish which one Puma's talking about. Y'all try to figure it out:

It was really pathy today. We flew through those 14 miles. Made it to the A.T.C. (Appalachian Trail Conservancy) office and realized we are actually closing in on the midway point. Feels good making it this far.

After eating at the local pizzeria, we walked down to the Allenberry, which is a flyfishing resort right on the Yellow Breeches Creek (my brain pronounces it "yellow britches"). We were the only patrons of the entire establishment, and I'm pretty sure I only saw one or two staff members. It was like we had walked onto a dusty production set of *The Shining*.

They advertised a dinner theatre, and it would have blown my mind if we had gotten to see that, especially as the only customers. The tennis courts were empty, the courtyards were empty, the restaurant and bar were also empty. They even had a flyfishing museum full of old photographs of sportsmen holding their trout, all covered in a dusty film. Mannequins were posed in flyfishing apparel from the 60s all around this room, and in the middle, there was a ping pong table with two paddles, no ball.

I could totally imagine this place full of people, but we were walking through a ghost town. It was definitely eerie, and why the person at the front desk didn't tell us to scram is beyond me.

The hotel room was tiny, which is totally fine, but I continued to feel like we were not supposed to be there. The floor was a dark forest green carpet, the bathroom had black and pink ceramic tiles, and the sink was in the bedroom. I felt like we had traveled back in time and stumbled into a mid-century modern apocalypse.

The trout were astounding and the creek was crystal clear. Very picturesque and I remember wishing I had my flyrod with me. Since then, this place must be under new management because now they are an Orvis-endorsed resort. Fannnncy! I guess they gave up on the dinner theatre idea.

Tuesday, August 27, 2013 – Warm Mountain Dew

Starting Location: Boiling Springs → Destination: James Fry Shelter
Today's Miles: 12 – Trip Miles: 919.80

Welcome to another day in paradise. We hiked through a couple of soybean plots and cornfields this morning, and I daydreamed about setting up on the edge of those fields on a crisp fall morning in all my camouflage waiting for a cheeseburger to walk by.

The fields ended and put us back in the woods with rocks and hills. We got to hike through a rock maze today and saw a couple of spots where people had been bouldering. We saw their chalk marks on the rock faces. Puma and I cannot wait to get our climbing gear out again when we get home.

My muscles were just plain worn out by the end of the day. I guess the hills and rocks make a big difference. We settled in and just had dinner – which was cold pizza and warm Mountain Dew...jackpot! Yep, we came across a box of Mountain Dews early this morning and carried two cans all day to enjoy them with our cold leftover pizza from the day before. Now when I say "cold leftover pizza" you understand that I really mean smashed warm pizza that we wrapped up in a plastic bag and carried on our backs for seven hours in the heat of the day. Yum. But it really hit the spot this evening.

I hope I haven't made y'all sick with today's menu descriptions. With that said, thanks for reading.

Love,

Number 2

Gearing up for the Half Gallon Challenge tomorrow (contents: ice cream of her choice), the greatest spoon operator, Puma:

After these first eight miles, my feet were hurting. The final four miles made me work. I am pumped about the Half Gallon Challenge tomorrow. Another 7.6 miles and then I can go nuts on some ice cream. After that, it'll be another four miles before we're done.

I remember seeing the box of warm Mountain Dews propped up against the blaze post. I hadn't had one in years. Some of y'all might know that we call ALL non-alcoholic carbonated drinks "Coke" down in the South. Example situation would be if you went to a Waffle House and the server asked you if you wanted a Coke, you would say, "Yes" and then the server would then ask you, "What kind?" And only then are you cleared to say, "Mountain Dew." Pepsi is the maker of Mountain Dew, but it doesn't matter. It's crazy how a warm can of Mountain Dew and a sweaty piece of pizza could be exactly what my body needed. If I had that meal today, I'd be in trouble...or whoever's close to me might be in trouble.

Wednesday, August 28, 2013 – Pine Grove Furnace and the Half Gallon Challenge

Starting Location: James Fry Shelter → Destination: Toms Run Shelter
Today's Miles: 11 – Trip Miles: 930.80

In today's episode of Puma vs. Food, Puma won! That's right folks, Puma conquered the famous Half Gallon Challenge with her choice of black cherry ice cream in only 37 minutes! It was exhilarating to watch, and I knew that this was her arena, not mine. She was so cold by the end that she had to put on her jacket, but she finished strong and that's what counts. We were the only two people around for this event, and I cheered her on as I ate my cheeseburger and two bags of chips (there's no award for finishing two bags of chips).

My hats off to Puma for taking on and completing this challenge; she then hiked another four miles up two big hills full of rocks. Just reading that makes me wanna puke.

In other news, we choreographed a small performance for y'all at the Mason-Dixon line, so keep your eyes peeled for the video.

We are thrilled to be meeting up with the Holy Smokes of 1990 in a couple of days (remember they're the couple we met in the White Mountains at Lake of the Clouds Hut). It's gonna be fun!

For dinner, we enjoyed some red beans and rice with cheese and crackers and a fruit punch drink. It's cooler tonight than I expected, and I love it because it makes me think of fall weather and football. Everybody gets a free hoodie sweatshirt tonight.

Love,

Number 2

Tolerating her lactose intake, the ice cream champeen, Puma:

Today was worth it. The midway point is officially happening tomorrow. I can't believe it.

The home of the Half Gallon Challenge is at the general store located in Pine Grove Furnace State Park. This is a rite of passage for those hiking the A.T., and Puma had been excited about this challenge for months. Again, *nobody* was around, but she still completed the challenge. Made me cold just watching her.

The state park was interesting, too. These furnaces looked like skinny stone pyramids that seemed about 20 feet tall, and their purpose was to manufacture cast iron stoves, kettles, and military weaponry way back in the mid-1700s. We also stopped in the Appalachian Trail Museum and saw pictures of the one and only Grandma Gatewood who was the first woman to complete a solo thru hike on the A.T. She made her own backpack, slept in the leaves, and hiked all those miles in Keds tennis shoes. Lordamercy!

Pennsylvania brought us a lot of stories for this adventure, and I don't think I gave it the credit it deserved compared to other states. The trout alone are worth writing home about.

Thursday, August 29, 2013 – Caledonia State Park, James Taylor, and Mark Knopfler

Starting Location: Toms Run Shelter → Destination: Caledonia State Park

Today's Miles: 15.80 – Trip Miles: 946.60

Got up early this morning, packed up camp (never gets old, we love our tent), and hiked out to this year's official halfway point just a couple miles past our campsite. This morning was cool and a little overcast which made for perfect hiking weather. All the leaves are changing colors and it's just gorgeous out here.

The first six miles flew by, and we got to meet a section hiker by the name of Old Timer at one of the shelters along the trail. He was in impeccable shape at 70 years old. I saw his biceps curl when he was putting his hair in a ponytail; Puma and I both paid him a compliment under our breaths as we watched him head back down the trail.

Hiked another 7.4 miles to the Quarry Gap Shelter, which was the cutest and most awesome shelter to date. This place had flowers, a wind blocker, a skylight, and a stone fire pit; and an innkeeper who should be commended on his efforts and dedication to such an oasis on the A.T.

While we were there, we met another section hiker named Wild Bill 129 (or was it 921?), and we sat and enjoyed his campfire for about an hour, sharing Oreos and summer sausage. He shaved down a stick and recommended roasting the sausage over the fire for a nice treat. It was soooo good! We thanked him and headed out for the final 2.6 miles into Caledonia State Park.

This is a nice state park with a big ol' pool and a twisty water slide. The slide and concession stand were closed, but the campground is open and so

are the restrooms! We love when that happens, even though I had to dry off with that daggone tiny Sham Wow again.

All in all, today was perfect. The even better news is that we meet up with the Holy Smokes of 1990 tomorrow morning bright and early! I LOVE being on this adventure. Thanks for checking in.

Love,

Number 2

And now, please give a warm welcome to the person who did not invent the Sham Wow, Puma:

Today we found a bunch of water jugs on the trail. Thank goodness. We closed out the day with pizza and Mellow Yellow. Had it all brought to the campsite. It was awesome.

This was the perfect Pennsylvania day. All that was missing was the song "Sailing to Philadelphia" by James Taylor and Mark Knopfler playing in the background. I've always liked that song for many reasons, but mainly because it's a good storytelling song about the Mason-Dixon line.

Hiking the Appalachian Trail made me feel like I was walking through my history classes. Such a great way to see the country, just walking.

Quarry Gap Shelter was such a nice shelter. I remember it had hanging planters full of brightly colored petunias and there was a breezeway with a picnic table that divided the two sleeping quarters with three-walled rooms.

The firepit was made of stone walls that were at least two feet high, and it was such a treat to share that roasty toasty summer sausage over the fire with Wild Bill 129 or was it 921? Damn. Since that day, I prefer my summer sausage to be fire roasted, and I have shared that delicious snack with my dear friends, The Pirate Witches, on backpacking trips.

The Pirate Witches is a very exclusive and elusive group, sacred and mostly secret. This group or "coven" was born out of a need for adventure, and the like-minded members of this adventure club are some of the most inspiring, supportive, kind, funny, and intelligent people I have ever met. I don't know how I got to be in this group, but I'm sure glad I am! I wish everybody could have their own group of Pirate Witches; whether ocean or land, the quest for adventure is at hand.

Friday, August 30, 2013 – Dill with it, Bill!

Starting Location: Caledonia State Park→ Destination: Dahlgren Campsite

Today's Miles: 1– Trip Miles: 947.60

I woke up around 5:30 this morning with excitement similar to Christmas morning because I knew our friends, the Holy Smokes of 1990, were headed our way to pick us up and spend the day with us. They pulled in around 8:00 a.m., and it was such a great reunion. Y'all remember this is the couple we had such a great time with in the White Mountains, and bless their hearts for coming to see us again!

We caught up on our travels since we'd last seen each other and then we all went bowling. Yep, bowling! Got a couple beers, some potato chips and bowled two games just for the heck of it. So much fun; and Bill and Melody are both darn good bowlers...natural athletes, I guess.

We spent the rest of the day on the Mason-Dixon line production. Thank goodness we had their help, too! I mean, this is Grammy winning footage, and I'd hate to miss out on an opportunity like that. Puma will have to figure out how to post the video, but I know y'all are just gonna love it! Might even be a little emotional for some (that is not even true).

We had a ridiculous amount of fun with the Holy Smokes of 1990, and we're so thankful to them for spending the day with us. Really great time.

Wait, real quick, funny story: We did a quick re-supply in town and Puma picked up a cute roll of duct tape, which is coming out in super fun patterns these days. Well, this one had a pickle with a message bubble by its mouth that said, "Dill with it!" Get it? Puma grabbed it off the shelf, tossed it in the basket, and told Bill to "Dill with it!" But he hadn't read what was on the tape yet. I saw the whole misunderstanding happen right before my very eyes and cracked up. Bill was all, "Okay...?" And I was all, "No no no no, look at the duct tape!" Puma was so embarrassed. It was glorious.

Alright folks, that's a wrap! Stay tuned.

Love,

Number 2

Serious about her duct tape (a little too serious), Puma:

What a great day! Up next we will see Number 2's parents and sister.

The Holy Smokes of 1990 a.k.a. Bill and Melody became such an important part of our A.T. story. Looking back, I think it'd feel pretty cool to hold that honor for those working on a thru hike of the Appalachian Trail. They knew everything we were about to experience, and the excitement we shared with them was the absolute best. As I've mentioned, they completed their thru hike of the A.T. back in 1990, and I was still in grade school.

We never knew what was in store for us, and I love how our paths intertwined on this adventure. One thing's for sure, though, the Appalachian Trail gets into one's soul. Whether completing a thru hike, a section hike, just a tiny section, one step, or reading about it, this thing can become an obsession. We only have today, folks; I'm asking for at least another year so I can get back out there to scratch the missing miles off my list (more about these miles later in the story). This need to complete the accomplishment is nagging at me more and more every day.

We looked up to Bill and Melody and appreciated their generosity and sense of humor. It was easy hanging out with them, and they made us feel confident and comfortable. I lost touch with them over the years, but I bet they are still the same adorable outdoorsy couple.

To Bill and Melody, thank you for all of your support and all the laughs. We truly enjoyed the time we got to spend with you two. Let's catch up again sometime soon!

Chapter Twelve

Maryland and West Virginia

Saturday, August 31, 2013 – Harpers Ferry, West Virginia

Starting Location: Dahlgren Campsite → Destination: Harpers Ferry

Today's Miles: 18.10 – Trip Miles: 965.70

We're in Harpers Ferry, West Virginia. Can y'all believe it? I'm thrilled! Today was a long day, but it was absolutely packed with interesting points.

Here are the highlights:

We got an early start and hiked past a couple of Civil War battlegrounds, Battle at Fox's Gap and Battle at Crampon's Gap. I was reading one of the displays and it quoted one of the generals quoting Shakespeare saying, "Hell is empty and all the devils are here." Oooo, it sent a shiver down my spine when I read that because I could just imagine all the soldiers in the heat of battle out in those fields. I bet it's even more powerful in the wee hours of the morning before the fog lifts.

We walked through history today, remnants of old stone houses and barns of the mid 1800s, cemeteries with headstones dated back to 1770s, old fences that are still marking the territory of Union and Confederate camps, and monuments telling the gruesome story of how our country literally came together under bloodshed. It's totally different to walk through it than to read about it.

Harpers Ferry is the neatest historical town/park. It's got cobblestone roads, and everything has been preserved from the 1800s. Lots of stories to read about this place. It's worth a trip up here, for sure!

I thought we were in a movie walking up the canal to the iron spiral staircase that lead us to the old timey railroad bridge where the Potomac and Shenandoah Rivers collide. Just as we reached the staircase, I looked behind me and saw this huge tunnel on the side of the mountain that had "Harpers Ferry" carved in stone and heard the train blow its extremely loud whistle as it emerged in all its glory. What a rush! I was right there for the whole thing. Just awesome (and very loud and very fast). Helllloooo, America!

Today's long miles have put us in position to watch some college football this evening, Alabama vs the Hokies. What a great day, but I am totally, totally pooped.

We sure do live in a beautiful country, and I feel very fortunate to be experiencing it in such a way out here on the Appalachian Trail.

Walking through my 6th grade history class (but paying a lot more attention this time).

I am,

Number 2

Guess who's decided to hike the rest of the trail in an authentic frock from 1862? It's Puma (very impressive, ...unnecessary, but impressive):

*Guess what we saw on the trail? The phantom mountain goats of Mary-
land. Found some really good trail magic on our way through Gathland
Park. There were bags of grapes, some bananas, a big bag of Fritos, and
another bag of M&Ms. Thanks for the snack. We met another hiker
named Applesauce today and had fun talking with him. The video for the
dance party on the Mason-Dixon line is coming.*

Ah, the Mason-Dixon line dance party video. We *did* do it. We made
paper instruments; I did some cloggin', and Puma was lip singing to the
Osborne Brothers version of "Rocky Top." She throws some pretend
moonshine in my face while I pretend to play a paper banjo; it wasn't
nominated for an Emmy or anything, but it was artistic with some tech-
nical merit involved. There is an actual sign that says "Mason-Dixon" out
there, but somebody had moved it, so we made our own.

Sunday, September 1, 2013 – Lunch in Harpers Ferry

Starting Location: Harpers Ferry → Destination: Campsite in the woods
   Today's Miles: 5 – Trip Miles: 970.70

*We took some time today to really take in the town of Harpers Ferry,
West Virginia. Got our picture taken at the A.T.C. (Appalachian Trail
Conservancy) headquarters by a staff person. In the photo for their record
books, I'm doing my usual air guitar move, and Puma opted for the air
flute in honor of our friend, Sahara Divine. The A.T.C. was a great stop
for us, and we really enjoyed talking with the two guys running the place
this afternoon, Old Man and Tart Pop.*

*We met up with our new friend, Will Percy, for lunch at this cute little
hole in the wall inn that served a full menu. We sat out on the back porch
and gabbed for a couple of hours about the Appalachian Trail. Good food,
great company. Thanks for lunch, Will!*

Hit the trail this afternoon before the thunderstorm came rolling in. I sleep pretty dang good in our tent, especially in the rain. It relaxes me. We are officially in the wonderful state of Virginia. I've never been to Virginia before (heck, I'd never been to any of these places before this trip), and I'm really looking forward to seeing what Virginia has to offer.

Lots more to share with y'all. The Mason-Dixon line video is coming to a theatre near you in just a couple more days.

Thanks for reading our journal,

Number 2

Cue lights, cue smoke, cue Puma's background dancers, y'all get ready for this, Puma:

I enjoyed sharing lunch with our new friend, Will. Wishing him and all future hikers the best on their hikes in 2014. It's really fun!

It was like feeling "Almost Famous" having lunch with our friend, Will Percy. He messaged through the online journal asking us to have lunch with him in Harpers Ferry because he wanted to talk about the trail and get some pointers for his planned attempt the following year. He'd been keeping up with our journal, and we were in the same place at the same time, so we agreed, and there was food.

Speaking for myself, this lunch felt a little awkward, and I have a feeling that it was all my fault. I don't think he could decide if I was a trip, a riot, a pill, or a hoot. So, I just got quiet. I remember him getting Puma and I mixed up because she was the one doing all the talking.

I was also a little perturbed that we waited until noon to eat lunch and still had to do our miles for the day. With such a late start, I felt like I couldn't find my rhythm. Thinking back on this lunch with Will, I feel like a brat but I have to tell ya, I don't think it was what he expected either. I ate my food really fast and spent the rest of the time looking at my watch. One of my weaknesses is being impatient, and why in the world

I was being fussy over a luncheon is hard to explain, even for myself. I was just in a mood. Hey Will, let me know if you want to have lunch sometime.

Chapter Thirteen

Virginia

Monday, September 2, 2013 – Tired and Cranky and Only Halfway There

Starting Location: Campsite in the woods → Destination: Blackburn A.T. Center

Today's Miles: 8 – Trip Miles: 978.70

Not too much to report today, y'all. We found the state signs for both West Virginia and Virginia. Real pretty signs.

The water situation here in northern Virginia is pretty scarce, but Puma manages to find places with spigots that allow us to fill up our bladders and water bottles.

I feeeel like we are definitely getting closer to home. The woods and the trees and the hills remind me of familiar hikes in my beloved Tennessee. Friends and family back home better believe Puma and I will be sending all kinds of invites for y'all to join us on as many hikes as possible after this adventure.

I'm excited to see my mom and dad and little sister, Number 3, in a couple of days. Yep, they are gonna spend a week with us out here to slackpack us through Shenandoah National Park. Mom's got tomatoes, and Dad's bringing Cheez-Its! My world is complete.

Number 3 is very excited to be hiking with us during the day, and I'm sure there'll be some silly pictures taken of us out there on the trail. The weather is cooling down in the evenings, and I'm looking forward to fall colors. Best time of the year. That's all I know right now, but please stay tuned for a word from our sponsor.

Yours truly,

Number 2

Yuma, duma, pneuma, Uma, and summa; there, that's all the words that rhyme with Puma:

I heard from my right foot this afternoon and it's ready for a break from the rocks. Number 2 is imagining cooler weather. It's simply not true.

You can't really tell that I was cranky from this entry, but I was. We had our moments of tiredness and our moments of crankiness out there, who wouldn't? This was one of those days. The daunting thought of over 500 miles in the same state was getting to me. Plus, with my family coming to town, missing my dog Peejay like crazy, and feeling uninspired, my battery was running low. This is the very real mental element of the trail that can play a huge role in either staying on or getting off. By this time, we already been out there for three and half months. There are hikers who can finish this thing in three or four months. I think we had so much fun in the first half and we expended our energy a little too much. We compensated for it with what thru hikers call the "yellow blaze." See, the double lines on the highway are yellow, and when one calls for a shuttle and rides along the double yellow lines, we call that a huge "yellow blaze." There's a stigma around anything that deviates from the white blaze on a thru hike.

I'll tell ya right now, we did not do a very thorough job of Virginia. In fact, I'd say we got less than half. We are not in the 2,000-Miler Club; but I sure plan on going back and having a do-over of Virginia so I can apply. Prolly redo Virginia and North Carolina just to be sure I hit the mark. Our total mileage for the A.T. came to in just under 1,400 miles. So, yeah, I'm going to thru hike Virginia and North Carolina in a couple of seasons. Maybe I'll see ya out there! And you better believe that when I complete those missing 600 miles, I will be submitting my application to the A.T.C. for the 2,000-Miler Club. I want that patch so bad...oooo, I want that patch! Prolly take me about three months to finish it, but hey, at least I can say I finished.

Tuesday, September 3, 2013 – Bear's Den Hostel and Ben E. King

Starting Location: Blackburn A.T. Center → Destination: Bear's Den Hostel

Today's Miles: 7.90 – Trip Miles: 986.60

The leaves are falling and crunching under my feet. Such beautiful weather, and I am lovin' every day out here.

Today was a short day because we wanted to check out the Bear's Den hostel and their "hiker special." This includes a bunk, shower, laundry, a pizza, and a pint of Ben & Jerry's ice cream all for $30. That's a great deal, folks.

We got in early enough for me to drink two orange Fantas and one Dr. Pepper, then I sat on the couch and watched "The Rookie" and ate from my food bag like it was a trough.

Tomorrow we hike what is known as the "rollercoaster," lots of back-to-back hills. I'll just pretend I'm at Opryland and everything'll be just fine.

It's time to hit the night night trail.

Love y'all,

Number 2

Welcome to Puma's Corner:

A shorter hike today, and that's okay with me. Bear's Den is a good stop; especially since there's ice cream.

Bear's Den hostel is a stone mansion from the 1930s that is tucked away in the Blue Ridge Mountains. It's got a huge kitchen, like something every summer camp needs, and they let us grab one of the frozen pizzas and pop it in the big commercial oven. If there had been a big rush of customers, I could have taken all the orders and cooked all the pizzas, no problem. I think there were only three of us staying there at the time. The bunkroom was nice enough, and the free ice cream was a real treat.

They had a lovely sitting room with a big fireplace (no fire) and a guitar available for the guests. I couldn't help myself and sat down with an old classical guitar that was badly out of tune. The pegs were almost seized, but it didn't bother me one bit. Ben E. King's "Stand by Me" is unmistakable and sounds good on anything.

Wednesday, September 4, 2013 – The Rollercoaster and FEMA

Starting Location: Ashby Gap → Destination: Bear's Den hostel

Today's Miles: 13.30 – Trip Miles: 999.90

Took us six hours to hike the "rollercoaster" and it wasn't too bad at all. Again, the weather was just beautiful. At one point, Puma said, "There's

not a cloud in the sky!" Then after twirling around to verify her statement, I said, "Well...there is ONE." She smacked my backpack with her trekking pole.

The rollercoaster definitely lives up to its name; we went up and over at least 10 peaks in 10 miles, and there's plenty of ankle buster rocks on the trail. Just adds to the excitement, if you ask me.

Word has it, we hiked past a Federal Emergency Management Agency (FEMA) facility hidden somewhere inside those 10 miles. Just as a fun game, I asked Puma what else FEMA could stand for, and she thought for a second then said, "Feeling Every Muscle Ache." My brain went the other direction with, "Fart Eloquently Momma's Around." We laughed about that for at least 30 feet.

Today was just awesome. The best part is my mom and dad and sister, Number 3, will be arriving tomorrow in Luray, Virginia, to slackpack us through Shenandoah National Park. We are gonna have the best time. There's gonna be plenty of pictures to share from this reunion.

Life is so so sweet right now, and I'm taking full advantage of it.

Love y'all,

Number 2

Eloquent farts should definitely be respectful. And now, back to you, Puma:

Today was compared to a rollercoaster. I'll say Maine was like riding Kingda Ka at Six Flags nonstop for a month. Happy to be in Virginia.

Was there a FEMA headquarters hidden way back in the trees of Virginia? Well, there was no sign announcing the purpose of these buildings inside this chain link fence with razor wire curling all around the top, but I suspect this was an important location for some serious decisions. That's all I can say about that.

Thursday, September 5, 2013 – Caves, Peejay, and Wineries

Starting Location: Luray → Destination: Fox Den Cabin

Today's Miles: 0 – Trip Miles: 999.90

My internal alarm clock went off way too early again this morning in anticipation of seeing my dad, mom, and sister. Puma started to get up, too, but I was like, "No no no no, it's not time yet." I played the scene of what it was going to be like to see my family over and over in my head. The excitement had been building for six hours and it wasn't even 10 a.m. yet.

We decided to go check out the town of Luray, Virginia, and the Luray Caverns. Man, was that something. The group tour was lovely, but my heart was set on the "stalag-pipe organ" that was set up 164 feet under the surface of the earth. There it was, with its grand seven million year old cathedral behind it.

The tour guide said, "Now, you will hear a live performance." She then walked to the side of the crowd and pressed a hidden button.

All my dreams were coming true; I waited for the grand symphony to erupt, this was my "Goonies" moment! T'was not the case. It's my own fault for expecting "Great Balls of Fire" to be cranked up to eleven.

A meditative tone came from the ceiling that I could hear if I didn't breathe too hard. Very faint, beautiful, and more appropriate than "Great Balls of Fire," I guess. The Tibetan Monks were singing along the way at spots during the tour, and Puma and I thought that was really cool. I wanted to sing in that cavern, too, but left it to the experts.

Y'all, we got to the cabin my parents rented for the week to slackpack us through Shenandoah, and I knew my mom, dad, and sister were coming, but I did NOT know my dog, Peejay, was coming!

Yep, they got me good. Puma took a video of my reaction when I saw his cute little face through the car window, and I think she's gonna post that in addition to our Mason-Dixon line dance video.

Today was a REALLY great day! I love my family.

Amen,

Number 2

Sneaky, bad, and downright awesome (like my mother), that would be, Miss Puma:

Number 2 crumbled when she saw Peejay's face through the window, and it's all on tape. Today was fun. I can now say I've been to caves in three different states. Sounds like I need to make caving across America my next big thing.

In anticipation of seeing my family, I remember pacing the front porch of that lovely cabin waiting for the first sign of the family car. Not having any idea that my sweet angel baby dog would be included in this visit, I was just ecstatic to see my family.

There they were coming up the gravel driveway, and I hollered and ran around the side of the porch to meet them in person. Running in place, waiting for my dad to park the car, that's when I caught a glimpse of little baby Peejay's face in the window, and I was immediate mush. While I collapsed in tears, my sister brought Peej over to me, and I just hugged him for a good while. It was the sweetest gift, and it was *also* nice to see my family.

I had a ball being with my family that week. We went to several wineries, made multiple grocery trips, cooked dinners, played cards, did a good bit of porch sittin', talked about everybody who wasn't there, and solved world problems. We did slackpack a little bit, but we did a lot more wine and food tastings, and it was glorious.

Friday, September 6, 2013 – Feeling Guilty with My Wine

Starting Location: Fox Den Cabin → Destination: Fox Den Cabin

Today's Miles: 0 – Trip Miles: 999.90

There's nothing like being back in the midst of family after some time apart. I've stood back taking in lots of moments and loving on them without them even knowing it.

We spent the day going back into Luray and wandered around the town stopping in at the little sandwich shops and the local outfitter. My dad was real cute walking Peejay in and out of the dog friendly stores; people walking by kept complimenting Peejay's manners (he is a reflection of me).

We had the pleasure of meeting up with our dear friends, Keith and Kathy, at a restaurant up the way in Front Royal, Virginia. It was so much fun to relive the memories of when they helped us out in Rangeley, Maine. They are wonderful people, and I do hope our paths cross again.

Tomorrow, we hit the trail with my sister and check out this blackberry milkshake we keep hearing about.

Life is wonderful, and I can't believe we're at this point already in this adventure. Thanks for reading.

Love,

Number 2

Guess who figured out how to link videos to our trail journal? It definitely was not me; it was Puma:

Yet again, we are having fun.

Let the guilty feeling set in. Yes, I was having a wonderful time with my family, but I also felt guilty for having all this extravagant fun. I mean, we had our hotel rooms along the way, and we were definitely not roughing it the whole time, but this was extra. A whole cabin for a whole week! We shopped and dined and wined, and after spending a good three months or more doing this adventure by ourselves, it was now a group effort. Just a bit overwhelming. Puma was, of course, being such a sport by going along with all it. I'm sure it wasn't easy.

I was grateful to have my family within arm's reach for a week, and appreciated all their efforts, including Puma's, to coordinate the timing of our hike with the cabin rental. We *always* have a good time when we get together; that was not the problem. My problem was feeling homesick and guilty at the same time. I was frozen in my emotions after they left, and it was hard for me to get back to the hiker mentality.

Tuesday, September 10, 2013 – Heavy Packs and Getting Back Out There

Starting Location: Fox Den Cabin → Destination: Daleville

Today's Miles: 0 – Trip Miles: 999.90

Hey y'all! My family headed back home to Tennessee this afternoon after a week of fun in Virginia.

We had more fun than I can explain, but here's a brief synopsis:

We ate lots of food, found the Wolf Gap Winery, played cards, hiked the trail, watched football, went sightseeing, attended the local Catholic church, put lots of miles on the front porch swing and glider, drank lots of coffee, sat around the campfire, talked about everybody who wasn't there, and listened to a Ray Charles record. I'm telling you, we just had the very best time.

We also planned the finale tailgate party for when we finish at Springer Mountain in November. More details to come for those who wish to join us for the event.

Here's one funny story from the visit: My parents wanted to visit the A. T.C. in West Virginia, so we ventured back up there to check it out. My sister and I were perusing the t-shirts and taking turns reading them out loud in exaggerated Southern accents. After about four or five inspirational t-shirt slogans, my sister holds up the last shirt and says, "I...No wait!...That's a white blaze!" I about doubled over from laughing so hard! Oh my goodness, it was so funny. She thought the blaze was the letter "I" like a profound statement was about to happen, but naw, it was just a blaze.

Puma and I are super pumped to hit the trail again, and I'm seriously looking forward to hiking in the fall colors. I hope y'all will hang out with us and follow along as we keep on heading south.

In the words of Paul Simon, I'm "Homeward Bound,"

Number 2

Leading the way, she is Puma:

I'm glad we got to see everybody. We're now further south and are geared up for more miles. Our packs are heavy, but it feels good.

I can feel the heaviness of my backpack right now. The muscle soreness was rough when we got back out on the trail, but nothing a little "Vitamin I" (Ibuprofen) couldn't fix. However, I was in a difficult mental state at this point because my body was tired, but I didn't want to quit. I was letting myself get distracted too easily. Don't get me wrong, I was elated to see my family and my dog, but I lost my momentum with my daily hiking.

As I write this, I am thinking about the logistics of my re-hike of Virginia and how I am going to hike every inch of every mile. It was not that important to me back then, but it is now because it will help me heal my hiker conscience. I long to feel the completeness of the experience and all that goes with it. This is just an excuse to get back out on the trail for a couple of months, but it will also allow me to finish what I started.

Wednesday, September 11, 2013 – Feeling the Aches and Pains

Starting Location: Daleville → Destination: Lambert Meadows Shelter

Today's Miles: 9.50 – Trip Miles: 1,009.40

Ladies and gentlemen, kids of all ages, how's it going?

We are feeling the aches and pains of putting those heavy backpacks on again after a brief break from the trail. The first day back is always a little rough, but the second day seems to make everything alright.

We are headed for the iconic MacAfee Knob tomorrow and will try our best to get a good photo. We might luck out and have a few hikers ahead of us who won't mind taking our picture.

What else, what else…We are VERY excited about our finish date, November 9, at Springer Mountain. I hope you all will join us for some Whit's bar-b-q and a couple games of cornhole. Post on our guestbook if you would like more information.

We are getting closer and closer to the Tennessee border, y'all! You know I'm looking forward to that one. Won't be long now!

For dinner, we had chicken flavored fried rice, two packs of fruit snacks, a brownie in the shape of a flying bat, one tuna salad packet, and washed it all down with some of that awesome peach tea.

Puma successfully hung our bear bag this evening, and I've got Gloria Estefan songs stuck in my head. That's about it for today, folks. Won't you stay tuned for another journal entry, and we'll keep on hiking and doing the same thing tomorrow.

Turning in for the night.

Love,

Number 2

Will the person who picked out the flying bat brownies please come to the customer service desk to write your part of the journal entry:

An important lesson I experienced on the trail today is not to sit on my backpack because I burst my water reservoir. Felt the water trickling down my backside. We need to get to town so I can pick up a new one.

The soreness I felt in my hips, knees, and shoulder blades felt like an appropriate penance. My hip bones stuck out pretty good and were bruised from my hip belt on my bag. The weight of the freshly packed backpack made me involuntarily wince with every step for the first hour of the day. My body did get used to the pain, and it became tolerable after a few miles.

I'll tell ya though, it felt good. The pain reminded me that we were back on the righteous hiker path. I was earning my keep again with every step. All was forgiven...mostly.

It's not easy for me to open up about this guilt I have been dealing with for 11 years. Year after year, thinking about those missing miles, and not having the means to accomplish them. So much has changed in my life since then, but I think my window of opportunity is finally getting closer. I have all the gear and inspiration. I'm confident it will happen.

Thursday, September 12, 2013 – Water Rations

Starting Location: Lambert Meadows Shelter → Destination: Catawba Shelter

Today's Miles: 9.60 – Trip Miles: 1,019

Hey y'all! We had some long climbs today up to the Tinker Cliffs and then over to McAfee Knob. Lucky for us there was a group of Baby Boomers (that's what they called themselves) hiking and we crossed paths with them

at McAfee Knob. Perfect timing for our coveted picture! I mean, this is a spot no one wants to miss on the trail, and I'm so glad we got ours.

The water situation is a bit scarce. I mean it. All the springs have dried up, and we are having to forgo cooking dinner tonight because we have to save our water for tomorrow's hike. You better believe I'm gonna be a glutton for water when we reach the next town. Two glasses of water for me, sir!

Tomorrow we hike up to the Dragon's Tooth and take silly pictures with this particular monolith. Can't wait!

I hope everybody is doing well and welcoming the fall season through their windows at night. Tomorrow at 3 p.m. the temperature is only supposed to be 68 degrees, I love it!

Thanks for keeping up with us, and we will see y'all soon.

Love,

Number 2

"Full" on a pack of fruit snacks and a handful of Goldfish crackers (I can hear you getting skinnier), the almighty, Puma:

Happy to have the iconic McAfee Knob photo. Just one more spot left for the Christmas postcard.

I was so thirsty! The water sources were all dried up, and we reached the point of having to ration our water supply. You know how hard it is when someone tells you that you can't eat or drink anything before surgery, and then all of a sudden all you want to do is drink 64 ounces of water in one sitting? That's how it felt. I switched from thinking about food to thinking about water.

We made it through. I mean, we were fine, just thirsty, and we did manage to find some not so great water sources like stagnant muddy water with bugs. Good thing I had done a ton of research and found a good water filter system.

I also found that it was helpful to slowly dissolve one of those Swedish Fish gummy candies in my mouth. But when we had the green light for some water, I was so grateful. It's times like those that have stayed with me the most. The harder lessons seem to be the ones that stuck. Story of my life.

At this time, my relationship with the trail needed some extra tender lovin' care. It felt like I had come home from a night out with some friends and tried to be all sweet knowing I was in the doghouse. I felt the distance between me and my purpose – the trail. I got the picture at McAfee Knob, but I didn't know the trail in Virginia like I *know* other sections. It was that feeling I had when I cheated on my sixth grade math test about measurements; wrote the answers on my hand. I made the grade, but I didn't know the material. I still can't tell you how many ounces are in a quart without looking it up.

I'm not mad about the experiences I had or how they happened. I love this story, but I am so inspired to get back out there. That's the point of this whole thing, to get inspired to get out there and have the experiences. It's time to get inspired by nature and go have an adventure to write home about. There's so much I want to see.

Friday, September 13, 2013 – Beer and Bar-b-q Chips

Starting Location: Catawba Shelter → Destination: Pearisburg

Today's Miles: 9.70 – Trip Miles: 1,028.70

If you want some endurance training, come hike the Appalachian Trail in Virginia. Today was an awesome hike with perfect backpacking temperatures and a constant breeze that helped keep us cool. Good thing, too, because the only downside to today was there wasn't any WATER!

Puma and I finished yesterday with just a little bit of water, which means today we actually ran out of water. We did about seven miles dry, and by the sixth mile, my brain was coming up with elaborate images of drinking fountains, larger than life fountain drinks, coolers full of ice and cold cans...it was almost too much.

Then we finally came across a footbridge with a tiny trickle of water and dropped our packs and started filtering. I had to scare all the tiny crawfish and snakes away from my water bottle to get a clear shot at the "flow." We spent at least 20 minutes filtering enough water for both of our water bags and a couple Gatorade bottles. Just sat on our packs and ate snacks while we drank the bottles of water. It is no fun being thirsty like that, and we will definitely never take water for granted.

Got all packed up, turned the corner, and THERE was the most beautiful creek full of clear, cold flowing water. It was just a muddy trickle where we had stopped minutes before. Didn't bother me one bit, but I did wish I'd had my fishing pole. Dangit.

We ended the day with some Mexican food, some sweet tea, cheese dip, and a couple of movies. I am so excited for the Tennessee game against Oregon and the Alabama game against Texas A&M. Puma and I are dedicated to the SEC, and we are far enough south to catch the SEC games we want to see. It's time to relax. Life is so good!

Now, if you'll excuse me, I'm going to get another glass of water.

Love,

Number 2

Y'all ever heard of P-ESPN? It stands for Puma Enjoys Sports, Pickles, and Naps:

The only thing missing today was a little bit more water. At the end of our hike this afternoon, we got the pleasure of meeting "The Lift." They were

picking up our new friend Barry who we met out on the trail last night. The
Lift also shared a bunch of beer and bar-b-q chips. Now, I'm tired.

"The Lift" was a lovely couple who were friends of Barry's. I believe
they were dropping him off and picking him up from his section hike
along the A.T. They had a variety of beer inside the cooler in the back of
their SUV along with a bunch of big bags of bar-b-q chips. Why does all
the bad stuff taste so good? I'm no scientist, but my body said that beer
and those bar-b-q chips were everything I ever needed in life. Goes back
to exerting a good bit of energy and needing to replenish those calories
with high calorie goodness. It all tasted so amazing, and I was grateful for
such a delicious snack.

I loved meeting people out on the trail, and I miss being in that
position. Crossing paths with strangers who become friends and a part
of the story; I crave that again. I want to become a part of someone else's
story, too.

Saturday, September 14, 2013 — Football and the Pace of Freedom

Starting Location: Pearisburg → Destination: Pearisburg

Today's Miles: 0 – Trip Miles: 1,028.70

What a grueling day of football, y'all! We started watching College
Game Day on ESPN this morning, and I love reading the silly signs people
make for that show. There were some good ones this morning. Somebody's
always hating on the band Nickelback. Cracks me up!

We ventured out down the street to the Hardee's for a breakfast sand-
wich, and man, this place was hoppin'! The only other choice was Dairy
Queen, but I think they catch the lunch crowd. Everybody was adorned with
their beloved college colors; such a perfect day for football.

We swung by the grocery and grabbed a little six pack and some chips before heading back to our room for MORE football. I'm sure glad we took the time off today to enjoy the games.

We hit the trail again in the morning, and it's crazy how close we are getting to my home state of Tennessee. I can't believe it.

Thanks for reading about us watching football. Now, please pass the Funyuns!

Your pal,

Number 2

Puma has four different cups of four different drinks next to her (and I thought I was being excessive):

Hydration is very important during football games. I'm happy we took this zero. We got word from the Holy Smokes of 1990 that Buddy Bear did some bouldering over the weekend.

I remember walking back to the motel from our grocery run and thinking about how I could feel fall in the air. This really was the perfect day for watching football, and that's what we did. I was also thinking about how we were getting closer to home and weren't going to be able to live this freely for much longer.

Pearisburg was small and friendly; the kind of place where the high school football team is the talk of the town. The motel room had white painted cinder block walls, linoleum floors, and an old box television. The front desk lady was very sweet, but I wouldn't want to cross her. We were living in the moment of *every* moment out there, and come what may, we were ready. Just cruising through life. I miss that pace and the freedom more than I can put into words. What a gift to have taken the time to slow down and simplify to that degree.

Buddy Bear was a prize that we won at one of the restaurants we went to while hanging out with Bill and Melody, the Holy Smokes of

1990. Puma and I were very skilled at winning claw games full of stuffed animals. I would take the side view while Puma ran the control unit. I'd gauge the precise distance for the winning drop position, and Puma would hit that red button, and dammit if we didn't win these little stuffed animals all the time. So, that's how we acquired Buddy Bear, and we gave him to the Holy Smokes as a parting gift. They, in turn, took him on a fun hike somewhere up north, staged his rock climbing pose, and sent us a picture; it was sweet.

I really liked traveling light and keeping things simple. We made it almost six months with just what was in our backpacks. Sure, we upgraded shoes along the way, and I acquired a fleece from Madison Hut in the White Mountains, a true godsend. But that was *it* by this point. I look around my house all the time and try to purge stuff, prolly get that from my mother. It's important to me that my things have purpose and function; I literally have three small knickknacks the size of my palm or smaller in my home: a cast iron turtle, a wooden pig, and a wooden frog, that's it. I follow the minimalist movement on social media; just another way I am trying to stay connected to this lifestyle. I still dress like I'm ready to hike at a moment's notice. I still eat trail foods for my lunches at work. Over 11 years later, and I miss it more than ever.

Sunday, September 15, 2013 – The Green Tunnel

Starting Location: Pearisburg → Destination: Doc's Knob Shelter

Today's Miles: 8.30 – Trip Miles: 1,037

The hike up and out of Pearisburg was a real good one – lots of switchbacks and there was a beautiful view at the top.

The rhododendron are HUGE on this part of the trail! They form a perfect tunnel for us to hike through, and it totally takes me back to my

*years of soccer when we'd all run through the tunnel of our peers at the end
of the game. A celebratory tunnel brings such joy to any situation, and I
think we should bring it to the workplace, America! It's simple, fast, and
fun for all ages.*

*After we set up camp this evening, I started thinking about our Hal-
loween costume ideas. I think my mom is gonna make us costumes, which
I am very excited about. I also started thinking about the holiday season
coming up and could have sworn there was a Christmas song with the
words "pumpkin pie" in it, but Puma kept saying there wasn't such a thing.
THERE IS, TOO! Everybody find "It's the Most Wonderful Time of the
Year" on your iPods and you'll hear Karen Carpenter sing about pumpkin
pie. Glad that's settled.*

*The trail is just awesome here in southern Virginia, and we had a great
day even though I made the mistake of singing "On the Rhododendron" to
the same tune of Willie Nelson's "On the Road Again." Now, I can't get it
out of my head.*

*Y'all are awesome, this trip is awesome, and we thank you for taking the
time to read our trail journal. Thanks for your support.*

Love,

Number 2

*Making a Carpenter's Christmas mixtape for everybody. You're wel-
come, from Puma:*

*I am still frustrated by switchbacks. They get on my nerves. Why should
it take four miles to gain a thousand feet of elevation? I get it, though. Saw
the New River on our hike today. We learned it is the oldest river in the
country. Cool.*

Some folks say hiking Virginia is like hiking through a "green tunnel"
because of the tree coverage. The green leaves and all the green vegetation
curl towards each other painting the picture of one long green tunnel.

Some hikers preferred to hike at night, and I certainly wouldn't consider that up in the New England sections. Virginia seems like it might be an okay choice for that, but I'm not doing it. There were people out there who were literally beating themselves to the brink with all the miles they were pushing each day. Not sure if it was necessary because of the allotted time off, shortages of funds, or personal achievement goals? I've clocked myself at a consistent three miles per hour, but I'm not really concerned with that measurement. For me, it's the joy of being immersed in nature, carrying everything I need, and the simplicity of letting my legs carry me from point A to point B while living daily life in the woods.

The fastest known time (FKT) in 2013 was 58 days, nine hours, 38 minutes. He likely passed us in the night while we were in our tent or in town somewhere. Way to go, Matt! I remember seeing his name on a piece of paper hanging up in the bar at The Doyle and thinking, "Damn, he's fast! Must have long legs."

Monday, September 16, 2013 – A Variety of Animal Poop

Starting Location: Doc's Knob Shelter → Destination: Campsite by a stream

Today's Miles: 11.60 – Trip Miles: 1,048.60

The water sources have determined our mileage so far in this stretch, but I'm good with it because we are STILL out here hiking the trail. Coming up on four months on this adventure, and I can almost see Tennessee.

Puma calculates miles for the days ahead pretty much every evening; she's been doing this every night for close to four months. Poor girl's not gonna know what to do with herself when she gets back home. Me, I'm just

chillin' and enjoying what time we have left out here. I definitely would not have come this far without Puma's guidance.

We hiked through dark tunnels of rhododendron again today and saw some horse poop on the trail. Haven't seen too much horse poop out here, but I don't mind it one bit. We've seen lots of moose poop, some bear poop, a little bit of coyote poop, a few dog turds, cow patties, and NOW horse poop. Thank you very much!

Dinner was awesome. We had beef stew, some Goldfish crackers, one of those flying bat brownies, and some fruit snacks. The weather is definitely getting cooler, which makes these hot dinners even more enjoyable.

I'm so happy and peaceful out here, and I just want to make the most of what time we have left. Looking forward to seeing more friends along the trail in Tennessee.

Y'all have a great evening, and we'll holler at ya tomorrow,

Love,

Number 2

Still on the lookout for porcupine poop (say that 10 times fast), that would be, Puma:

The other evening we met a section hiker, and he listened to us talk about our hike. Then he said, "Almost there!" It made me realize how close we are to being done. I grabbed the map and started crunching numbers again.

I was feeling the changing of the seasons from summer to fall, as well as feeling the emotional shift from starting this adventure to getting closer to the end. I had an ache in my heart thinking about this experience coming to an end, but I was also so excited to see family, friends, and my bicycle.

Change is inevitable, and it's good for me. It keeps my interests, which helps me pay attention to my surroundings and learn a thing or two. By this point, I had started looking at the trail from a mountain biking perspective, and it was fun to think about. I was thinking about it a lot. Fast forward a little bit, and I ended up going to bicycle mechanic school in Ashland, Oregon, in February the following year. I figured if I could make it through the A.T., then I could make it through anything.

Tuesday, September 17, 2013 – Hunger Drives the Agenda

Starting Location: Campsite by a stream → Destination: Bland

Today's Miles: 7.50 – Trip Miles: 1,056.10

I think we are gonna have cold mornings from here on out, which makes the early climbs a lot easier. My metabolism is kind of crazy right now because of all the hills. We were debating stopping by this place called Trent's Grocery, and when I heard it had a hot order kitchen, there was no more debate about it.

For lunch, I had a crispy chicken sandwich with lettuce and tomato and mayo, a slice of pizza, four potato wedges, most of Puma's French fries, one of those Zebra Cakes, six little chocolate doughnuts, and a bag of Funyuns. Washed it all down with some orange Gatorade and a large Dr. Pepper.

I could have stayed in Trent's Grocery all day long. Not to mention, I could have done all my Christmas shopping in there too. I love little places like that; everything under one roof, from new hardwood flooring to the perfect fishing tackle and some groceries.

Well, I hate to tell y'all this, but I'm getting' hungry again.

Stay tuned for tomorrow's menu!

Love,

Number 2

Dragging me out of Trent's Grocery, that would be, Puma:

The hiker hunger is in charge at this point. We plan our stops around food.

There was some kind of primal shift when the hunger hit me. I had little to no self-control in those convenient convenience stores. All the high calorie foods right at my fingertips; Little Debbie was my bitch. I could slam three boxes of her oatmeal cream pies, wash it all down with a 20 ounce Dr. Pepper, and not five minutes later be hungry again.

I wish I could still eat like that, but I cannot. What I really need is a reason to eat like that again. Burning more calories than I could consume was fun but something I needed to watch after coming home. Everything was processed. Hardly any fresh fruits or vegetables were consumed for almost six months.

I remember being back home and having to shift my brain from trail food supply to normal life food supply. I load up my grocery basket with fruits and veggies, but I still reach for the tuna packet and trail mix for my lunches. Today, when I eat my trail mix at work, there's this little voice inside me whispering, "It's time to go on another adventure."

Wednesday, September 18, 2013 – Kenny Chesney Says Hello

Starting Location: Bland → Destination: Jenkins Shelter

Today's Miles: 13.20 – Trip Miles: 1,069.30

By now y'all might have heard that my sister, Number 3, bumped into Kenny Chesney in downtown Nashville the other day, and she told him, "My sister is hiking the Appalachian Trail, and your music is all she has on her iPod."

I could not believe my ears when she told me this story. I guess that's one of the perks of living in Nashville, Tennessee; I would like to thank my sister for telling Kenny Chesney about my iPod playlist. This is a true story! Can't wait to rehash it all over again when I get home. (Mermz, I swear to tell Grace Potter that you love her style if I ever run into her, but we're a good ways past Vermont.)

Y'all! Re-supplied at the Kangaroo Express/Dairy Queen, and again, I am so good at re-supplying at gas stations (prolly could have done my Christmas shopping in there, too).

We had an awesome hike through the hills with some great weather today. The trail is SUPER nice down here, and I'm looking forward to Grayson Highland Park. Wild ponies, y'all. Should be some good video footage. And Mount Rogers. These will be coming up soon.

Please check in with us again tomorrow for more captivating entries from,

Number 2

Puuuuuuuuma! Your friends are all on the phone for you:

I swear we only turned to the left today. I thought for sure we were going to land back at the beginning. Thankfully, we did eventually turn right and made it to our destination. Everything is running together.

Even Kenny Chesney has a role in my story. This is what happened, my sister goes downtown with one of her friends, and they wind up at The Stage, a bar on lower Broadway, which is the heart of downtown Nashville. She was standing outside the restrooms waiting for her friend to come out, and when he does, he walks up to my sister and says, "That's Kenny Chesney."

When she turns to look for him, she really only sees who she believes to be "a big bodyguard," but then Kenny walks up to *her!* She says that while her brain was registering Kenny Chesney approaching her, she is also noticing that he has the sweetest smile and is really short. She shakes his hand, and tells him about me hiking the Appalachian Trail and how his music is all that's on my iPod.

When I called her to have her tell me every single detail, she admitted that it was really loud in there and there were lots of flashing lights and some liquid courage going on so he may not have heard her tell him about me being on the A.T. They had a sweet exchange and that was that. I still take full ownership of this experience considering I am only once removed. I'm so close, I can almost smell the restroom.

Thursday, September 19, 2013 – That's Really All I Need

Starting Location: Jenkins Shelter → Destination: Chestnut Knob Shelter

Today's Miles: 10 – Trip Miles: 1,079.30

The rain started coming down as soon as I woke up this morning. Heavy fog and rain pretty much all day today with zero views and lots of long climbs. It was great!

We stopped at the McChesney, I mean McChestnut, I mean Chestnut Knob Shelter, which is a stone shelter with four walls and a door! Puma already vetoed us staying in the shelter because of the possibility of spiiiiders. I didn't say a word.

We found a nice little spot to pitch our tent under some trees and warmed up with some snacks while it continued to rain on us. I snacked on Raisinets, and Puma had some "puppy chow" (Chex Mix with peanut butter and powdered sugar). Thought of some great pranks to play on my family at Thanksgiving with the Raisinets. Wink, wink! Like I'd eat deer poop out here; I ain't that hungry yet. YET!

Oh mercy, I'm just having fun, and we are working on our Tennessee border dance party video. Y'all don't want to miss that nonsense, that's for sure.

Okay, America!

Thanks for reading, and don't change that dial! We hit the four month mark out here as of today.

Love,

Number 2

"It burns and it itches, when it gets in your britches. When it gets in your britches, it burns and it itches." (A little ditty my Pappy taught me a loooong time ago.) And now back to you, Puma:

It rained today, and it's been a while since that happened. Tonight our camping spot is the highest elevation between Mount Moosilauke and Mount Rogers. Maybe we can catch a clear view in the morning.

I still randomly sing that little ditty to myself. Don't know why, but I do. I always imagined the subject of that song to be fire ants. Only once in my life have I had the unpleasant experience of being bitten by fire ants. It was in college, and me and my friend were smoking cigars and drinking chocolate milk at the outdoor amphitheater on campus. I started having this itchy stingy feeling on my lower back and then my butt, and the second verse goes on to say, "It'll make you jump and shout, 'til you finally shake it out." True story. There were no fire ants to speak of at Chesnut Knob Shelter.

Chesnut Knob Shelter would be a perfect tiny home. It's built of stone with a tin roof and exposed wooden beams. Actually, any of the shelters, with a little tender loving care, would be perfect tiny homes. Secluded enough to get some good writing sessions in, but close enough to your neighbors for a full moon pickin' party. That's really all I need, a tiny home with a fireplace.

Sunday, September 22, 2013 – You're All Invited to Brunch

Starting Location: Chestnut Knob Shelter → Destination: Marion

Today's Miles: 11.30 – Trip Miles: 1,090.60

Hey y'all! We had a good hike on Friday. Stopped for some water at Lick Creek, which was a good size creek, prolly about four or five feet deep in the middle. That's where we met Jud and Ollie. Jud was a nice guy, and Ollie was his super sweet big yellow Lab.

Puma was filling up the water bag for us to filter, and guess who did a belly flop into the water? It was Jud! No, it was Ollie! He was in heaven and walked around biting the water taking in huge gulps, loving life. Such a sweet baby.

We got into Marion, walked to the Walmart for more re-supply, and watched some football. I've been eating beer and drinking chips all afternoon.

Puma has planned out our next stretch on the trail and we're comin up on the wild ponies in Grayson Highland Park. I'll prolly end up takin' one home with me. It's whatevs. Y'all know I'm just having fun, and we're Tennessee bound.

Thanks for keeping up with us all this way. I think I'm gonna invite all of you to my townhouse for a nice brunch when we get back.

Truly Yours,

Number 2

Counting down the states we have left on one hand, please give a warm welcome to Puma's secretary:

The remaining miles are all planned out. I'm pumped that my brother is going to join us through the Smokies. We'll see another friend in

Knoxville. Number 3 is planning on making another appearance. And our dear friend, Jess Leigh, is going to be with us on the last part of our journey.

For those who have this book as their first experience with this story, I made a big deal out of this planned brunch for all of us to attend at my townhouse in Nashville, Tennessee. The idea kind of took off in the guestbook entries, and it brought me so much joy and entertainment. I think that was one of the best gifts of my life, keeping up with all the daily journal entries and the responses in the guestbook. We had people from all over the country reading this online trail journal, from New Brunswick, Canada, to Kodiak, Alaska, and everywhere in between. That's a pretty far reach! One of my favorite entries is from a reader in Virginia who says he's excited about the brunch at my townhouse, but regrets that he'll only be able to stay for nine days.

Monday, September 23, 2013 – Entitled Wild Ponies

Starting Location: Fox Gap → Destination: Thomas Knob

Today's Miles: 13.40 – Trip Miles: 1,104

Started my day off with a chicken biscuit from McDonald's and it was soooo good. We didn't know what to expect from today's hike, but I have to tell y'all that it was possibly the best hiking we've had on the trail thus far.

This Grayson Highland Park is just spectacular. We had the most beautiful weather from morning until evening, and Puma snapped the most pictures in one day since we started this thing. We witnessed a bonafide longhorn cattle fight right in front of us and then had to hike within four feet of both of them – gotta' follow the white blaze! There's video of said fight and it's intense!

Puma started to lose hope that we weren't gonna see any wild ponies... BUT WE DID. I got an exclusive interview with one of the ponies.

Mount Rogers is just beautiful and with this clear weather, I'm pretty sure I could see all the way to Springer Mountain or Atlanta, Georgia. Just row after row of mountains in the distance, and the sunset was really awesome. Our campsite is grassy and everything smells like our campfire...not too bad for a Monday.

Today goes down in the books as one of THE best days on the trail. I hope we encourage more folks to GET OUT HERE to check this stuff out. It's worth the trip.

Oh, and last night I dreamt I was hiking up this long climb picking up sledgehammers along the way. What am I gonna do with 12 sledgehammers? Christmas presents!

Thanks for reading y'all.

Love,

Number 2

Puma dreamt we were walking over a bridge made of pork chops:

I had the best time hiking today. I'm so proud of us for all the preparation and planning we did to make it a reality. What a fantastic day.

A word about wild ponies, if you haven't ever hiked with wild ponies before, I think you're missing out. But a word of caution – these ponies are smart. They know how to work the zippers on your jackets and backpacks, they know how to open Ziplock bags; they are friendly, but I would recommend being assertive around them. They want your food. Even if you don't have it out, they want your food. Too many snacks have given them this entitlement, and it only makes it worse if we all give in to them.

They are short in stature, and most of them have "emo" haircuts, which I found hilarious. Like the park rangers always say, do not approach any wild animals; however, these dudes will approach you, so be on the ready. It's like walking past the perfume kiosk in the mall, just keep it movin'.

This was the most perfect hiking day yet thanks to the weather and scenery. Grayson Highlands is a gorgeous hiking area. The Highlands have big beautiful rock outcroppings and grassy balds offering views that go on for miles. The wild ponies were fun to experience, and I was cracking myself up singing Green Day songs inspired by their "emo" bangs. We cranked through a good number of miles (by our standards), and still had energy when we finished.

I love a good dream interpretation. I believe my dream of carrying 12 sledgehammers may have signified my desire to slow down and possibly live full-time on the A.T. Or I was feeling the heavy weight of responsibility related to rejoining society and the workforce lurking in my future.

Puma's dream about walking over a bridge made of pork chops could have been a fabrication of mine in order to keep with the tradition of my ridiculous intros to her two cents. Or if she really did have that dream, it could signify she was thinking about the upcoming transition back into society and was feeling salty about it.

Tuesday, September 24, 2013 – Damascus, Virginia

Starting Location: Thomas Knob → Destination: Damascus

Today's Miles: 10.60 – Trip Miles: 1,114.60

Again, what a great day of hiking! Y'all have got to come to Damascus to ride bikes or hike some trails because it is just gorgeous this time of year. I hear the fly fishing is really good, too. But you didn't hear that from me.

We got into Damascus this afternoon with a little help from Gypsy Gene, and he gave us a tour of the town. This town has more character than you can shake a stick at, and it's easy to see why some people visit and never leave.

We were hoping to stop in at a restaurant called L-Boe's in honor of my friend Baby Lewis because he dislocated his elbow at a church league softball game recently, but the restaurant had gone out of business.

So, we checked out this place called Blue Blaze Cafe, and I had the most amazing slice of pumpkin cake. I love pumpkin flavored stuff. We sat in there for a long time listening to their awesome selection of 90s jams. Some of those songs just stick with ya forever.

I wish you a wonderful evening, America!

Singing along,

Number 2

Hey Puma, does it "Smell Like Teen Spirit" in here to you?

I'm still basking in the fun of our hike from yesterday. Today was just as awesome. The current obstacle is to stay on our feet because all the leaves have us slipping and sliding all over the place. Number 2 fell once already. I believe that brings her total to two falls on this whole trip.

I remember my second fall. We were cruising along, and Puma's right, the ground was absolutely covered in orange, brown, yellow, and red leaves. It was like a never-ending blanket of pumpkin spice and everything nice until I slipped on a root which then had me spinning, midair, in the fetal position. It was the softest landing I could have imagined, and we laughed so hard about that because it was accidentally awesome.

I felt like I had just completed some crazy cool kung fu move like a character from the 1987 Street Fighter arcade game. You know? Like, when you stick the landing and are just as surprised as all the people watching? It was like that, but in front of Puma and the usual wildlife.

Damascus was great. A tiny little town with a huge amount of character, lovingly referred to as "Trail Town, USA." This is where they host the annual Appalachian Trail Days Festival every May. I have yet to attend this soiree, but y'all better believe that I will be there soon. The Blue Blaze Cafe was entertaining. The local outfitter was excellent, similar vibe to that of my beloved Cumberland Transit in Nashville. I bought some Mountain Hardwear long johns, and I still have them to this day.

The food options in town were pretty limited back in 2013; there was a brewery, a little coffee shop called Mojoe's Trailside Coffee, and the Blue Blaze Cafe. I loved the name of the cafe; it was basically a small diner. The food was good, but the pumpkin pie with whipped cream was delicious. I also seem to recall the owner of the Blue Blaze Cafe and his lady friend standing at the tall counter. She was obviously under his spell, and they were having some sort of lovers' quarrel. All my senses were glued to that situation as I stared off to the slight right of their general direction pretending to be a million miles away, but I was right there with them. It was like one of those grocery store romance novel covers coming to life. His white half buttoned shirt made his dark skin tone shine like warm caramel drizzle. His long black hair was thick and healthy, just like a horse. She was tall and thin and cut just right for her high wasted jeans. Her fair skinned hand draped on top of his rough man hand looked like the piece of pumpkin pie on my plate.

On the edge of town is a lovely park, which I'm sure fills up with tents and vendors during the Appalachian Trail Days Festival. I really want to go to that next year. There's also a red caboose parked out in the yard, but we couldn't go inside because it was closed.

The hostel in Damascus, Hiker's Inn, was wonderful. A quaint little mother-in-law's quarters behind this white bungalow on the cutest street you ever saw. The bunks were comfy and it felt calm, quiet, and clean while we were there. We walked everywhere, and I remember thinking that I could definitely see myself coming back to this town to settle down, work at one of the bicycle shops, and enjoy daily chats with the locals over a cup of coffee at Mojoe's Trailside Coffee. What a life.

Wednesday, September 25, 2013 – A Zenful State

Starting Location: Damascus → Destination: Hikers Inn

Today's Miles: 0 – Trip Miles: 1,114.60

Spent today walking around Damascus and letting the rain pass on through. This town has made me miss my bicycle something awful. Y'all gotta' check out the Creeper Trail; it's a bike trail that goes from the Virginia/North Carolina line down to the town of Abingdon, Virginia. I think it's something like 34 miles, and it's definitely on our to-do list.

I got a pumpkin spice latte this morning after my first cup of coffee, which was kind of a mistake because I had the coffee jitters until late this afternoon.

We met some great people who were also just passing through this wonderful town and spent some time with them solving all the world's problems. The Blue Blaze Cafe served us well for dinner. I strongly recommend the shrimp po' boy, French fries, their homemade ranch dressing, and the sexiest slice of pumpkin pie you've ever had in your life.

Hitting the trail in the morning and crossing that glorious Tennessee state line! Can y'all believe it?

Love,

Number 2

Here to hum "Rocky Top" for you now, please welcome, Puma (she's been humming her whole life):

I can see why people come here and make it their forever home. We cross over into Tennessee in the morning.

There were a handful of bicycle rental places, which makes sense because so many biking and hiking trails intersect in this little town. The Virginia Creeper Trail is an old railroad track turned into a gravel biking trail of about 34 miles. It's part of the lovely Rails-to-Trails Conservancy project and is open to runners, bikers, hikers, etc.

There was this tall fellow on his bicycle who looked like a thru hiker, same kind of easy-going eyes and grime. His name was Jasper Keeper, and he was the defender of the Creeper Trail. This guy was picking up trash all along the trail every day. What a great service he provided.. After some research on the internet, I found out that by the time we'd met Jasper, he'd been living on the Creeper Trail for years already. I hope he's still out there protecting the trail. I'm also deciding here and now that I, too, will sell all of my possessions and travel around on the Rails-to-Trails system picking up trash with my dog in tow. I *would* keep a tidy trail.

I wish I could have left a comment card for the whole town of Damascus, Virginia. The hiking, the biking, the coffee, the people (especially Jasper), the hostels, Mt. Rogers Outfitter, the restaurants, and the red caboose are just a few reasons to visit Damascus. But you've been warned, this place will make you want to stay. Be sure to bring your flyrod and hammock when you visit, and you'll be all set to be whisked away to a zenful state of inner peace surrounded by nature.

The Hiker's Inn has closed, but it was a cozy little spot. A small home that was perfect for a hiker hostel in the perfect hiker town. There's several hostels listed in Damascus now. I love the feeling of a small town, especially one that is central to so many outdoor activities. Damascus gets my vote as one of the best small towns in America...that I've seen. Who knows, maybe I'll wind up there someday.

Chapter Fourteen

Tennessee (and North Carolina)

Thursday, September 26, 2013 – A Sophisticated Lady

Starting Location: Hiker Inn → Destination: Abingdon Shelter

Today's Miles: 11.10 – Trip Miles: 1,125.70

Grabbed a cup of coffee and a sausage biscuit on the way out of Damascus, and said so long to our new friends at the Hikers Inn. Such a great place, and we vowed to come back for some bike riding and fishing adventures. Can't wait.

The hike out of Damascus is a steady climb for what seemed like most of the day. It levels out towards the end for some real nice ridge walking.

Guess where we are, America? That's right! The great state of Tennessee. Yep, my personal favorite and wouldn't you know about four miles into Tennessee we see a big momma bear slide down a 30 foot tree like a fireman coming down the firepole about 10 yards in front of us. And after one verse of "She'll Be Comin' Round the Mountain When She Comes," we see two bear cubs slide down a 20 foot tree that was opposite the momma's tree. They were very fuzzy and cute, but we kept our distance and continued an even more exciting second verse of our song. It was crazy to hear their claws scraping down the tree bark.

We're in for the night, and I just can't believe we are already in Tenne ssee...with lots of stories to tell. I love it. I hope y'all will finish this thing out with us and keep on posting on our journal. I can't wait to read it all over again when we are finished. Thinking about what a great trip it's been and how there's still more to go.

Thanks y'all!

Love,

Number 2

Glad we hung our bear bag up in a TREE, that would be, Puma:

We crossed the 12th state line this morning. I'm impressed. Can't believe there's only a couple more to go. I'm really excited to see my family soon.

I remember the climb up and out of Damascus. Being on top of the ridge and seeing the wooden sign for the Tennessee/Virginia border was surreal. It had been a long time since I'd seen something familiar, which was a bizarre feeling because I had gotten used to having no idea where I was or what was coming up next. I did not stare at the map like Puma had been doing for the previous four months; I just kept on walking and let it happen, come what may.

I had my Tennessee Vols hat on by this point to showcase to my fellow Tennesseans that I was a proud card-carrying member. We started seeing Tennessee Vols flags well up into Virginia, and I felt inspired.

Let's talk about these bears. It had been a good while since we'd seen a bear, I mean I feel like we saw at least one in Virginia, but we should have seen more. Anyway, there we were hiking along, and Ms. Momma Bear stopped us in our tracks. She was a sophisticated lady with long nails, not to be underestimated. I will never forget the sound of her nails scraping the tree bark all the way down. That was a very special "nature moment" that made all my senses come alive. I don't think my eyes could have gotten any wider.

Then to see and hear her fuzzy little cubs come sliding down the opposite tree put us in super caution mode. They were cute, but we were more focused on the fact that we had come into her territory. We always hear about being not getting caught between a momma bear and her cubs, and we were *close* and in *that* situation. We started backing up slowly while cautiously singing. I think I was repeatedly bowing my head to add another element of peaceful and respectful communication. Thank goodness it worked. Namaste.

Friday, September 27, 2013 – Protein Pockets and Tales of Fishhooks

Starting Location: Abingdon Gap Shelter → Destination: Elizabethton
   Today's Miles: 11.30 – Trip Miles: 1,137

Another great ridge walk today, folks. I still can't believe we are in Tennessee. I did a double-take on a Tennessee license plate just because I hadn't seen one in so long.

We got some amazing views hiking through farmland and pastures – got real close to some more cattle, too. At one point the entire herd was blocking the trail, but they don't make a fuss if you talk to them like they're adults. They were very nice (and very fragrant, but it didn't bother us one bit).

I had a hunger attack on the trail today. It came outta nowhere and pretty much stopped me in my tracks. I told Puma, "I gotta' eat something!" So, I dropped my pack, dug out my food bag and created what I call a "Protein Pocket."

It's a packet of tuna, a bunch of jalapeno Cheetos, and a couple of Slim Jims wrapped up in a tortilla. Eat about three of those then wash it down with a Nutty Buddy (with extra peanut butter), some more jalapeno Cheetos, two more Slim Jims, and a pack of Sour Patch Kids – and a few sips of warm water. If I ever get a menu board, it'll be the Number 2 Combo.

We got a hitch into town from a father and his two sons who we met out on the trail this afternoon. I spotted a Lone Star Steakhouse on the ride. I am really, really full right now, but it was soooo good.

Life is great (and after I digest some of this food, it'll be really great).

Love,

Number 2

Hoping for more funny ESPN John Clayton commercials, her majesty, Puma:

Watching Number 2 eat like that was scary. The cattle were our biggest obstacle on the trail today. Just happened to be the area with all the shade. It was fine.

I give you, the Protein Pocket. Yes, my friends, the number one protein product of our lives has arrived. Let's just jump to the recipe, shall we! Ingredients list: one flour tortilla, a packet of tuna salad, some jalapeno Cheetos, and two Slim Jims. It's got everything you need to satisfy the sneakiest of hunger attacks. You got your salty, you got your sweet, you got your creamy, you got your crunchy, you got your spicy, you got your chewy, and you got your calories. You thought the Gold Bar was great; try the Protein Pocket today! Available in all stores and gas stations (you just have to buy the ingredients separately and then put them all together). If somebody turns this into a legitimate product, I'm gonna scream. When that hunger attack hit, I scarfed three of these bad boys in what felt like less than a minute. Even Puma was alarmed. I'm kind of in the mood for one right now!

Another story that never made its way to the online journal. There's not one mention or even a hint at what had happened to us our first night in Tennessee. It was the night of September 26; we had the lovely ridge walk into Tennessee, gave Ms. Momma Bear and her cubs a respectable distance, and successfully hung our bear bag in a tree. All was well until it wasn't.

On the previous night outside the Abingdon Shelter, we put our tent up maybe 30 yards from the shelter because we felt more comfortable in our own space. No other hikers were there that evening, but we still like to set up down the way, you know, to avoid sharing our space.

We were all tucked in for the night and had been asleep for a few hours when we awoke to the sound of shattered glass. Our eyes shot wide open, and we laid very still listening to every detail, which seemed to paint a dangerous picture.

I never saw what happened, but I know what I heard. It was the middle of the night, and I heard at least two men slurring their words down by the shelter. I believe they were drunk and heard them throwing and smashing their empty bottles. I remember hoping they would keep their distance and not see our tent, but no such luck. They smashed one more glass bottle, then one hopped on a four-wheeler and the other on his dirt bike. I could tell by the engine pitches. They drove all the way up to our tent and shined their headlights directly on us. I could feel the rumble of the tires on the ground next to my face. We never moved. We never made a sound.

They circled our tent a couple of times and spoke to each other, but I couldn't make out what they were saying. I don't like thinking about all the what-ifs. Thankfully they buzzed on out of our vicinity, and no one was physically hurt, but my feelings were hurt. I felt betrayed by my own people, my own state that I had been so proud of the whole trip, and it was a struggle for me to let it go. The "boys will be boys" excuse only infuriated me, but I worked hard to move on from it because I was not going to let fear rob me of my love for the trail.

We talked about all of it the next morning and remembered how in our research prior to starting the trail this was the exact location that alumni hikers had warned us about. Tales of fishhooks hanging from the trees, invisible tripwires, ghosts, fights, harassment, etc. Wouldn't you know that's exactly where we set up our tent (eye roll). In a way, though, it kind of woke us up – jarred us to remember that we needed to be smart and not get lazy.

Saturday, September 28, 2013 – Let's Do Something

Starting Location: Elizabethton → Destination: Elizabethton

Today's Miles: 0 – Trip Miles: 1,137

Did y'all watch any of those games yesterday? We sure did, and I'm real happy we got to do that.

In addition to watching football, we did our re-supply at the local Big Lots, and I have to say that I just love seasonal decorations. I saw a hundred cute Thanksgiving and Fall decorations that I would love to put up around my future camper and/or campsite. I love the sparkly spray-painted pumpkins that have one word printed on the front, like "Harvest." I'd make my own plastic glittery orange pumpkin and put the word "Tired" on it. That'd be hilarious on someone's front porch. I appreciate the honesty. It's relatable.

I ordered a large pepperoni pizza and watched more football for the rest of the evening. Puma planned out our next blip, and I am thrilled to be

*in these beautiful mountains and hills of Tennessee and upcoming North
Carolina. This is some beautiful country!*

Y'all are doing great, stay with us all the way!

Love,

Number 2

Puma's pumpkin would have the word "Focused" on it:

*I needed this time off to nurse my left foot, and watching football makes
the time off enjoyable. Next up, Roan Mountain.*

We were still a little spooked from the night before. Not wanting
to have a repeat, we put a little distance between us and "the visitors."
Decided to move ahead a little ways for safety purposes. I've seen this
kind of harassment before, and it's disappointing when it gets in the way
of a goal.

One of the worst times, I was manning one of the bicycle mechanic
stations for a charity bicycle ride called the Jack and Back, where people
ride 75 miles one way from Franklin to the Jack Daniel's Distillery in
Lynchburg, Tennessee. Someone thought it'd be fun to scatter a bunch
of tacks on the road causing a great number of flat tires. Come on, now!

However, we cannot live in a bubble of protection because it will
deprive us of our personal growth. Let's do something! It's time to go out
there and do the things that we've been putting off for whatever reason.

I feel extremely fortunate to have had my A.T. experience. Period. I
prepared and all the windows and doors opened for me to make it a reality. I do not take it for granted. I am forever changed by this experience
of freedom, and like I've already said, I'm desperate to have it again. I
know a guy who's hiked the A.T. not once, but twice.

We never quite knew what was in store for the day out there, and it
took some adjustment to be okay with that shift of mindset. Keeping
things positive is one of my defense mechanisms.

Sunday, September 29, 2013 – Don't Get Mad, Just Bear Bag

Starting Location: Elizabethton → Destination: Campsite in the woods

Today's Miles: 12.90 – Trip Miles: 1,149.90

Oooo, what a good climb out of Elizabethton it was today, and we saw a gorgeous waterfall to boot.

The trail is awesome down here with twists and turns and rocks (but not too many rocks), and I just love it. More ridge walking today, too, which might be my personal favorite because of all the views.

We saw lots of weekend warriors out on the trail, and I remember saving up all my time at work for a long weekend so that I could go backpacking until Monday morning arrived. I'll be honest with y'all and say that I have thought of a couple of things that I would like to do after the trail, but my focus is still on the trail right now.

Puma and I spent about 30 minutes trying to hang our bear bags in this particular tree. It was a tall tree. Puma started to get frustrated, and I said, "Don't get mad, we either do this or we go to sleep...that's all we have to do out here." The very next throw was hugely successful, and all was right with the world again. I bet I'll have the urge to hang my food even when I get home.

Looking forward to tomorrow's hike. Now, I gotta' go ice my pitching arm.

Love,

Number 2

Puma has generously donated her top-of-the-line bear bag kit as a give-away for anyone in the audience tonight. Plus one of those instrumental meditative flute cds:

Laurel Falls had a ton of steps today. I was very impressed with the trail maintenance in this area. We appreciate all the work and effort. Looks like a tough job.

Puma was always impressed with the trail maintenance. I remember even up in Maine, we'd cross paths with some trail Maine-tainers (get it?) with the bright orange chainsaw chaps on, covered in saw dust, bugs, and sweat, and they'd be as happy as could be. I bet Puma would like to have that job. I was impressed with their work, but I'm not much for heavy lifting. Getting a shovel down into the dirt takes everything I've got. These people who volunteer their time to work really hard on the trail maintenance are all aces in my book. It takes some creative engineering minds to build those steps, and I'm sure it's incredibly hard work. Thank you for all you do!

Monday, September 30, 2013 – Camping Along the Elk River

Starting Location: Campsite in the woods → Destination: Beside the Elk River

Today's Miles: 10.70 – Trip Miles: 1,160.60

Hello friends!

We got a considerably late start this morning and paid the price for it this afternoon. I don't seem quite as sore when we get an earlier start. Against her better judgement, Puma took a nap this afternoon when we stopped; now she's gonna be counting sheep and whatever else she can find in this tent for a long time. Poor thing.

The trail crossed a few steady streams and passed through a bunch of rhododendron tunnels. For some reason, I swear I can smell stewed tomatoes in those tunnels.

We're looking forward to our climb up to Roan Mountain and all the bumps along the way. It's gonna be a long climb, but we are actually really good at those.

I can't believe we are already in the home stretch of this trip. The other day we were visualizing all the state line crossings and discussing our favorite parts of each state thus far. A big THANK YOU to all the friends we've made on the trail and to all our loved ones back home. This is truly a trip of a lifetime.

We got a party waiting for us in just a few weeks! I'd bring a casserole but it's just not feasible from the trail. I'll see what I can do, though.

Protein Pockets for everyone!

Love y'all,

Number 2

Puma makes a mean homemade salsa, and pigs in a blanket, and grilled pork chops, and loaded mashed potatoes. ENOUGH! And white beans, and pickles, and:

I do not like a late start to the day. It makes the rest of the day drag on and on.

Camping along the Elk River was lovely. It was not a designated camping spot, but we made it our own. Made me feel a little bit like a homesteader. Hung the paracord as a clothesline, went and filtered some water, shook out the tent, boiled some water to use for dinner, and crafted a homemade broom for the pretend cabin. It's a simple life, but we love it.

Oh, and by this time, we had also heard the cry of some elk. I don't think we ever saw any, but we heard them. Such a high-pitched sound for such a stout animal. I reckon the grunt makes up for it. Can't tell y'all how many times I tried to mimic the elk call. I got the grunt down pretty good, though.

I remember hiking around Edgar Evans State Park, in Silver Point, Tennessee, with my mom one time, and it is very hilly over there. One one steep hillside we came across an educational plaque describing how the homesteaders would have to go get water for the family meal. My mom and I immediately started griping about Mr. Homesteader and why the hell he picked the side of a hill to live happily ever after. We crack each other up.

Tuesday, October 1, 2013 – Roan Mountain and Her Grassy Balds

Starting Location: Mountain Harbour Hostel → Destination: Overmountain Shelter

Today's Miles: 9 – Trip Miles: 1,169.60

When breakfast is as amazing as it is at Mountain Harbour Hostel, I have no problem waiting until 11 a.m. to start hiking for the day. This kitchen was fit for a Southern Living Magazine spread, and the menu was the freshest we've had on the trail. Plus the owner puts extra cheese in her eggs! Holy Moly Marie, it was so damn good, and we joked about staying until the end of the season.

After breakfast, we hit the trail and went up, up, and UP to Big Hump Mountain. Puma said it was about five miles uphill, and it released us to these spectacular grassy balds. I'm talkin' bout it was amazingly beautiful and prolly MY favorite hiking on the trail. I mean it this time.

I can't wait to get up another trip through Roan Mountain. Who's with me? We'll ALL go. Yet another awesome day tomorrow, so I gotta' hit the night night trail.

Love y'all,

Number 2

Puma, Pumer, Pumed:

We are camping at Overmountain Shelter. It looks out onto Yellow Gap. The shelter is crowded, but this place is big and there's plenty of room. Looking forward to the rest of the area in the morning.

Still one of my top three favorite hikes in Tennessee. I absolutely loved this section through Roan Mountain. I have been back multiple times since then, and it is never enough. If you want an excellent backpacking experience, head to the Mountain Harbour Hostel and hike south to Carver's Gap. You will not be disappointed.

We fell in love with Mountain Harbour Hostel. At the time we were there, they had a bunch of goats and horses on the property, which was fun. I'd never spent a bunch of time looking into the eyes of a goat, but I sure got my chance. So wise.

This place is a bed and breakfast and a hiker hostel. The thru hikers typically stay in the upstairs of the barn, which was a working barn when we were there. There was a loft with maybe four bunks and then a single bedroom with a curtain. Everything was cozy and quaint with amazing country quilts draping over the bedframes. We sprung for the bedroom, and I have to admit that I got a bit of a headache due to the scent of animal poop rising through the floorboards. Other than that, I have no complaints. It's probably not like that anymore.

The breakfast was *incredible*. She had this massive table that was covered from end to end with the most picture perfect, over-indulgent breakfast spread I have ever seen. It was absolutely beautiful and felt like a dream – like some kind of Alice in Wonderland meets the The Muppets Ghost of Christmas Past cornucopia. I wish we had taken a picture, but I think we were too far gone under the spell of her food.

Overmountain Shelter is one of my all-time favorite shelters on the A.T. It is a big red barn with a picnic table in a small clearing in the most beautiful valley about 8.7 miles from Mountain Harbour Hostel. At night, off in the distance we could see the porch light of a perfect cabin nestled amongst the trees. There's plenty of room in the barn for several hikers to get comfortable. I have been back there at least four times since 2013.

Coming up to the top of the biggest grassy bald called Big Hump Mountain, I timed it just right with a NOBO hiker, and we high fived without skipping a beat. It was pure magic.

Wednesday, October 2, 2013 – The Mom Meal

Start Location: Over Mountain Shelter → Destination: Clyde Smith Shelter

Today's Miles: 14.70 – Trip Miles: 1,184.30

Today's journal entry is dedicated to our moms.

I would like to give a shout out to my mom because she has hiked this part of the trail. Standing on top of Jane Bald, I dedicated a moment to YOU. Thanks for being so supportive and so excited for us in this adventure. You are my wilderness guru.

Today's hike was spectacular; even with the bathrooms at Carver's Gap being closed, I loved the trail. We will definitely be back for this section again sometime next year. Y'all keep your calendars clear for the invite.

For dinner, we had a chicken and rice meal that closely resembles the yumminess of Puma's mom's famous "Mom Meal."

We wouldn't be here without our moms. And that's the truth. Now everybody hug the person to your left.

Sincerely,

Number 2

Here now to tell y'all all about her mom's "Mom Meal," give it up for, Puma:

Yes, a basic rice and chicken combo. It's the best. Love you, Mom.

It's true, the "Mom Meal" was very delicious. Puma's mom has some kind of magic (like most moms do) that takes rice and chicken breast and turns it into the most delicious meal of your life. Maybe it's a bouillon cube, I don't know, but whatever she does, it works because I could eat 100 pounds of that stuff in one sitting. Our dehydrated meal was good enough, but it was definitely not to the standard of deliciousness that Puma's mom has perfected.

My mom loves to tell stories, and she loves to retell her adventures of hiking on and around the A.T. over the years. Jane Bald is one from her collection. My mom is real outdoorsy; she's all the time going camping, scoping out secret fly fishing spots, or booking guided fishing trips in eastern Kentucky. I want to be like her when I grow up. She also makes a real good potato salad.

Friday, October 4, 2013 – Uncle Johnny, Himself

Starting Location: Clyde Smith Shelter → Destination: Erwin

Today's Miles: 6 – Trip Miles: 1,190.30

It was exceptionally dark this morning when we woke up, so instead of carrying on with our usual morning rigamaroo, we waited for the sun to come up a little bit higher.

To pass the time, we decided to name as many famous Canadians as we could. I think we had about 12; Puma threw out Kevin Bacon as her final guess, but I said, "No, you're thinking of Canadian Bacon."

We hiked as far as Iron Gap and got a shuttle into Erwin because, well ...I ate all our food. It was all good though because we got to Uncle Johnny's and rent a couple bicycles to ride to the grocery and the Apple Festival. That's right! A big ol' festival with lots of food, music, country knickknacks, and Tennessee orange. I mentally bought just about a hundred cute little things from painted wooden signs to leather wallets to duck calls to feather earrings.

We had such a great time. The bike path followed the Nolichucky River, which was FULL of really big trout. This is another place that we vowed to come back to with our fishing poles in the near future.

What a day! Looking forward to tomorrow's adventure. Thanks for reading, y'all.

Love,

Number 2

Puma loves Canadian Bacon and feather earrings:

Now that we are in the bigger mountains again, I realize I'm going to have to plan better for our re-supply. We'll need more calories to get over these hills. Number 2 has to keep a steady food supply so she doesn't lose any more weight.

Let's talk about Uncle Johnny's Hostel. This place is under new management now, but when we arrived it was still under the command of Uncle Johnny himself. Let's say he was not in the best of health, and neither was his establishment, but he shared his chili dog with me. It means more when we share what we have with others. He also had a sign out front advertising 40 cent Snickers – that's a deal!

There was a big wooden deck with a picnic table out front and some dusty camping gear for sale inside. The backyard consisted of a few small cabins and a firepit with a centrally located restroom shed. I took a shower, but kept my guard up for spiders the whole time. We camped out in our trusty tent for the duration of our stay.

I was so excited to see that we could rent bicycles at Uncle Johnny's. I remember walking up and seeing the yellowish single speed bicycles with big blue seats all leaning up against each other in the front area. These things were borderline death traps. The chains were loose, and the bolts were soft. I remember pedaling very gingerly, following Puma on the road, obeying all traffic laws, and the slightest thing would throw my chain. When this happens on a single speed bicycle, it means there is no way to brake. In one instance I hollered out, "Bailing!" and luckily rolled into a large open grassy field. I reset the chain and tightened the bolt on the rear wheel as much as I could with my hand. My hand strength isn't what it used to be. Had to do this a few more times on that excursion to the grocery store and the Apple Festival.

At the festival a good number of vendors lined the street selling home-made goodies like cookies, breads, pies and canned goods. Apple-every-thing. My family begged me to stop in at the Hawg-N-Dawg, an adorable little diner that served hot dogs and bar-b-q. My parents still have a koozie from when they went there years ago. It smelled amazing, but the line was already up the street and around the corner.

I got a caramel apple and was having a ball perusing the tents and touching all the feather earrings. They had everything there: wooden rubber band pistols, apple aprons, Blue Ridge pottery, biblical signs for every kitchen, airbrush stuff, homemade leather wallets, impressive cast iron pieces, apple art, and lots of Tennessee Vols merchandise. I was trying to see if I could find the ultimate trifecta prize containing a biblical reference, an apple, and something about the Tennessee Vols, but to no avail.

It was fun, and I have to say that I have thoroughly enjoyed my experiences in Unicoi County, Tennessee. The terrain is rugged, the rivers are enticing, the music is authentic, the food is delicious, the people are nice, and the trees are haunting. I can *feel* the stories in the atmosphere over there. Speaking of stories, just up the road in Jonesborough, Tennessee, happening at the same time as the Apple Festival was the International Storytelling Festival. I definitely want to experience that.

I felt bad for Uncle Johnny; I could tell he was not feeling well. His face was swollen, he had a cast on his leg, and frankly looked like he needed to be taken care of. I never asked him about his health, but it was evident that he was not okay. His voice was real raspy and weak, but I sat and talked with him about our adventure thus far. I enjoyed the time I had with him very much, and I'm grateful I had the honor of hanging out with such an interesting man. He was a man of adventure. He told me stories that sounded like scenes from a movie. I read that Uncle Johnny passed away in 2018. Thanks for sharing your stories and your chili dog with me, sir.

Sunday, October 6, 2013 – We Found Megan

Starting Location: Erwin → Destination: Erwin

Today's Miles: 0 – Trip Miles: 1,190.30

Hey y'all! Guess who we ran into in Erwin? That's right, it's MEGAN! Can you believe it? My good friend Megan joined us for some much needed Mexican food, and we just had the best time. What a great friend!

Since then, I've been watching some more football, and Puma's been reading up on the Smokies being closed. I guess we'll figure out what to do when we get there. Maybe they'll be open by then.

I'm telling y'all, I can almost taste that bar-b-q at our grand finale party! Don't forget to bring your chairs, hiking shoes, and be prepared for the award ceremony. Yes, I have prepared a small presentation for the top of Springer Mountain.

I hope you'll stick around for more of our antics, thanks y'all.

Love,

Number 2

Puma has prepared an interpretive dance to accompany my small pre-sentation, so:

It was fun eating lunch with Megan. That's the best part of being down here in the South; we can see friends and family a lot easier. There was no way we were going to hike north. I bet it's getting cold up there by now.

Being closer to home, what an absolute treat it was to see and hang out with my dear friend Megan. She's one of my best friends from high school, and one of the funniest people I know. Megan was in and around the area and met us for a few hundred rounds of chips and salsa. I could have stayed and talked with her for four days.

At this time we were also following reports of a government shutdown impacting parts of the trail. On the one hand, it didn't change much; we were still out there the same as when we started, pooping in the woods just like all the other animals. On the other hand, the shutdown closed all of the available bathrooms in the parks, namely the Great Smoky Mountains National Park (Shaconage). When it's rainy and cold, a real bathroom break is a fabulous recharge. I'm not getting political here, but I bet neither side considered my bathroom breaks.

We kept looking to see if the Smokies were "open," and wouldn't you know it, just like Katahdin, the park ranger told us they were closed. A.T. hikers were allowed to continue on with the trail, but it was like "swim at your own risk" because management had locked all the doors and headed home.

Monday, October 7, 2013 – We Found Blue

Starting Location: Erwin → Destination: No Business Knob Shelter

Today's Miles: 6.20 – Trip Miles: 1,196.50

Well y'all, we got out of Erwin this afternoon, and once we reached the campsite there was this beautiful dog that looked just like Smokey, the Tennessee Vols mascot. He's gorgeous and sweet and a real hunting dog.

We waited about 20 minutes thinking his owner would come walking up the trail, but 20 minutes came and went. So, we checked his collar for a name and found one. Called the phone number on the tag, and the owner said the dog's name is Blue and, "He's a long way from home." Blue had a radio tracker collar on, but his nose had gotten him so far away that the owners couldn't get a signal on him.

Here's the happy ending: we are meeting his owner tomorrow morning just a few miles down the trail. Poor Blue gobbled up what beef jerky we had left, and we have him snug as a bug in a rug in our tent with us tonight.

We've been loving on him, and I've been singing to him. He just looks back with these heavy sweet, lovey eyes and pushes his head down in my hands. What a sweet baby.

Puma said we might turn this hunting machine into a big ball of mushy love bug. I have that effect on animals when I sing to them. Naturally, Blue's favorite song is Carl Perkin's "Blue Suede Shoes." I believe he also enjoys Kenny Chesney Christmas songs. I'll prolly end up putting together a list of his favorite songs to give to his owner tomorrow.

In other news, a couple of guys came into camp a little bit after us and they, too, had a dog that ended up following them. It's a German Shepherd named Zeus, and he and Blue weren't too sure about each other. Zeus also had a collar with his momma's information on it, and we gave her a call. She's in Knoxville. Long story short, Zeus will be safely returned to his owner in Erwin tomorrow. I tell y'all, make sure you put your name and number on your puppy's collar because we WILL call you if we find your baby. I'm thinking of my sweet Peejay tonight.

Thanks y'all,

Number 2

Puma's Dog Rescue has a nice ring to it:

It's nice to have Blue inside the tent tonight. Zeus is good with the other hikers by the shelter. I'm happy we get to help reunite everybody tomorrow.

Finding Blue in the woods I was like, "Well, hi!" He was one of the most impressive dogs I'd ever seen. The haunches on that dog were incredible, and his collar had some serious technology going on. I didn't realize that people use dogs to hunt for bears, and I can't really think about it too much because I don't like violence. Plus, I picture all wildlife living as Beatrix Potter portrayed them in her artwork. You know, like the momma bear is hollering at her cubs to come downstairs while she is serving up the piping hot stew around the table.

Pretty sure we only met two hikers who brought dogs with them on their thru hike. The first thru hiker dog was up in Connecticut at Bearded Woods Hostel. The human thru hiker had been at the hostel for four days waiting on his dog to heal from Lyme disease. The dog was a big beautiful Golden Retriever, and he was toast. I mean, this poor dog could barely move and looked extremely exhausted. I petted his forehead and let him rest.

Everyone encouraged the human hiker to get his dog off the trail and go back home. Not sure how all that ended, but it hurt my heart to see this dog suffering like that. The human hiker was also suffering in a different kind of way. I reckon he was torn between accomplishing his goal and caring for his pup, but his canine companion was not fit to stick with him. I like to think the human hiker made a decision that was best for the dog.

The second thru hiker dog we met was in a shelter somewhere in Vermont. It was a crowded shelter night, like 10 or more hikers. Everyone had settled into their sleeping bags and drifted off into a deep sleep. I don't know what time it was, but all of a sudden, the dog, German Shepherd-like, franticly barks like five times and then leaps off the front of the shelter to rustle with *something* in the night. It was darker than the darkest night, as usual, and my heart was racing. It sucks not being able to see what's going on, and my brain was piecing together the worst case scenario just from the sounds.

The human thru hiker woke up and hollered his dog, fumbled for his headlamp, and thankfully the dog minded his owner well. I cannot confirm if the scuffle was with a bear, a bobcat, or a squirrel but it ended rather quickly. I can confirm that my eyes were wide open for a couple hours after that, even though I couldn't see a damn thing.

I remember reading in one of the journals in the shelters that this same thru hiker made it through Virginia in less than a month. I wondered if he still had his dog with him. By my calculations, the total miles for Virginia back in 2013 were somewhere around 550 miles, so to finish in a month would mean a minimum of 18 miles a day or something like that. No doubt that young man made it, but I wonder about the dog.

The Appalachian Trail Conservancy recommends keeping your dog on a six foot leash at all times. They also request that folks bury their dog's poop since the dog is not a natural inhabitant of the woods, and lastly, they state that it is the owner's responsibility to maintain the dog's health and comfort for the duration of the hike. I've read some horror stories about thru hiking with dogs, but I've also felt the emotional support of a constant canine companion. One thing I do know, I could barely carry and eat enough food just for myself out there.

Tuesday, October 8, 2013 – Dogs on the A.T. Continued

Starting Location: No Business Knob Shelter → Destination: Big Bald Mountain

Today's Miles: 11.70 – Trip Miles: 1,208.20

I hate to tell y'all this but today kicked my butt. I'm not exactly sure why because it's not like we haven't hiked up steep hills before, but I was totally gassed a couple of times today. Oh well, I just keep on putting one foot in front of the other.

We got Blue safely delivered back to his owner this morning, and Blue was so excited to be going home. I am so happy that all worked out; the owner said Blue had been missing for a couple of days. Dang Blue.

Our reward was this beautiful 360-degree view at the top of Big Bald Mountain. We thought about hiking on, but this spot is just way too beautiful to pass up, so we're camping here tonight. Perfect sunset and sunrise views. I'm gonna remember this spot as one of the best campsites on the trail.

I'm tired and hungry and very happy. Talk to y'all tomorrow.

Love,

Number 2

Puma's made so many divots in the ground from spinning around getting her panoramic photos, people are gonna think there's moles up here:

We were sitting outside of our tent when Zeus' owner came walking up. He's meeting up with Zeus in the morning, and he thanked us a bunch. I felt good about that.

Blue was so far from home that his owner said he'd be able to meet up with us the following day. So, we kept him in the tent all night and tied some paracord around his collar the next day. Boy was that an adventure. With every little squirrel or chipmunk, Blue went berserk. Did I mention how strong this dude was? He took me down the bank a few times and was obviously way stronger than me. Puma took a turn with him along the trail and had the same experience, but we managed to hang on to him all the way to the meeting spot.

His owner was a nice young man of few words. Had a sweet ass first generation Tacoma with a really nice kennel box built into the truck bed. Blue knew exactly who it was when he saw the truck, and my feelings were a little bit hurt because I thought we had bonded. I moved on quickly, as I do. The guy thanked us, dropped the tailgate, Blue eagerly jumped in, and they drove off. That was it.

I had forgotten about meeting Zeus' owner on top of Big Bald Mountain. We settled into our camp for the afternoon and were chillin' out when this guy came by and asked if we were Number 2 and Puma. That happened to us a few times on the trail, and every time I was amazed. I thought for a second, "Oh, another faithful follower," but then I realized there was no one else around and this guy had coordinated with the other hikers for where to meet to pick up his dog.

He was so very appreciative of all of our efforts to get Zeus back where he belongs. Zeus was one of those breeds that looks very similar to a German Shepherd, and either way he was a good baby dog.

Saturday, October 12, 2013 – I Could *Not* Eat *Enough*

Starting Location: Big Bald Mountain → Destination: Hot Springs
Today's Miles: 0 – Trip Miles: 1,208.20

We finally got into the town of Hot Springs, North Carolina (or "Nort Carolina" as my brother would say), and found the greatest little diner known to man called the Smoky Mountain Diner. I've already had three orders of country ham and a bucket of black coffee.

The town of Hot Springs is packed with mountain charm and motorcycles. We walked up and down the main drag and went into every store meeting lots of nice people.

Don't be mad, but we skipped the natural hot springs. I can't help but feel like a lobster in those things. I really love the people in this town (ultimately the diner). They keep on "blessing" everything, and I feel right at home.

We're getting real close to the next big piece of this adventure, the Smokies. I sure hope they open up, like tomorrow. Y'all better be breakin' in your hiking shoes so you're ready to hike that last mile to the top of Springer Mountain with us! You got four Saturdays.

We're meeting up with family again in a couple days. Have I told y'all how happy I am to be down here?

Thanks for sendin' us your messages of encouragement. They mean the world to us.

Love,

Number 2

Looking forward to an upcoming Shoney's salad bar, that would be me AND Puma:

Only four more weeks. I bought another pair of shoes, and hoping there's no new blisters. I reached the point of being tired of hiking.

I was wrestling with hiker fatigue, too. I'm trying to be vulnerable here, which is a hard place for me to sit still because I like to be on the move. What bothers me about this point in the trail is that we got tired. I take responsibility for my actions, and looking back on this, I have to admit that I am disappointed in my lack of commitment to the trail.

How do I put it all into words? This was definitely the adventure of a lifetime; I got to see and do so much, and I had a lot of time in the woods, which is my ultimate happy place. I think the hard pill to swallow is that we had the time to cover all the miles and we didn't. This has been gnawing at me for years, and I'm ready to cross it off my to-do list. I want to at least hit the 2,000-Miler mark.

The Smoky Mountain Diner was delicious. I got a skillet scramble with eggs, sausage, mushrooms, bacon, hashbrowns, and cheese, with a few sides of country ham. I could *not* eat *enough* food. I think my body was burning calories non-stop, like I could eat an enormous meal and somehow my body would burn it all off before I left the establishment.

Thinking back about food storage on the trail, I didn't see anybody with a bear canister on the A.T. back in 2013. It seems to be the popular choice now. Seems a lot easier than slinging the bear bag rope, but also that gave us our evening entertainment. Thankfully, we didn't have any issues with bears coming after our food; hell, I was the nuisance. Puma was bear-bagging the food from me! Pretty sure I can't get into a bear canister either.

Back to post-trail life, I've stayed fairly active since the trail, nothing extreme, and I watch what I eat, but I also started smoking cigarettes, again. Quit (again) this year, but that's a whole other story. It's time to stop wasting time, y'all. So many plans have been inspired by this retelling of the A.T., and I needed to feel this inspiration again more than I can explain.

Sunday, October 13, 2013 – A Spark of Magic

Starting Location: Lemon Gap → Destination: Brown Gap
Today's Miles: 8.90 – Trip Miles: 1,217.10

Hello, America! I'm here to tell y'all about our adventure today. We got to have one more time breakfast at the Smoky Mountain Diner, and it was delicious. I had a "skillet," which is a pile of potato wedges topped with sausage, mushrooms, peppers, onions, cheese, and two fried eggs over easy. I also had one big pancake and two big mugs full of black coffee. Puma had a couple of bites of my skillet and two pancakes with two big cups of sweet tea. We were absolutely stuffed and ready to go.

A very nice gentleman named John gave us a hitch up to Lemon Gap so we could get a head start on meetin' up with my sister by tomorrow night. John drove a sweet ass Ford-150 with a camper top, and we had great time riding down the winding roads of North Carolina. I noticed all the fall colors and mountain streams and old barns as we passed by, and I also noticed Puma's face turn green from carsickness.

John thought Puma was resting her head in the back, but I knew she was holding on for dear life trying not to blow chunks all over the backseat of John's sweet, sweet F-150. We successfully got to our destination, and I swear I coulda' poured her out of that truck. She was taking deep breaths and coming around slowly.

We prolly hiked two miles and then she puked. All was right with the world again after that. I won't give y'all the details but I'm pretty sure I smelled that skillet for a second time. Enough of that!

Max Patch Bald was really beautiful, even with the heavy fog, and it made our list of places we'd like to revisit in the near future with friends.

I want to thank everyone for their support and encouragement on this adventure.

We're having the time of our lives out here. I hope you'll stay with us!

Thanks y'all,

Number 2

Puma does her best Louis Armstrong impression when she pukes. Take it away, Puma:

All I needed was some food, a small break, and a re-up on some hiking shoes. Puking doesn't stop me from having a good day.

I failed to mention that John took our picture by a tree when he dropped us off. Puma's face was all-telling of what was to come. Nothing like putting on a pretty face when you're green from carsickness and have to keep it together until company leaves. My mom still has the photo on her fridge.

Max Patch *was* awesome. I could spin all the way around and see mountains as far as the eye could see. This is a dedicated area for studying a diverse number of bird species, and we saw a group from Birdlife International catching little warblers to study their nests and feeding spots.

There were a good number of people hiking that day, and we even got asked if we were "Number 2 and Puma" by a few people who I guess were keeping up with our journal. We stopped and chit-chatted about the trail, all the preparation, and what was next. I loved talking with people, especially out on the trail. There's a spark of magic when we connect with people outside. I could see it happen in people's eyes. I love being in that moment with someone, and I will be your biggest cheerleader for any adventure.

I was never an actual cheerleader, just the mascot in eighth grade, but I have spent the bulk of my working career encouraging others with hope and resources for what's next. Let's take that next office meeting outside on the trail or out on the water, friends. I bet we can find a lot more inspiration that way.

Monday, October 14, 2013 – In the Arms of I-40

Starting Location: Brown Gap → Destination: Newport

Today's Miles: 11 – Trip Miles: 1,228.10

Hey y'all! We came up to the top of Snowbird Mountain just as the fog lifted and guess what we saw – The Great Smoky Mountains (Shaconage). They really do look great. Puma got an awesome picture of the entire mountain range, and I'm pretty sure we saw Fontana Dam, too.

Coming down Snowbird, I heard a highway and as I got closer and closer, Puma said, "That's I-40!" It caught me off guard, and I actually teared up JUST a bit because I recognized it. I hugged the sign. Won't be long before we head west on I-40 back home. That's just crazy.

We got a shuttle at the base of Snowbird at Davenport Gap into Newport, Tennessee. My sister, Number 3, met us in town and we had a great time at Ruby Tuesday's. Shut the place down. We always have fun with Number 3.

My parents met up with us the next day at Cracker Barrel. Did y'all know they discontinued their steak and biscuits entree?! I'm just as upset as you are. Still, it was delicious food and good coffee.

Our dear friend, Jenny, met us at Cracker Barrel and brought us into Knoxville for a day where we will meet up with Puma's parents and brother. Her brother has more awesomeness in his pinky finger than I do in my entire left leg, true story. He's going to be hiking with us for a few days, and we're excited to see him.

Puma has gotten a plan of action together for the Smokies. This just in, Governor Haslam worked it out for the Smokies to be open from Thursday through Sunday. We'll take what we can get.

Thanks for sticking with us, y'all. Your trail journal endurance has been appreciated and impressive. Keep it up!

Love,

Number 2

Okay Puma, tell everyone what they've won:

Number 2 lunged for the I-40 sign. I enjoyed seeing my family and friends. Still a few more guests to come.

Sometimes I am just like my dad; we like to visit. I had seen my sister and my parents a couple of times already, and here we were having another good visit. I highly recommend going out to eat with my sister if you get the chance. She is so much fun no matter what you end up doing.

Seeing the I-40 sign, that was something. My eyes got wider as I visualized how close I was to home. It was like I could almost see my townhouse and my dog. That was a special moment for me. Recognizing the sign and my location also made me think about how far I had come and what a sizable journey this had been. Distance really does make the heart grow fonder, and it was like the I-40 sign was standing there with its arms spread wide open for a big hug, just like my mother.

Friday, October 18, 2013 – Hiking with Tuff Ribeye

Starting Location: Gatlinburg → Destination: Derrick Knob Shelter

Today's Miles: 10.80 – Trip Miles: 1,238.90

Well, I don't know if anybody told y'all that the Smokies are open, but they are and they are beautiful. Lots of folks were out around Kuwohi [formerly known as Clingmans Dome] and on the trail. Puma's brother is in fantastic shape already and hiking right along with us, no problem.

I totally want to come back to Gatlinburg sometime around Christmas because there were TONS of Christmas lights already up. Not turned on, but already in place.

We've met some really great folks who are out for the week enjoying the Smokies. It's been tough obeying the "no tent" rule, but I'm sure we can make it. Crowded shelters, here we come!

It's way colder up here at 5,000 feet, which is fine because we hike a lot faster. My hands are cold.

Gotta' go!

Love,

Number 2

Having more fun than you can shake a stick at, please welcome, Puma:

I'm so happy my brother, Tuff Ribeye (Tuff for short), is hiking with us for the next week. This will be good.

Hanging out in Gatlinburg, I'm sure glad Puma got the chance to be with her family on this adventure. It's a special feeling when you see your family like this, similar to that of running into one of your parents at the grocery, but a little bit more exciting. We all went out to eat (one of my favorite pastimes at the time), and then got dropped off at the trail for our hike through the Smokies.

Puma's brother was an excellent addition to this experience. He's one of those people who is always in great shape, and he has a great sense of humor, so it worked out well. Like his sister, he likes to get shit done. So, that meant we could keep our pace without any worry.

We were cruising through that section with Tuff Ribeye right there with us every step of the way. He slept out under the stars every night, no tent, a true outdoorsman doing a little cowboy campin'. We laughed a lot, talked about anything and everything, and it was easy. Truly a great hiking companion for us, and I think it meant a lot to him and Puma to hike together.

Monday, October 21, 2013 – "Rocky Top" On Top of Rocky Top

Starting Location: Derrick Knob Shelter → Destination: Cody Gap

Today's Miles: 41.80 – Trip Miles: 1,280.70

Hey guys! I have so much to tell y'all! Like I said before, it's daggum COLD up here in the mountains, and I just couldn't get the journal going again until my fingers had a chance to thaw out. We've had some fun times with Puma's brother, Tuff Ribeye. He's a riot and loves to make campfires at night. We're trying to figure out a way to force him to finish with us.

So, a lot has happened: we've seen amazing views, the trail through this area is just plain badass, we've laughed more than ever, and got to check out the Fontana Village in North Carolina. This place is begging for a family reunion.

We caught up on all the crazy SEC football that we missed on Saturday. Go VOLS! Go Vandy! Go Bama! Plus, we had the most amazing steak dinners and drinks. That's where a lot of the laughing took place, never mind that Puma and I both accidentally pooted at the dinner table...I said never mind!

We're hiking real strong right now and really enjoying what little time we have left out here on the trail. This has been the best adventure of my life, and I'm so thankful that we did it. Sometimes we all just have to go for it.

Looking forward to what tomorrow has in store for us.

Thanks for reading our journal. See y'all soon!

Love,

Number 2

Harmonizing to "Rocky Top" on top of the actual Rocky Top, that was me. Okay! Take it away, Puma:

I had a great time this week. I loved hiking with my brother. Makes us want to do more trips together. This adventure isn't over yet. It does seem like everything is moving faster, though. Hope to see everyone at the finale.

Remember when you were young and your parents tried to take the family out to dinner, but things got out of hand? Having this dinner at Fontana Village was like that, sans the parentals. Too much fun! The large bench seats weren't doing us any favors. I mean with that much food, wine, laughter, and exhaustion, all I wanted to do was lay down. Never mind, I had forgotten my manners and ripped one that ricocheted off that vinyl seat and soared around the room. Was I raised in a barn?! No, but I had stayed in a couple fairly recently. My, my, my, and *then* Puma had the same lapse of judgement and that sent us all right over the edge of that booth.

Oh, dear, dear, dear, dear, we laughed so much during that steak dinner at the restaurant in Fontana Village. Yes, the red wine was flowing, and everything just got funnier and funnier. It's a wonder they didn't ask us to leave. I think what saved us was the complimentary bread rolls, but also the tables were sunken down in the floor which gave us somewhere to hide.

This place was nice, like a lodge, but instead of taxidermy deer heads, they had *huge* wild boar heads. I'm talking, 200 pound beasts with magnificent tusks, and they were everywhere. Pretty sure three heads were watching me eat my steak dinner. Maybe I was delirious, but I recall there being a massive wild boar on every wall and stationed at every corner.

Coming out of the woods, we walked over Fontana Dam, which was this sizable stretch of road that made up the Tennessee/North Carolina border. I could see the fall colors and, of course, had to spit over the side. Long way down. It was a beautiful and fun hike with Tuff Ribeye in the Smokies. I really enjoyed that time with him.

Camping in the Smokies, we saw not one bear! But we did see lots of bear bag cable devices. The A.T. was pretty crowded through the Smokies, but it was for good reason because it was also leaf season. Gorgeous color palate everywhere you looked. I loved walking by Kuwohi and talking with all the tourists. We even saw the secret little closet of a room at the base of the observation tower. I'd stay in there if I had to, but only if I had to. There's a "no tenting" rule in the park which requires hikers to obtain a permit for a spot in the shelters every night. I believe its purpose is to protect the biodiversity of all the plants and animals. Nothing like cozying up next to 12 strangers and making small talk in the morning.

I love the Smokies so very much. I try to get back there as much as I can, and I think it'd be a wonderful goal to hike every mile through there in order to earn a spot in the 900-Miler Club. It used to be the 800-Miler Club, but now it's 900. That's a *wonderful* goal, and anybody who wants to do it, just give me a shout, and I'll go with ya.

I remember being on the A.T. and seeing the spur trail to Mt. LeConte called the Boulevard Trail. Puma and I blew past that opportunity with zero consideration back then, but I recently bagged Mt. LeConte with my good friend, Leah, via the Alum Cave Trail. Excellent day hike! Leah and I hadn't spoken to each other in 10 years or more, and she contacted me out of the blue to see if I wanted to join her. It went like this:

Leah: Hey mayn, wanna go hike Mt. LeConte with me next weekend?

Me: Yep!

Leah: Wanna campout close to there?

Me: Yep!

Leah: Meet ya there?

Me: Yep!

And we had the best time. It was so easy to coordinate. Her timing was impeccable, and I needed it more than I could ever explain. I got off the phone and hollered out to the Universe, "I'm going to Mt. LeConte!" It's pivotal moments like these that get me closer to my next big trail adventure.

Chapter Fifteen

North Carolina

Tuesday, October 22, 2013 – Land of the Noon Day Sun

Starting Location: Cody Gap → Destination: Sassafras Shelter

 Today's Miles: 12.30 – Trip Miles: 1,293

 Hey, North Carolina! Y'all got some steep mountains and hills and gorgeous views. We hiked real strong today, and my legs are adjusting to these climbs again.

 The fall colors are in full swing with brilliant reds and yellows making the photos look like Bob Ross paintings. I highly recommend a backpacking trip on the A.T. through North Carolina. We'll definitely be coming back.

 I can't believe how close we are to the finish line; we've just had so much fun, met some excellent people, seen a lot of the country that we've never seen before, and made a lifetime of memories. I love telling stories, and now I really have some great storytelling material. We haven't put everything in the trail journal, and you better believe that I'm going to sit down with a big cup of coffee and edit the entire thing when I get back home.

 We hike down to the N.O.C. (Nantahala Outdoor Center) tomorrow.

Heard there's a pub next door, and that's where I'll be sipping on a cold beer keeping my eyes peeled for another storyteller.

Tuff Ribeye, Puma, and I are having the best time together out here on the trail. Thanks to everyone for your support and awesome posts on the journal. I kind of wish we could continue the journal for the rest of our lives.

We love you, America!

Singing off (I did just sing a little),

Number 2

Please welcome some of the hottest bands and artists from 2013: Pumo Mars, Fall Out Puma, Imagine Pumas, and the Pumineers:

I have always been a fan of Top 40 hits. I think Tuff Ribeye hiked slower on purpose to avoid my singing. I had fun, though.

The mountains of North Carolina felt endless, rugged, and haunted. I want to go back. Per the Nantahala National Forest website, the Cherokee word "Nantahala" means "land of the noon day sun," which makes a lot of sense to me because the sun finally reaches the hollers and valleys for maybe an hour and then is gone again. These mountains are plentiful and thick, and I love them. I go back and forth between professing my love for the ocean or the mountains, and right now, it's mountains. It'll change as soon as I go to the ocean, but for now, it's the mountains.

At work, I'm not listening to Top 40 radio; I'm listening to my searches on YouTube for things such as: "thunderstorm in a tent" or "hiking through the rain" or "campfire sounds." My favorite right now is "thunderstorm in a tent" because it takes me back to the coziness of the tent on those rainy mornings, and I tell you what, I got some of the best sleep of my life out there on the trail in that thing. Some of the worst, too, but mostly the best.

Wednesday, October 23, 2013 – Campfires and Automatic Hand Dryers

Starting Location: Sassafras Shelter → Destination: Nantahala Outdoor Center

Today's Miles: 6.90 – Trip Miles: 1,299.90

It sure was cold this morning! I had to put on another layer just to go use the outhouse. Once we are up, it doesn't take us long to break camp and hit the trail. A hot breakfast isn't on the menu for us in the morning if we aren't in town.

It's a good thing we bundled up because the wind was whipping across the ridges and cutting right through the first layer of clothing. The sun was shining, but it was still pretty darn cold.

We were hiking along and out of nowhere came about four guys all decked out in camouflage with their rifles and hunting dogs leading the way. I'm pretty sure I told them they looked fantastic, in a rugged sort of way, you know. That brings our total number of hunters to seven (that we've actually seen). Good thing we got on our orange on out here.

Besides the hike, the most exciting part of the day was walking into the Nantahala Outdoor Center. They got a real nice place up here near Bryson City, and I'm certain we'll be back for some mountain biking and kayaking in the near future.

We watched the Nantahala River rise pretty quickly as all the paddlers got out in their kayaks to play around in the rapids. It made me shiver in my seat thinking about the temperature of that water. Then I thought about how happy I am not to be fording rivers anymore like we did up in Maine. Y'all remember that, don't ya!? No, thank you.

We're getting down to it, America! I hope you'll stay with us for just a short while longer until we finish this thing.

Thanks for reading all about our adventures.

Love,

Number 2

Puma got stung AGAIN today about a mile and half from the NOC. It didn't bother her one bit:

I will miss having Tuff Ribeye with us on the trail. The temperatures have dropped, and we enjoyed his campfires. Those six days flew by.

People assumed we made fires every night out on the trail, and we did not. Let me clarify that this was not because we couldn't; I pride myself on my fire-making skills, but it took too much energy. If we had been in a survival situation, then that would have been different. Tuff Ribeye made campfires during his stay, and we came across a couple of other borrowed fires along the way. They were all a welcomed sight. There was *one* super-secret fire that felt kind of survival-ish way back in the 100 Mile Wilderness, but we don't talk about that one.

By this point, I was really struggling with the cold temperatures. If I got too cold, I couldn't function. The temperature teetered on the fence for me for all of North Carolina. It gets cold up in those mountains, y'all! I didn't have enough clothes or meat on my bones for insulation. I walked down the trail and went straight into the restroom at the N.O.C. and slapped that automatic hand dryer button like I had the winning answer on *Family Feud*. I filled my shirt, my little fleece, my neck gaiter, and my shorts with that recycled warm air. It was glorious.

Just before that, Puma got stung *again*. She really was the best sport through thick, thin, and sting-y situations. I always hiked in front, and wouldn't you know it, I passed by the hornets' nest unscathed, but Puma got *got*! She started hollerin' and runnin', which of course made me holler and run, too. My bravery came into play when she realized she had dropped her Buff on the trail back in the danger zone.

I put on my stealthiest persona and ninja-turtled my way back through that hornet zone. Grabbed the Buff and ran back like I was a contender on *American Gladiators*.

Puma was the real hero in this story, though. If I had been the one to have gotten stung, we'd prolly have to call the government and shut down the whole operation again until I was good to go.

Thursday, October 24, 2013 – Cold Weather Camping

Starting Location: Burningtown Gap → Destination: Bartram Trail Campsite

Today's Miles: 4.70 – Trip Miles: 1,304.60

Well, I am just no fun when the temperature gets down to 27 degrees. Sure, I'm still singing silly songs to myself like "If You're Cold and You're Hungry, Clap Your Hands," but the camping part gets a little rough when the temps drop this low. We heard it's just a cold snap and it'll be over soon. Works for me.

We passed a spot called Wayah Bald, and I keep pronouncing it "Why-Ya-Bald?" I know my dad's answer would be that he didn't eat his green beans when he was little. He's been telling me that since I was little, and it really had an effect on me. So, for dinner we had long grain wild rice pilaf with green beans, broccoli, portobella mushrooms, red peppers, and onions all mixed with a creamy parmesan sauce. Too bad we didn't have any of those white wine to-go bottles...you know that's a good pairing.

Real soon we'll be cruising into Franklin, North Carolina, to watch Tennessee play Bama. Happy timing.

It's still gorgeous up here at 5,000 feet, and we are getting so close to the end. We think about our party at Springer Mountain just about every day. I hope you'll join us.

Thanks for keeping up with us. Y'all have really been great.
Love,
Number 2
Puma's turn on the mic, won't you say a few words for us tonight:
It's cold out here.

Per the Cherokee Nation website, the word "wa-ya" means wolf. I read numerous articles telling of packs of red wolves roaming the Wayah Bald area prior to the arrival of the Europeans. Back in 2013, clearly I wasn't thinking about how these places got their original names from the Cherokee Nation. I cringe reading some of these journal entries, but they have sparked a hunger for knowledge, action, and conversation to foster a deeper connection and understanding of the land I love and its people.

I love camping any time of year. I've camped out in the cold numerous times in my life, namely in late November, when temps have gotten down into the teens. The hard part is not having enough layers, and once I get too cold, it's hard for me to come back.

At this point on the trail, I wasn't going to buy a bunch of other clothes, but the temps teetered on too cold. At night, I'd change into my long johns and crawl into my silk liner inside my sleeping bag. I love my sleeping bag. It's a Mountain Hardwear 32 degree bag.

Is there anything better than a cozy camping setup? Especially in the cold weather months? You can't beat it, and I want to be out there in the woods no matter what time of year. Just be prepared. Whether car camping, backpacking, bikepacking, or kayak-ping (an original term), all you need to do is research and compare gear to prepare.

My parents started our camping traditions very early on, and I reckon that's one of the reasons I love it so much. Either that or I'm part hobbit.

Friday, October 25, 2013 – I *Had* to *Do* It

Starting Location: Bartram Trail Campsite → Destination: Franklin

Today's Miles: 10.50 – Trip Miles: 1,315.10

So, there I was at 4:30 a.m. shivering in my sleeping bag thinking about how great it would be to have an electric blanket and a hot cup of coffee. It was so cold that there was condensation on the outside of my sleeping bag from my breath (bad breath, I'm sure).

Puma started to stir around 7:20 a.m., and we laid there for another 20 minutes prolonging the inevitable. We layered up and knocked the frost off the tent before breaking down camp. Man, it was really cold this morning!

It was so cold that my hands and feet went numb, and I HAD to put my hands in Puma's armpits. This cold snap was biting me so bad that we decided to take the weekend off in Franklin to let the temps warm up again. It's just no fun hiking when I can't get warm enough to enjoy it. The temperature goes back up this week and everything will be fine.

I hope y'all will stay with us for these last few days. I have to tell you how much we have loved keeping up the journal. It's really been fun and funny and encouraging. Thanks for your support.

This thing ain't over yet, so stay tuned! Homemade costumes coming soon.

Love,

Number 2

No, she's not a medical doctor, but she did stay at a Holiday Inn Express: I believe Tuff Ribeye got off the trail at the right time. If he was still here, we'd have to squeeze him in the tent. This has definitely been the coldest weather we've experienced out here so far.

I remember the pains in my hands. I sound like such a baby, but I was hurting. I knew it was not going to be good for me, and I did *try* to push through the stinging pain. It just got too painful. I can't quite describe it other than a very painful, stinging sensation in all my fingers. I did put my hands in Puma's armpits hoping that would help, but it did not, and poor Puma's prolly scarred from that, too. Have you ever made the mistake of playing in the snow with no gloves on, and then come inside to wash up for hot chocolate and burned your hands in the hot water? Or tried to play frisbee in the winter months? It was like that but 10 times worse.

The dangers of being too cold and/or too hungry were the only things that tried to keep me down out there in that second half of the trail, and thankfully, we had the means to work around those issues.

Sunday, October 27, 2013 – Torn Between Happiness and Sadness

Starting Location: Franklin → Destination: Franklin

Today's Miles: 0 – Trip Miles: 1,315.10

We are so looking forward to seeing y'all on November 9th!

Get there early and enjoy a Whitt's bar-b-q sandwich, some limited-edition Mountain Dew in a camo can, maybe some chips, a little rock n' roll via Number 3's iPod, and a rousing game of cornhole.

Puma and I shall emerge from the woods around 2 p.m. and will be ready to party. Y'all be sure to wear your hiking shoes for the last mile.

Here's Puma with more directions:

The starting point is from Ellijay, Georgia. Take GA 52 East for about 19 miles. When you come to the traffic circle at Amicalola, take the second exit onto USFS 42 for about 6.5 miles. Best of luck.

I remember feeling torn between happiness and sadness realizing the end was near. It's real easy for me to feel multiple feelings all at the same time. Sometimes I can't make up my mind on how I really feel so I stay frozen in time.

We'd come a long way, and it was not going to be long before our pace of life was going to change again.

When my only job was to wake up and hike, I felt so alive. Every day was new. I had just enough information for the day, and my mind could go anywhere it wanted to go. I could stay present or astral project myself to who knows where. I had a lot of the "if I had a million dollars, what would I do with it" daydreams that usually resulted in giving most of it away because I wanted everyone else not tot have bills so we could all travel and play together.

One of the things I loved most about this experience was literally moving forward every day, moving through the changes of scenery, moving through the seasons, and doing it at my own pace.

Tuesday, October 29, 2013 – Like a Sherwood Forest Drama

Starting Location: Franklin → Destination: Muskrat Shelter

Today's Miles: 10.50 – Trip Miles: 1,325.60

Do y'all remember the animated version of Robin Hood from the early 70s with the cast full of animals? Roger Miller played the guitar pickin' rooster who narrates the whole story. It's probably one of my all-time favorite movies, and I can't help but imagine that we've walked through a hundred little Sherwood Forest dramas without even knowing it. Pretty sure we've seen two chipmunks stealing acorns from each other out here, but who am I to judge. I don't say a word.

Today's weather was eons better than a couple days ago. That cold snap blew on through, and it just makes hiking so much more enjoyable when we have these warmer temperatures. All the leaves are barely hangin' on out here. Another strong windy day and these fall colors are toast. I give it another week, tops.

The anticipation of our finale party at Springer Mountain is on our minds daily. I just can't believe how fast this trip has gone by. I swear we were drinking Guinness at the pub inside the Inn at Long Trail in Vermont just a week ago.

A few more journal entries to go and then we bid y'all adieu. I'm going to miss our witty banter and your encouraging messages. Seems a little selfish, but in all honesty, I'd like to take you with us on our next adventure (like to the car wash or the grocery store or the library...that's all I've got lined up right now).

We thank you from the bottom of our hearts, and we truly look forward to seeing you on Springer Mountain.

I have to give a shout out to my Great Uncle Aubrey who turns 84 today! Happy birthday, Uncle Aubrey! I hope you ordered a juicy steak and a bottomless glass of iced tea. I'm still telling your "BLT-NT" joke every chance I get.

Thanks for reading our journal, America! We love ya.

I am,

Number 2

Forgot to tell y'all that Puma almost fell today, but she caught herself on a rock with her knee. She never made a peep. Not one stinkin' peep. They're all yours, Puma:

I basically rammed my knee into a 50 pound rock. It was sore for a minute, but then I moved on. It'll bruise before the dawn.

Thinking about the Sherwood Forest dramas, I witnessed birds in a lover's quarrel, squirrels in an all-out dual, and mice and rats scrambling to find the freshest ingredients for the night's ratatouille. It was alive out there. I can still picture the squirrels running back and forth stealing each other's nut collections. They do that. I watched a whole documentary recently about how these squirrels work hard to store enough nuts away for the winter, and then the neighboring squirrel, we'll call him "D-Wayne," is waiting in the wings to steal the family's nuts. Hey now, it's for the children!

Saw a diverse group of wildlife in their natural habitats, and I am certain there were a good number of animals who saw us, but we never saw them. Like this one time, we were sitting on a log back-to-back to keep a lookout for anything suspicious. I remember feeling like we were being stalked like prey while taking our leftover pizza lunch break. This was a fast break; took big bites. Couldn't really see very far into the distance because the vegetation was so thick.

We scarfed the leftover pizza and as we stood up to get the hell outta' there, *something* made an enormous rustle in the bushes. Still couldn't see anything. The branches moved like a 250 pound *something* had fallen. There was no animal cry, no meow, no growl, no roar, but it was *alive*, it was *big*.

We frantically packed it all up and shoved off with our trekking poles. I can really scoot when I need to, and that was one of those times.

On the flipside, nary did we have any trouble with the wildlife. I cannot confirm or deny that we were in danger in the above situation, and all animals are innocent until proven guilty. They did not approach us, and we did not approach them (intentionally).

Humans are the biggest caution, and I am happy to share my leftover pizza with a human. Alls ya gotta' do is ask.

Wednesday, October 30, 2013 – I Walked Right Past the Most Important Sign

Starting Location: Muskrat Shelter → Destination: Plum Orchard Shelter

Today's Miles: 7.30 – Trip Miles: 1,332.90

We were in no hurry to get going this morning, and it was really nice to mosey through the morning ritual of packing up camp. Another couple and their dog, Stetson, were staying at the same shelter. Stetson was the same size as my dog Peejay and had similar eyes, so you can bet that we were instantly friends.

A few miles into our hike and I passed right by the North Carolina/Georgia sign. Puma was like, "Are you serious? You just missed the most important sign." About 10 steps into Georgia is when it really hit us, and we had a dance party to a Donna Lewis classic hit from the 90s. Just google Donna Lewis and you'll find the song I'm talking about. It's a karaoke MUST!

Puma and I are absolutely elated to be in Georgia right now. We bought a one-way ticket to Maine and now we're in the 14th state on the trail. It's an incredible feeling, similar to the feeling when we successfully hang our bear bag.

Thanks to all of you for your support and encouragement. There's no way we can repay you. So, thanks. But seriously, you all made this journal experience a lot of fun.

Now, we got our hands on a People magazine, and this headline just caught my eye: "What's Trending Now, Big Eyebrows!" I gotta' go.

Love,

Number 2

Staring at pictures of a P.F. Chang's advertisement (damn that looks good). Give it up for, Puma:

Today was the last time we hollered "DOG SHIT" on this adventure. What a rush!

I walked right past it! I was in another realm. A big shift was about to happen in my life, and if there's one thing I love, it's change; any kind of change, changes of the seasons, changing of the guard, pocket change, a good change of clothes, you name it.

By this time, fall weather was in full swing, and my head was full of ideas and daydreams. I was really focused on my future aspiration of becoming a bicycle mechanic. Barely knew how to change a tire at this point, but I wanted to learn everything. The second thing I love most is learning new things, although I'll admit I was never a great student in my "traditional" school years. However, I have always been good at researching, preparing, observing, and adapting.

When figuring out my next move, I like to dissect all the options, even go as far as claiming one of those options and trying it on for size. I'll stick with it until it becomes clear that it's not the right choice and change my mind. I'm impulsive and move too quickly, a blessing and a curse, but I'm okay because I'm making progress.

Being this close to the end of the journey on the Appalachian Trail was giving me great inspiration. I was already thinking about turning the trail journal into a book; didn't know it would take me over 11 years to cross that one off my list. It was pretty intimidating breaking into the bicycle mechanic industry, but I did it and made some lifelong friends.

Here's the bottom line: Going through my experiences on the A.T. gave me the courage to face the unknown.

Chapter Sixteen

Georgia

Thursday, October 31, 2013 – Faithful Followers and Pumpkin Pack Covers

Starting Location: Plum Orchard Shelter → Destination: Hiawassee

Today's Miles: 4.50 – Trip Miles: 1,337.40

Y'all just aren't going to believe this; I don't think we believed it at first. When we got to the road at Hiawassee wearing our Halloween costumes, there waiting for us was one incredible family, Norma and Edward and their daughter Wendy.

These folks traveled up from Augusta, Georgia, with "#2 & Puma" written in shoe polish on their van windows! They had fresh fruits and veggies and chocolate in addition to their warm hugs and laughter. They were very generous and helped us greatly. They picked our brains about this adventure because it's Wendy's turn for an Appalachian Trail hike next year. We laughed and told stories and thoroughly enjoyed each other's company. Puma and I were blown away by their tremendous generosity and kindness. What an incredibly awesome family. They definitely made our Forever Christmas Card List.

Folks, we are staring down our finish date for Springer Mountain. Y'all know this. Our dear friend, Jess Leigh, is coming to hike with us in this last little bit. Don't worry, Jess Leigh's in great shape and will do just fine. Kudos to her for making the trip!

I cannot tell y'all how excited we are to be at this point. I've been lying awake at night rehearsing my speech for Springer. That marks the spot of Puma's last introduction. Noooo!

Won't you stay with us just a little bit longer to the finish line? Most of the key players in this adventure are making an appearance, which means the world to Puma and me.

Thanks for reading, America!

We love ya,

Number 2

Protein Pocket mouse pads. This was all Puma's idea:

I am blown away by the incredible friends we have made during this adventure. I've said it all along. The A.T. brings people together. Be on the lookout for our festive costumes.

I never thought something like that would happen. I daydreamed about it before, for sure. Coming out of the woods and seeing this lovely family waiting with such excitement to see us walking down the path towards them. Seeing our names written in shoe polish across the side of their van windows made me feel crazy special. I, of course, had imagined this same scene before, but with 10 more vans. Norma and Edward had been following our journal from the start, and I guess once we got closer down to their neck of the woods, they asked if they could meet us. They had been commenting on our trail journal and sending lovely messages of support and encouragement for months.

They hugged us and mentioned so many things about the journal entries, and I could tell they were faithful followers. We all loaded up in the van and they took us to the quaint little motel they were staying at for a couple of days. Norma was probably our biggest fan, and Edward was the nicest guy. Their daughter Wendy was asking us great questions about the trail in preparation for her hike planned for the following year.

They paid for our room, our laundry services, and I believe our dinner, too. I remember Puma and I having a moment in our motel room questioning if this was really happening. This family was showering us with the most elaborate trail magic we'd experienced on this whole adventure. Norma and Edward were also very encouraging of Wendy going out for her A.T. hike.

At dinner, we found out they had traveled up from Augusta, Georgia, which was about a three and half hour drive. They lived real close to the Master's golf course and were telling us all about how crazy it gets down there during the tournament. They said people rent out their homes and even driveways for parking for at least that week. This was before I had become familiar with Airbnb, so it blew my mind. I remember thinking to myself, "How can people just up and leave their own homes and all their possessions for entire week?" Never mind, I had done the exact same thing but for close to 6 months.

Staying at the same motel was our friend, Will Percy. You remember, the guy who invited us to have lunch with him way back in Harpers Ferry, West Virginia. I believe he was out doing a section of the A.T., and we all happened to land at the same place.

Looking back, I can now see that the trail journal was inspiring all of us. It was a two way street of inspiration, and I'm so grateful for all that was shared through the experience.

My mom had sewn adorable little pumpkin stem beret hats to go with our pumpkin face orange pack covers. I thought this was brilliant. Just a big ol' pumpkin walking down the trail. Norma and Edward got a kick out of that.

Tuesday, November 5, 2013 – Old Friends and Wild Pigs

Starting Location: Hiawassee → Destination: Low Gap Shelter

Today's Miles: 9.70 – Trip Miles: 1,347.10

The leaves have fallen. I repeat, the leaves have fallen!

Jess Leigh has joined us for a couple days, and we can't even enjoy a friendly conversation while we're hiking because the crunch of leaves is so LOUD. After repeating ourselves multiple times, we all just stopped hiking to finish our sentences. Puma finds the loud continuous crunch maddening at times, but I just tune it out...or pretend it's a bunch of potato chips (pronounced "poe-tay-tuh" chips).

We cruised through the miles, set up camp, filtered some water, and made supper: pasta primavera. Delicious. Jess Leigh had never seen anyone hang a bear bag before, so that was fun. It's a bit chilly tonight, but nothing like it was back in Franklin, North Carolina. Judging by the forecast, we are looking real good for Saturday's Springer party! Looking forward to eating a Whitt's bar-b-q sandwich. It's my favorite. There, I said it. It won't disappoint.

It's been a real treat hearing from our families and friends and your excitement about hiking the last mile with us up to the top of Springer. I'm gonna slap that rock and roll out – after my speech, of course. Puma's preparing a special rendition of Miley Cyrus's "The Climb" while holding sparklers, or maybe y'all are supposed to hold the sparklers? I can't remember. And yes, you all will be receiving your very own victory sausages on top of Springer Mountain.

If you can't tell, we're excited. Thanks for reading, America!

Love,

Number 2

And now, everyone's favorite party animal, Puma:

We are stoked to have Jess Leigh with us on the trail. Every day is happening faster than the last. The weather is holding up. Bring a blanket for the finale party. Looking forward to it.

It was a lot of fun having Jess Leigh with us during that last leg. She has a great sense of humor, and we all moved at the same pace. That part was cool and fine. However, something scary did happen during her visit. One of those wild boars came to visit us at night.

That's right, we were all laying in the tent because Jess Leigh had forgotten her rainfly, when we were awakened by the sound of a wild boar sniffing the tent, grunting, and rootin' around the ground with what I imagined to be a big nasty snout. I read somewhere that these animals have caused millions of dollars of damage to the landscape nationwide, and they can be dangerous. All the taxidermied boars that decorated Fontana Village were giving me the creeps, and there we were laying down next to one. I mean our thin nylon tent was the only thing between us and that pig.

Glad we had our food up in the tree! I've heard these things will eat anything – including each other. We were dedicated to hanging the food bag every night for almost the entire trail. I didn't want any trouble, even when trouble was in the vicinity. We laid real still and listened to every move that wild boar was making. Seems like the area we were hiking through was a popular place for these animals because everywhere we looked, there were these long deep ruts scraped through the soft ground. Just tore up! I'd be sick if that were my mother's garden, and I'm sure landowners had to come to terms with these animals more than a few times.

Thankfully, we were sniffed and that was it. Maybe circled a few times, but nobody had to fight a pig. Also, I can't help but tell this next story anytime a pig is the subject of conversation. A pig was named after me one time, true story. My cousins had a sizeable pig on their farm and named her "Margie the Pig." I like pigs, and I think it's funny how they have appeared in different chapters of my life. I even refer to my present-day dog, JayJay, as "Piglet." He pooped the letter "K" on the floor one time, and I thought we had a *Charlotte's Web* situation on our hands.

Wednesday, November 6, 2013 – Random Acts of Kindness and a Very Large Knife

Starting Location: Low Gap Shelter → Destination: Neels Gap
Today's Miles: 11.70 – Trip Miles: 1,358.80

It was early Wednesday morning, like 1 a.m. early, when Puma heard Jess Leigh say, "Oh Shit!" An unauthorized rain shower was upon us, and Jess Leigh didn't bring her rainfly, so everything was getting wet.

We quickly made room for her and tested out our three-person tent that's comfortably made for two. No problem! We were all snug and cozy in the tent until morning. We've said it a hundred times, but we love our tent. I'd buy it again and again.

The weather didn't ease up at all for the remainder of the day: heavy cross winds, thick fog that collected on our eyelashes, and steady rain. Didn't bother me one bit because all I have been thinking about is how close we are to Springer Mountain.

Coming up to the top of Levelland Mountain, we were met by a group of gentlemen who offered us gourmet turkey sandwiches and vine ripe tomatoes that were absolutely divine. Jess Leigh was like, "Does this happen all the time?" That's one of the best parts of this adventure, meeting generous people who don't think twice about random acts of kindness. One guy said, "Congratulations! Your parents are really proud of you." I said, "You got to cut that out before I start crying again."

The wind stayed at our backs all the way down to Neel Gap, which has a sweet little outfitter/hostel right on the trail. We grabbed some microwaveable cheeseburgers, a couple Coca-Cola Classics, and staked out in the hostel for the night. Got to watch the Tom Hanks classic "Big" on VHS.

Happy to be inside tonight; it's rainy and cold out there. Gives us more power to conquer the great Blood Mountain tomorrow! Can't believe we are at this point on the trail. It's truly amazing!

See y'all soon.

Love,

Number 2

Puma's not telling y'all that she has new blisters. Like Milli Vanilli said, "Blame It on the Rain (Yeah, Yeah)":

I laughed pretty hard when Jess Leigh was cussing about not having her rainfly. It's true; I have two additional blisters, but there's no use crying over them at this point.

Also staying at Mountain Crossings hostel was another hiker, I can't remember his trail name, but I'll tell you what I can remember about this fellow. He was a little bit older than us, maybe mid thirties (I had turned 31 on the trail back in June). He wore a very large knife tied to the side of his shin. This knife was tactical. It stretched the length of his lower leg and all the way down to his ankle. We didn't ask about it, and he didn't mention it, but my eyes were glued to it all the time.

This guy was a world traveler; he talked about how he *had* to be in Dubai in a couple of weeks and told us more stories about his travels. He'd been everywhere and done everything. Don't know if he was in the military or what, but I certainly wasn't trying to challenge him in any way. I guess he heard me talking about how nice a cup of coffee would be on that rainy evening because he gave me one of his instant dark roast coffee packets from Starbucks. I'd never seen these before, and was like, "Damn, I could have had these the whole time." He was a nice fellow, but I was keeping his whereabouts and my wits about me.

Mountain Crossings hostel (currently known as the Walasi-yi Interpretive Center) was built by the Civilian Conservation Corps way back in 1934 and finished in 1937, which coincidently is the same year the A.T. was finished. How about that! They have a lovely outdoor gear store, rivalling our favorite Cumberland Transit store in Nashville, Tennessee.

The bunk room was long and skinny with probably four bunks lining the back wall and two more flanking the entrance. We claimed the opposite side of the room from our fellow hiker. It was like sleeping in a cave down there. I had no trouble falling asleep, but Jess Leigh and Puma woke me up a couple of times notifying me of my snoring. I hope I didn't disturb that guy with my snoring either. He could have easily carved me an extra breathing hole.

Thursday, November 7, 2013 – No Guilt Eating Style One Last Time

Starting Location: Neels Gap → Destination: Suches
Today's Miles: 10.90 – Trip Miles: 1,369.70

I could hear the rain coming down outside this morning, and the wind was whipping through the historic breezeway of the Mountain Crossings hostel. Nothing a little procrastination can't fix.

The first order of business was the climb up Blood Mountain. We kept a steady pace through the wind, the rain, and the fog; the climb up gave us flashbacks to Maine with the trail traversing exposed rock surface to the top. I think we surprised ourselves by how fast we got to the top; I guess we still got it. The stone shelter is surrounded by boulders that I'm sure are a lot of fun to climb around on in dry weather. Raincheck!

After we hiked down Blood Mountain, the weather broke, and the sun came out. I feel like I blinked, and we were already at Woody Gap.

A gentleman by the name of Hot Coffee had a huge spread of fresh food under a couple tarps. I ate three sloppy joes, one apple, one banana, a bunch of Ritz crackers, a handful of Pringles, drank two cups of coffee, and one cup of Kool Aid. So many hikers got to enjoy the same indulgence during the season, and Hot Coffee is a testament to the amazing trail magic one can experience out here. Thank you, sir, for your tremendous efforts; they are very much appreciated.

Will y'all believe me when I tell you soon after that feeding frenzy, I ate three slices of pizza, a cup of ice cream, and drank two more root beers and a bottle of water? What's the deal, Lucille? I guess I had to take advantage of this no guilt eating style just one last time. Too bad I didn't throw in some chicken wings, right! Who's with me?

Just a tiny little bit more to go out here, folks. I do hope you know how much we have enjoyed your posts on the journal. This has been an adventure of a lifetime, and the journal was the icing on the cake. Thank you so much for your encouragement, support, and humor. Y'all are clever and should consider writing a book.

Just a couple more journal entries, and then...it's your turn, America!

Thanks for reading; I miss you already.

Love,

Number 2

Thinking about her cats, no doubt, the great and powerful, Puma:

This is when the journals begin to mention the ending of everything; the end of the trail, the end of the hike, the end of this experience, etc. I bet Number 2 could keep this going.

Once again I was going through some big emotions all at the same time. Trying to process the end of this experience and moving on from what had been my job for the last six months. I was feeling all of the emotions at once, excitement for what was next, sadness for leaving the trail and ending the trail journal, and nervousness for how I was going to handle these changes.

Part of me wanted to slap that finish plaque, turn around, and head back to Katahdin like a "YOYO," but that wasn't in the cards. I think my biggest struggle was knowing that we skipped a good bit of the trail, and we didn't have time or resources to go back. It still irks me to this day.

The trail journal was a major accomplishment and friend to me during this adventure. I am still amazed by how far it reached people in the country and even outside of the United States. The best part for me was the routine. It became my therapy, along with my personal journals, which were much more private. I have spilled most of the beans, but not every single bean. My cousin is a farmer, and he tells this story about having to count some soybeans and put them in a cup. His dad was helping count the beans one time and accidentally spilled them in the truck. Such is life. It's okay to spill some beans, and it's okay to keep some things private. It's personal, you know.

Friday, November 8, 2013 – Reba McEntire Tribute Concert for the Soldiers

Starting Location: Suches → Destination: Almost to Springer!

Today's Miles: 0 – Trip Miles: 1,369.70

A wise man once said, "Don't start nothing, won't be nothing." My sister changed it to, "Better quit 'fore I start!" The moral of the story is that the beginning and the end are interchangeable. So, even though tonight is our last night on this adventure, our next adventure is about to begin.

I've had a thousand daydreams about what I'm going to do next: everything from bicycle mechanic to writing uplifting fiction for preteens, but one thing is for sure – I'm going fishing!

Hiking the trail was so surreal because I kept telling myself that it was the last full day out here. After almost six months, that's hard to believe. Puma said it also hit her today that we are actually heading home. Our appreciation for everyday appliances and "flushers" is skyrocketing right now, and I hope we don't lose that mentality too quickly when we get home. I WANT to watch my bread get toasted in the toaster, I WANT to grow my own vegetables year-round, I WANT to ride my bicycle as much as possible. There's so much to do.

We got a surprise visit from a friend we met way back in Stratton, Maine; Waterman found us on the trail this evening and made us a wonderful campfire for our last night in the woods. What a great guy! We wish him all the best with his future A.T. hike!

The stars are beautiful, the moon is super bright, and it is butt ass cold out here tonight...I love it.

Camping is in my soul. I have my family to thank for that. Now, I have to try to pretend to sleep tonight. We will see y'all tomorrow! Can't hardly believe it.

Love,

Number 2

P.S. The Army Rangers train on this part of the trail, and we saw them today. It's a really great story! We acted like we didn't see them in their full camo, helmets, and rifles, and I can't imagine what they thought when they saw two bright pumpkins come bouncing up the trail. All I know is if they come too close to the tent tonight, we might give their positions away with all the farting that's going on.

Puma said we could eat everything in our food bags tonight. Turn that food bag bottom up:

We're camping in our tent down the way from the shelter tonight. We can hear other hikers talking about finishing around mid-day tomorrow.

Oh yes, I remember seeing the military in the woods. This story makes me laugh. We were hiking along, singing the old Reba McEntire classic "Little Rock" when all of sudden my eyes caught another pair of eyes. I stopped right then and signaled to Puma to be quiet. We stood there for a few minutes in total silence waiting for our eyes to focus. It was like seeing the hidden dolphin in those posters we'd buy in grade school during the Scholastic book fairs. Once I could see them, I couldn't unsee them, and we were absolutely surrounded by soldiers. They stayed in character mostly and did not make one single sound. Not one cough!

I caught this one soldier who I could tell was struggling a little bit with controlling his laughter, likely due to my ridiculousness and watching me figure it all out. He had to divert his stare elsewhere and keep it together. I had gone from singing so loudly to being so quiet having realized the situation. I bet there were 20 people in the woods right there, maybe even more!

We made it to the road crossing and saw these two very large military trucks parked on the shoulder. The two officers looked at us, and I'm sure they were wondering if we had messed up their whole training operation. I could have put on an entire Reba McEntire tribute concert for them in the woods, "WHOAAAAooooOOOOO, Little Rock!"

Saturday, November 9, 2013 – Crossing the Toilet Paper Finish Line

Starting Location: Almost to Springer! → Destination: SPRINGER!
   Today's Miles: 8.10 – Trip Miles: 1,377.80
   Hey everybody! We made it back to Nashville this afternoon. I'm sitting on a blow-up mattress trying my best to recall the crazy awesomeness of the last 24 hours. What an awesome experience we had on Springer!
   I have to backtrack just a bit to capture it all for you:
   My eyes opened at 5:58 a.m. on November 9th, and I thought to myself, "Today's the day!" Since we only had seven miles to the parking lot where our friends and family would be waiting to walk the last mile to the top of Springer, we decided to enjoy our first morning campfire and powdered doughnuts courtesy of our good friend, Waterman.
   I'm pretty sure the sun was shining a little bit brighter and the sky was just a little bit bluer for the last few miles. The pep in our steps was hard to hide as we got closer and closer to the parking lot; that might also be because we had these amazing beards that we'd been saving for the perfect occasion, and this was it! Mine made me look exactly like my brother, and Puma's beard made her resemble the likes of Bob Seger – that's a win win in my book.
   As we approached the parking lot, I could see a crowd of folks and heard a familiar jock jam blaring from a loudspeaker. People started cheering, familiar faces came into focus, and I'm pretty sure I had the face of a warrior as we ran and broke the toilet paper finish line that was stretched

between two trees. Everybody was so great out there with tons of support and cheers.

We took a few pictures and didn't waste any time passing out victory sausages to everyone who was going to hike up to Springer for the finale speech.

I forgot my speech in my backpack that was already in my parents' car, but it was all good because I memorized the entire thing. We got to the top of Springer and monopolized it for maybe 20 minutes as I gave my speech, and Puma chimed in perfectly with thank yous that I would have almost forgotten.

It was an incredible feeling and the most amazing thing to see everyone there with us for the final moment. I forgot to tell y'all that my mom had been working on collecting patches from different spots along the trail since we started back in May, and then sewed them all on a green vest. We looked...like REI employees with lots of flair! These vests are treasures for life, and we'll probably wear them if we get asked to do a speaking event about our trail experience (hint, hint!). Thanks to everyone for your tremendous support and efforts for making the trip to Springer Mountain!

Being back home is pretty crazy, but the Holy Smokes of 1990 assured us that we'd be fine. So far, I've tried on about four different jackets, two pairs of climbing shoes, played guitar for maybe 15 minutes, hung out with Peejay in the backyard, thought about making a campfire, called my siblings, opened the mail, and scooped the cat poop. It's just going to take some time to settle in again, but that's just fine. We got the time, and it all feels so wonderful.

Have y'all decided what you're gonna do now that the journal is over? It's been such an incredible experience for us to read your posts from all over the United States. You've given us such a gift that we will cherish for the rest of our lives. So, THANK YOU for being a part of all this.

Feel free to send us your email, and we'd be more than happy to send you a copy of our finale postcard.

I wish all of you the very best. We wouldn't have had as much fun without you.

Yours Truly,

One more time,

Number 2

Roll the credits, Puma:

Just as before, here's my two cents – thanks to all the people who supported us along in this journey. This was an adventure of a lifetime. Looking forward to whatever comes next.

Waterman was this young lad we had met way back up in the Mid-Atlantic area or maybe even further north. I think I remember correctly that he hurt his knee or foot and had to come off the trail. He must have lived close to Springer because he found us on the trail, made us a lovely campfire, *and* left us some powdered donuts. What a nice guy!

We got up early the next morning, and I was listening to "A Pirate Looks at Forty" and a few other Jimmy Buffett songs on my iPod. Totally happy, hyper, and hungry. We were hiking so fast that we had to take a two hour break at this shelter and fill our time with making silly videos. We tried on our beards. Mine was red and Puma's was black. I really did look like my brother.

Crossing the toilet paper finish line, I saw so many familiar faces that I had not seen in months and some even in years. I felt so loved and important. There was so much laughter and congratulations. We threw our backpacks in the backseats of our parents' vehicles, passed out the victory sausages (extra long Slim Jims this time), and everyone hiked up the last mile ahead of us.

We hiked up to the top through the makeshift tunnel made of extra long victory sausages that everyone held up like swords. I gave my speech, Puma made helpful interjections, we took lots of photos, signed the final A.T. logbook, and then everybody headed back down to the parking lot and ate Whitt's bar-b-q sandwiches. Pretty sure I had four or five sandwiches while talking with my mouth open.

On the car ride home, I rode with my parents, and Puma rode with her parents. I was kind of quiet all the way back to Nashville, mostly because I was like a toddler asleep in my car seat. It was a lot to process in the moment, and when that happens, I just kind of shut down. Got a little numb. I'd been saying so much and then didn't really have much to say. My parents understood and let me contemplate and sleep.

Puma and I were lucky enough to have a spot on a local public television show called *Transitions* soon after our return home from the trail. I'm not sure if it's still out there in tv land or cyberspace, but we sure had fun doing it. The host was great, and she had us bring our fully-loaded backpacks to review each piece of gear for the audience. I hammed it up way too much. Still haven't caught the full episode.

Being back in my own home with all my *stuff* was bizarre. The minimalist life had changed me, and I didn't know what to do next. I was so used to moving every day to now not having anywhere to go. I felt kind of trapped.

I tried on shoes and jackets and went through my things. I remember getting rid of a lot of unnecessary items of clothing and organizing and cleaning my gear. My backpack had turned into a close friend, and I was sad to put it away in the closet.

We ended up going down to Key West with my sister, Number 3, for a little while. Did some fishing in the flats, explored the town, vowed to move there, etc. It was nice to get away again and to do it rather quickly. I needed to step away and think. What was I going to do next?

I did my research, as I do, and finally decided to go to bicycle mechanic school in Ashland, Oregon. I got to visit with my brother and his family for a few weeks since they live very close to there. That was a great experience, and I did my best to absorb a ton of information about the mechanics of a bicycle. There's way more to those things than meets the eye. I love it so much, and it gave me a plan for my future. I finished bicycle mechanic school in February in 2014 and was hired on in the bicycle shop at Cumberland Transit.

I stayed at the bicycle shop for two years, got another "grown-up job" as a trainer at a background screening company and stayed there for five years. In 2020, I started working at a local nonprofit in Nashville and have been there ever since. When I tell y'all that my itch for adventure is strong right now, I mean it takes everything I have to stay the course that I have planned for myself.

I can hear my backpack calling my name from the closet, and it's all I can do to steady the call of *my wild*, if you will. I've been seeing the same numbers on the clocks repeatedly. It started slowly in late summer last year, and now here I am in early fall of this year, 2024, seeing these numbers more and more frequently. I take it as a sign that I am on the right path. I have a plan of action to have another grand adventure. It's still brewing at the moment, but the start of any adventure is the planning.

In the meantime, I am finally writing this book, starting a website to revive the travel journal, and working on my music projects. The purpose for all of this is to break free again, to leave behind the trappings of home and find my soul purpose. It's not an easy thing to do, but it's worth the effort. I'm lucky that I got to have this adventure, but it can't be all there is for me.

Thanks for reading, America. I hope you enjoyed reading it as much as I enjoyed telling it. I feel like we really did just catch up around the campfire together. I've missed you.

Appendix

Glossary, iPod Playlist, Gear List

Glossary

Aquablaze – when a thru-hiker hops in a canoe or a kayak to float down a river on the Appalachian Trail instead of hiking that section. I believe there's opportunity for this on the Shenandoah River in Virginia.

A.T.C – stands for Appalachian Trail Conservancy, which is a non-profit organization located in Harpers Ferry, West Virginia, dedicated to conserving the Appalachian Trail.

Bear bagging – when a hiker puts a couple of rocks into a zippered pouch attached to a long string of paracord and tosses that rock bag over the limb of a tree. The hiker's food bag is then tied to the end of the string and hoisted up into the air about 10 feet high off the ground and at least six feet away from the tree trunk.

Bigelows – a strenuous mountain range located along the Appalachian Trail in western Maine.

Bog bridge – a skinny bridge made of skinny logs with no hand rail that stretches over mud and water.

Boosting – a super-fast walking pace.

Breather – pausing for a moment to catch one's breath.

Buff – the name brand of a popular neck gaiter.

Cairn – a pile of rocks often used above tree line that takes the place of a blaze mark on a tree.

Chicken legs – the unfortunate description of human legs that resemble the skinny, bony legs of a chicken.

Combinations – a fun way of referring to the popular snack Combos.

Cowboy camping – sleeping out under the stars instead of in some sort of shelter.

Croo – the college kids who work at the huts in the White Mountains of New Hampshire.

Crow hop – this is a specific throw learned in softball that feels a little bit like a dance move from the music video "Thriller."

F.K.T. – fastest known time.

Flip-flop – when a hiker starts at Springer Mountain and hikes north to the halfway point at Harpers Ferry, and then goes up to Katahdin and hikes south back to Harpers Ferry. This is just one example of a flip-flop hike.

Flowy – a description of the trail being fast and slopey. (See slopey)

From the Outside – a frame of mind that has been with me my whole life in a very literal sense but also represents a positive embrace of individuality, creativity, and uniqueness to flourish.

Green tunnel – the term given to describe the endless green vegetation of the trees along the A.T. in Virginia.

Hike your own hike – a phrase mentioned by thru hikers who are taking ownership of their own experience out on the Appalachian Trail.

Hiker bubble – a large group of northbound hikers coming from Springer Mountain that usually thins out after a couple of months.

Hiker box – an actual box that is typically found at the hostels and sometimes in the shelters that is a place for hikers to offload unwanted gear, making it free for the taking by other hikers, if need be.

Hiker loaner clothes – a bin of clean clothes pulled together by the hostels with the purpose of providing a change of clothes while the nasty, stinky clothes the hiker was wearing get washed.

Hiker trash – a term of endearment used by long distance hikers who know the joy of wearing the same outfit for months.

Hut – this is the name of the off-the-grid buildings nestled inside the White Mountains in New Hampshire.

Kayak-ping – taking an overnight trip on the river and packing everything you need in your kayak. Similar to canoe-ping.

Leave No Trace – a standard environmental principle and practice for anyone who enjoys the outdoors, and in short means make it look like you were never there. Take your trash with you, and dispose of it properly.

Night night trail – another way of saying, "Hey y'all, I'm going to sleep now."

NOBO – a northbound thru hiker.

Norovirus – this was a particularly nasty virus that was running rampant through the NOBO hiker bubble in 2013 causing hikers to poop and puke...a lot. A horrendous experience.

Pathy – when the trail is clear of excessive roots and/or rocks.

P.C.T. Method – stands for the Pacific Crest Trail Method, and is the preferred method for hanging a bear bag using a carabiner and a toggle making the tie-off at the base of the tree trunk unnecessary.

Presidential Range – the mountain range along the Appalachian Trail in the White Mountains of New Hampshire.

Privy – a fancy word for an outhouse.

Ridgerunner – a paid employee of the A.T.C. whose job it is to maintain a section of the Appalachian Trail by picking up trash, servicing the privy, talking with hikers, and answering questions about the trail.

Section hiker – a hiker who completes shorter sections of the trail to piece together the the entire distance.

Slackpacking – a wonderful opportunity to leave the fully loaded backpack at the hostel in order to hike faster during a day hike, and being picked up at the agreed upon location to come back to the hostel at the end of the day.

Slopey – when the trail has easy rolling hills and makes for a faster hiking pace.

SOBO – a southbound thru hiker.

Switchback – a winding path that carves out the entire side of a mountain with the purpose of easing the ascent and/or descent.

Thru hiker – someone who is hiking from one end to other of a particular long-distance trail.

Trail angel – a person who voluntarily provides support and aide to thru hikers.

Trail magic – typically referred to the goods left behind for the thru hikers to find along the trail, but it could be as extravagant as paid room and board, a free offer of laundry, a fresh sandwich, jugs of water, or something as magical as a warm Mountain Dew.

Twofer – when two things are great at the same time.

Unlimited timeouts – a hiking principle that has no end to its gracious understanding of the need for a pause.

Up and overs – the practice of hiking all the way up to the top of a mountain and coming all the way down the other side.

Vermud – the name given to Vermont by thru hikers who have experienced the muddiness along the A.T. within that particular state.

Victory sausage – another word for a Slim Jim.

Vitamin I – another word for Ibuprofen.

Yellow blaze – when a thru hiker gets a ride down the highway.

YOYO – when a thru hiker completes a thru hike at one end of the Appalachian Trail and then turns around and immediately heads towards the other terminus.

Zero day – when a hiker does not hike any miles along the Appalachian Trail.

2,000-Miler – someone who completes the 2,000 mile plus journey of the Appalachian Trail.

iPod Playlist

1. *Old Blue Chair* by Kenny Chesney
2. *On the Coast of Somewhere Beautiful* by Kenny Chesney
3. *Back Where I Come From* by Kenny Chesney
4. *All I Want for Christmas is a Real Good Tan* by Kenny Chesney
5. *Be As You Are* by Kenny Chesney
6. *Boston* by Kenny Chesney
7. *Summertime* by Kenny Chesney
8. *The Life* by Kenny Chesney
9. *Nowhere to Go, Nowhere to Be* by Kenny Chesney
10. *Hemingway's Whiskey* by Kenny Chesney
11. *The Great Filling Station Holdup* by Jimmy Buffett
12. *Grapefruit-Juicy Fruit* by Jimmy Buffett
13. *Pencil Thin Mustache* by Jimmy Buffett
14. *Stories We Could Tell* by Jimmy Buffett

15. *Life is Just a Tire Swing* by Jimmy Buffett

16. *A Pirate Looks at Forty* by Jimmy Buffett

17. *Trying to Reason with Hurricane Season* by Jimmy Buffett

18. *Nautical Wheelers* by Jimmy Buffett

19. *Tin Cup Chalice* by Jimmy Buffett

20. *The Captain and the Kid* by Jimmy Buffett

21. *Havana Daydreamin'* by Jimmy Buffett

22. *Son of a Son of a Sailor* by Jimmy Buffett

23. *Growing Older But Not Up* by Jimmy Buffett

24. *One Particular Harbour* by Jimmy Buffett

25. *Frank and Lola* by Jimmy Buffett

Gear List

- Osprey Exos 58, 2 lbs. 7 oz. Number 2's backpack

- Big Agnes UL3 Fly Creek tent, 3 lbs. 3 oz.

- Therm-a-Rest NeoAir XLite Sleeping Pad, 13 oz.

- Mountain Hardwear Phantom 32 degree sleeping bag, 1 lbs. 7 oz.

- The Packa (rain coat and pack cover), 13 oz.

- Sawyer Complete 2 Liter Water Filtration System, 12 oz.

- GSI Pinnacle Dualist cooking pot, 1 lb. 5 oz.

- MSR Pocket Rocket camp stove, 3 oz.

- TOAKS Titanium Long Handle Spoon, .7 oz.

- Black Diamond Alpine Carbon Cork Trekking Poles, 1.4 lbs.

- Sea to Summit eVent Compression Dry Sack 13 Liter, 4.5 oz. (used two of these, one for my sleeping bag and the other for my long johns, one pair of socks, and my fleece from Madison Spring Hut)

- Leatherman Skeletool CX Multi-Tool, 5 oz.

- Outdoor Research Expedition Crocodile Gaiters, 12 oz.

- Black Diamond Spot Headlamp, 7oz.

- Sea to Summit Lightweight Dry Bag 8 Liter, 2.4 oz.

- Platypus Hoser 2 Liter Reservoir, 3.6 oz.

- Patagonia Ultralight Down Jacket, 11.4 oz.

- Crocs, 14 oz.

- Adventure Medical Kit Ultralight/Watertight Medical Kit Pro, 1 lb. 12 oz.

- Patagonia Capilene 4 Expedition Weight base layers, top and bottoms

- Darn Tough Socks